BEYOND LIMITS
THE STORY OF ULTRA RUNNER AND EXPLORER
LOWRI MORGAN

Dear Izzie

Don't let anyone or
team work harder
than you do.
Good luck with Hockey
Wales
Lowri

BEYOND LIMITS
THE STORY OF ULTRA RUNNER AND EXPLORER
LOWRI MORGAN

Gomer

To my son Gwilym.
To my husband, parents and brother who have given me such joy.
To all who have helped and inspired me on my life's adventures.
This book is for you.
Caru chi.

First published in 2020 by Gomer Press,
Llandysul, Ceredigion SA44 4JL

ISBN 978 1 78562 275 5

A CIP record for this title is available from the British Library.

© Text copyright Lowri Morgan, 2020

Lowri Morgan asserts her moral right under the
Copyright, Designs and Patents Act, 1988
to be identified as author of this work.

This book is published with the financial support of the
Books Council of Wales.

Printed and bound in Wales at
Gomer Press, Llandysul, Ceredigion
www.gomer.co.uk

CONTENTS

ACKNOWLEDGEMENTS

My life has been shaped by so many people. I have been extremely lucky to have been surrounded by some of the most inspirational, loving, supportive and encouraging people on earth. Some have been mentioned in this book but many have not. However I am thankful and indebted to each and every one of you. You know who you are because I tell you. Thank you for all the happiness and excitement we've shared. We only get one shot at life and it's too short to be miserable.

I am grateful to the teachers in my junior and secondary schools who inspired me to hope, fired my imagination and instilled in me a love of learning.

To S4C. Without the Welsh TV Channel's support and belief in me, I would never have been on the many adventures I have had. I am forever indebted and thankful to them.

Writing a book is harder than I thought and more rewarding than I could have imagined and I owe a world of gratitude to the talented Edward Butler. Without his expertise, it would have taken me even longer to complete and not contain the level of depth that it does.

Many thanks to my wonderful editor Rebecca John, to Meirion Davies, Sue Roberts and to the patient staff at Gomer; their tireless marathon efforts in bringing this book to life have been extraordinary.

My brother Roger who is always there for me with invaluable advice, support and training chats. Thank you for all you've done, and continue to do, every day.

To my husband and best friend. Siôn, your incredible heart and your endless support (and patience) have enabled me to pursue my dream of living a happy life without limits, and for that I am grateful. I love you.

My parents. Mam and Dad. Thank you. Thank you for fostering in me the confidence and passion to never give up and pursue my goals without boundaries. You're unwavering and selfless support and love have provided me with immeasurable inspiration and motivation. Whatever I am today is because of you.

The most important mark I will leave on this world is my son, Gwilym. I wrote this book because of you. A rainbow has seven colours, but the rainbow of our lives has a million, thanks to you. I wish you adventure on your journey, the strength to follow your dreams and keep going, because success only comes to those who attempt.

Picture credits
Lowri in Arctic wear: Warren Orchard
Planed Plant: S4C
Titanic Expedition: Deep Ocean Expeditions
Jungle Marathon: Christiane Kappes / Kappes Adventure Press
6633 Ultra Marathon: Alun Morris Jones
Lowri presenting at the Cardiff Half Marathon: Huw Fairclough
333 Challenge: Sport Pictures Cymru
Dragon's Back Race: No Limits Photography
Portrait of Lowri: Emyr Young

FOREWORD

I suspect Lowri thought this was going to be a book aimed away from herself. I think she was inclined to write a general guide to running as she knew it and give gentle encouragement to other runners to go a little bit further. A few tips here and a bit of advice there, based on her own experiences. She would happily have written about the running shoes best-suited to uphill repeats and about hammock weights and electrolytes. Of herself, by herself, she may have offered a little less.

Among many others, I have told her that, important as the quality of her equipment undoubtedly is, it is not quite as vital as the person inside it. Her shoes are not as interesting as her story. Well, they may be to somebody looking for a new pair of trainers, but they are not as extraordinary as the feet that wear them.

She has agreed – she has allowed herself to be persuaded – to turn her book a little more inward and let it do to her what her adventures have done: taken her apart and put her back together. She has yielded reluctantly. 'But I can't,' she has often said, when asked to go a little further in miles, or a little further about certain things and certain people.

'But you can,' says the voice inside her head.

This, then, is the slightly reconfigured story of an owner not so much of a good pair of shoes as of an inner strength that has carried her to some of the most testing places on the planet. It is also the story of a Welsh-speaking woman writing about her homeland. It is about going up and down and round and round in her small country and then leaving it. It is the life of a long-distance traveller, blessed with a fortitude – or perhaps cursed with an obstinacy – that has defied the advice of her outer body and the alarms bells ringing in her limbs and carried on.

Why? That's exactly the question, easy to ask and not so easy to answer. You must reach your own conclusions about the mind that has wrestled most directly with the question and the answer. I suggest it is a rare instrument. I wish I could say the same for Lowri's feet. I feel I should offer one of those warnings that accompany news reports: there are scenes in this story that some readers may find upsetting.

So, here she is, beyond advice on kit. Beyond toenails. Something ordinary has to give in the running of an extraordinary life ...

Edward Butler

PROLOGUE – MIND GAMES

I am on the Ice Road, trudging along to the relentless click-click, click-click of my walking poles. It is -72 degrees Celsius. The wind ploughs into me at 70 miles per hour. I am beyond the halfway point: 230 miles down, 120 to go. Just me – head down, eyes up, arms and legs pumping – and my little blue sled on wheels – a twin-axle 'pulk'. The Incredible Pulk. It rumbling along on its bouncy tyres and me almost out on my broken feet with their blistered toes and blackened, peeling nails.

Come on, feet. Keep going. You can do it. Just one step at a time. It's an old cliché but now it's so true. Look at the feet Lowri, don't look ahead at the never-ending road. Count the steps. Let's say 2,500 to the mile, what with all the wibble-wobbling all over the road. Multiply by 120. Just the 300,000 more of them to take, then. One at a time.

There is complete silence all around me. Just the click-click of my poles on the ice. The sound of the steps, the beat of the walk, the click-click of the seconds passing. I need them badly, to take the pressure off my bruised and fractured feet ... oh, what jaunty steps we took at the start of this race.

... oh yes. I'm in a race. I'm in one of the toughest races in the world. A 350-mile self-sufficient footrace above the Arctic Circle in Northern Canada. And this is but a blip. A rough patch.

I hate it. I love it.

I want to stop. I don't want to stop.

I am on the Ice Road to Tuktoyaktuk – my goal, my destination, my end. Tuk. And only 120 miles away. All I want is to sleep. I've slept 12 hours in total this week. I am exhausted. No, I am more than that.

I could lie down, stare up at the amazing glow of the northern lights, watch them dance. No one would think any less of me.

No! Don't listen to that voice in the back of your mind telling you to quit. Keep going. Focus. Come on, Lowri. Force the mind to obey. Think of why you're here. Think about all the training. The four years of training. Think of how far you have come: 14,000 miles of running in four years to reach this point. Don't throw that all away.

But here I am, exhausted. I need to sleep. What was I taught a lifetime ago during training? Right shoe off, get inside the bivvy, other shoe off, climb fully in. Prepare food. Boil snow for drinking. Sleep. Pack up. Back out. And repeat. Right shoe off ... I recite the words as I walk and walk.

And out of this mind-numbing routine comes clarity: not far along the ice tunnel, a lovely little mountain hut, with a curl of smoke rising from its chimney and skis standing neatly in a row outside the front door. The relief! What great timing when I'm fighting the urge to give up. I could call in, have a warm drink and a breather, recharge my batteries. Just what I need ... But, no. When I look again the hut, the skis, the curl of smoke ... Vanished.

Hallucinations during training. And more hallucinations here on the race, too.

But for the visions, I am empty. Beyond empty. Broken. Tears start to fill my eyes but as they fall onto my cheeks, they freeze. There is no point crying. Nobody can hear me. Nobody can see me. I am on my own.

'Rest if you must, but do not quit.' That's what my parents had told me just before I left home, and their words resound inside my head now. Their voices are louder than my walking poles, my footsteps. I listen.

I dig my poles harder into the ice, hoping they will propel me closer to the finish line.

'DO NOT QUIT, LOWRI!' I shout. 'YOU WILL NOT QUIT!'

The statistics are heavily against me. Only five people have ever completed the 6633 Ultra. I am facing the biggest challenge of my life, and I have confronted a fair few.

I am hurting. But this is supposed to hurt.

Giving up is not an option.

I just have to put one foot in front of another and keep going, in the hope that eventually my mind will find that white, quiet space where pain and worries go to disappear. I have to carry on. For me if not for anyone else.

I am 37 years old. I am, somehow, an endurance athlete.

And I am nearing the end. With every step, I am moving closer to Tuk. 100 miles. 70 miles. 50. The tiredness and fantasies give way to a sweet euphoria. I am my sensible self again. I'm on the home straight. 50 miles, a mere 50 miles from the finish line. I know this feeling and I know everything there is to know about what makes me love the Ice Road. I have just one small regret. Why didn't I pack that little fold-up chair and strap it on board the pulk? Just for this moment, to stop in the Arctic sunshine, to sit down and soak it all in. I am tired. My feet are sore. I just want to sit down but I can't sit on the ground. I'm afraid I won't get back up. Then again, there's no need. Just over there, thirty frozen steps away, someone has installed a park bench on the Ice Road. For strangers, perhaps, to sit a while and reflect; think of family; think of home.

I walk towards this last stopping-point and begin to undo the straps of the harness that locks me to my life-support pulk. I'll take one short rest before the finish. I'll savour the moment. I start to loosen my rucksack.

When I look up, the bench has disappeared.

There is nothing on the ice road but me – frustrated, frozen, alone. How on EARTH did I get to be here?

CHAPTER 1

EARLY YEARS

So, here I am, at the start. My mind is clear although I am a little nervous, as I always am at the outset of a challenge. But sometimes it's worth stepping outside your comfort zone. You never know what talents and abilities you'll find. So here I go. Attempting to go beyond my limits.

You see, I never set out to become an ultra runner. Somebody challenged me to do it, and I accepted. They say fools rush in. So call me a fool. But I tell you what, by rushing in, I have been introduced to a fantastic world of endurance sport – full of amazing people with inspirational and humbling stories.

I'd better start at the beginning and find my flow.

If you stick with this – and I hope you do because perseverance is such a huge part of covering distance – I hope you might find out something about me. I am not so sure about persuading you to do for yourself what I have done. In fact, it may be slightly irresponsible to encourage you to sign up for the 350-mile, non-stop 6633 Arctic Ultra race or the 220km Jungle Marathon because I freely admit that they are not for everyone.

So, what is an ultra? An ultra is anything beyond the 26.2 miles of a marathon. And a multi-stage ultramarathon is when you set out on daily stages day after day. Some are self-sufficient (i.e. carrying everything on your back); some are supported; some are not. Not, therefore, everyone's idea of exercise.

Why, then, have I done them? Well, I hope all will be revealed, but forgive me if I pause here at the very start. As I say, I am clear of mind and ready to go … except, I'm not. You see, I am writing this in the long weeks of preparation for my latest adventure: the Dragon's Back Race; an ultra that goes 200 miles (315 kilometres) down the spine of Wales, from Conwy Castle in the North to Carreg Cennen Castle near the town of Llandeilo in Carmarthenshire. Only 50% will complete it.

Much of my story is about running in far-flung, remote places, but this race is in my homeland and is dear to me on many fronts. The very name of the race, for example. The dragon is not only blessed with a tail and back that perfectly illustrate the ups and downs of the course ahead, but is also one of the national symbols of Wales, a mythical creature, an expression of defiance.

Where was I? The Dragon's Back Race. A distance of 200 miles over five days is not the most extreme, and my homeland, for all its mountainous beauty and secrets, is not Himalayan in height – at least, not in single climbs. But here's the rub. Add together the multitude of climbs along the Dragon's Back, and they come to 15,500 metres of vertical ascent (nearly 51,000 feet), which puts this race in the global top ten of difficulty.

Even so, it's not the physical punishment ahead that makes me hesitate at the start line. I know what I have done before and I know what it takes. I have been here many times and I know in my head that I can do it again, even if it means crawling to the finish line. I once wrote this about myself:

> *'Just to let you know, I'm not tough. I'm not fast. Nor am I strong. I'm just your average runner who completes quite respectable times in races, but I'm no world champion. I'm nobody.'*

I have revised my verdict slightly, having come to understand that I have, if nothing else, a high threshold when it comes to pain and fatigue. It seems, moreover, that even when I am feeling their effects most acutely, they do not induce the anxiety that for most people comes with agony. I press on. It is my thing. It is what *in extremis* my mind tells me – and allows me – to do.

No, the problem is not inside my head. It is my body, or one particular part of me. I must introduce you to my right knee. I have a tear to my cartilage. It's not sufficiently serious to have brought my training to a wincing halt or to have stopped me from uphill-slope torture (it doesn't like downhills much), but exercise causes swelling and, yes, I have to admit it, brings a certain degree of discomfort. I am a little worried, which is different from feeling nervous before a race. I know the difference. I know the difference between needing to rest the body and an injury that forces the body to rest.

When I approached the start line for the Jungle Marathon, for example, I was completely new to this world of the ultra and utterly out of my comfort zone in an Amazonian setting that struck me as unrelentingly hostile. I looked at all the other runners – at their body shapes and their equipment – and felt inadequate. Those were worries and a lack of confidence, that I have learned through preparation and repetition and experience, to overcome.

It wasn't always the case, but now I embrace nerves, that fluttering sense of anticipation that vanishes on the signal to go, as if it had never been there. To be nagged, however, by doubt and by the ache in this old swollen patched-up knee of mine is a less welcome sensation.

Shall I stop? Or rather, shall I not start? No. I can't begin here in Chapter 1 with a no-show. It may turn out to be a slow show, but whatever happens on the Dragon's Back, I shall let you know.

My knee is a big part of my story. We have history and, in an odd kind of way, if it hadn't been for this bit of my leg I might never have discovered long-distance running. Through early childhood and all my days at school, it left me well alone. I was brought up in Gowerton, which is in the hinterland of the Gower Peninsula to the west of the city of Swansea. To be more precise, we lived as a Welsh-speaking family in a house on the road to the village of Three Crosses. Ask anyone round there and they'll know where I mean.

Swansea has its own bay and the broad sweep of the South Wales coast from Aberavon to Mumbles is not without majesty on a fine day. To the east, the Port Talbot steelworks dominate the skyline. Swansea is an older centre of metal-making. Once, tinplate and copper poured from the works that stretched up the banks of the rivers – the Neath, Tawe and Afan – that feed into Swansea Bay. It's not until you have rounded Mumbles Head that Swansea Bay becomes Gower and the coastline and water quality change dramatically. The coves and beaches of the peninsula, from Caswell and Langland through Oxwich, vie with each other for splendour until they all yield before the incomparable Rhossili and Worms Head. It is a wonderful natural playground for an adventurous child – ready-made, that is, for me. I went from crawling to running with barely a step taken at walking pace. As soon as my balance allowed, I took to my bicycle. I ran, I cycled; I spent whole days lost among the sand dunes of Horton and Llanmadoc.

My parents, Richard and Ceridwen – or Ceri for short, were my pathfinders when Dad's work as a doctor in Gowerton and Mam's work as a school nurse allowed. A sense of adventure and love of sport seemed to run in our family on all sides.

My mother, Ceridwen, had been a very good tennis and squash player, and my early memories are of being her No.1 Fan Club and watching her compete in local squash tournaments, although she sacrificed her sporting activities when she became my taxi service, taking me from orchestra to athletics, from singing to swimming. Every night there was something and she was instrumental in supporting me and my brother Roger.

Next to our house is a slope leading uphill for about 400 metres to the farm. She would be in our garden and would call out the numbers of my hill-repeats as I went up and down on my training runs. I would moan and groan, and she would answer, 'You can give up now', but in the next breath she would remind me that if I wanted to succeed as a runner, then I needed to put in the hours and hard graft.

My parents took us further afield, too. I have clear memories of our old white Saab, with the caravan hitched to the back, my mother sitting in the front buried beneath unfurled maps of Europe, and Roger and I fighting for space on the back seat.

The Morgans were off on holiday. On an adventure, either with our close extended family or just the four of us. Wherever the road took us. Oh, the stories I could tell – the punctures, the getting lost. I remember one early morning, lost and parked up in the Saab, with our caravan and maps … in the middle of the Pope's Palace in Avignon, France. Could you imagine if he had walked out to point us in the right direction?!

My father came to running late, but he soon took to it with a passion, setting off on regular outings around the village – a doctor on a different type of rounds, with me alongside him. I cherished those moments when Dad would come in from work, change and we'd be back out again, pounding the tarmac and then turning into the surrounding countryside. There was often no talking at all. We'd just run, listening to the rhythm of our hearts, our breathing.

Age has caught up a bit with Mam and Dad. But, well into their seventies, they are reluctant to give up. Dad swims regulary, has rediscovered his bike and keeps me company when I go running. Mam, a keen skier, has now hung up her boots, but Dad can still keep up with us on the more challenging runs; a sign perhaps that if I have this capacity to keep going, to cut through pain barriers, it has come down the family line. What so many of my bloodline have given me is my family-support-group of genes, it seems. Even Dad, though, cannot ignore the reality that his knees are no longer what they were. It looks as if we share that, too.

My parents have been my rock and my inspiration. If Mam had to take a less active part in my sport, she was just as important and just as present. She was a theatre sister in the operating theatres during her working life, and gave up a successful career to stay at home to raise the family and to support my father's job. There were no locums or out of hours services then. She returned to work when I was ten and my brother eight years old.

She became a travelling companion on my trails: not in body, but inside my head; a supplier of little sayings that over many years have kept me going. I remember struggling through one particular training phase for a long distance race, in which I felt increasingly dejected by so much of what I was doing. Such doubts about the slog of it all are part of the process. I always knew these clouds were lurking, but being forewarned didn't make it any easier to fend them off when they did arrive. They did not launch an assault, but crept up on me, worming their way into my thoughts. I was growing more and more despondent and less and less able to motivate myself.

And then I heard the voice of my mother: 'Lowri, I can already see you crossing the finish line and getting that reward you've dreamed of for so long. Remind yourself how hard you have worked for this goal. All those hours. Don't let them count for nothing. You've got it. You will do it.' And those last few words became the beat to which I carried on training. 'You've got it. You WILL do it.'

I loved running cross-country at school, but the first competitive race I remember entering was over a shorter distance on the track. I must have been about eleven. The distance was the schools' county championship 1500 metres and I finished in second place. The coach told my parents I had some good running skills and technique, and asked if I would be interested in joining the local athletics club, the Swansea Harriers.

I wasn't sure. I knew I wasn't the quickest and suspected I never would be. I had to judge myself against a girl called Claire, who hardly trained, but who flowed over both track and cross-country with an entirely natural grace. I was the grafter who lost all form in my arms and legs when I grew tired. I'd stagger over the finish line and fall to the ground, panting and heaving. Claire, the winner, would stroll up, barely out of breath to offer a hand to pick me up.

I was the plodder. I never won but it made me keep going. I had a goal to chase. And I did make it to senior county and then national level with the school. And I did manage, over the years, to win races. How many times had my mother repeated out loud or in my head the virtues that a plodder brings to, well, just about everything in life? If they're willing to work hard, persevere, if they are determined enough, then the plodders do get to the finishing line, in the end. They can reach their potential. Nevertheless, I knew that whatever it was that gave me this doggedness would not help me reach the stars.

Besides, I had other interests – other 'talents', I suppose – that might serve me better if I continued to be drawn towards performing under the bright lights. As hard as I trained as a runner, I was already doing more in my quest to become a professional singer.

Wales is known as 'the land of song'. In Wales we have many festivals but the *Eisteddfod* is a leading cultural festival, a coming together in celebration of the performing arts.

Some start young. You can perform at the Urdd National Eisteddfod from the age of seven. The Urdd is the junior version of the Eisteddfod Genedlaethol (National), but is arguably the biggest cultural youth festival in Europe, held each year in the last week of May. The venue, traditionally an open field (*Y Maes*) with a large pavilion for the stage, changes each year, alternating between North and South Wales, and invites entries across a huge range of activities: singing, recitation, art, composition, dance and instrumental performance and sport. It is, perhaps above all, competitive. You enter at District *(Cylch)* level, go through to County *(Sir)* and, if successful, end up at the National *(Cenedlaethol)*. There, if the adjudicator places you in the top three, you perform in the pavilion, all shown live on S4C, the Welsh-language television channel.

I was nine when I first entered. Until then, I had sung only at Sunday School at chapel in Gowerton, but Gwen and Eric Jones, exceptional musicians and dear friends of the family, suggested to my parents that I try for the Urdd. My parents were fully on board and I'd like to say my nomination received universal backing, but at my school they weren't overly keen at first. The quotas for the competitions had already been filled. I was a bit of a late-entry headache.

My parents, with the backing of Gwen and Eric, managed to find me a slot in the Girls Under-10 Solo. It was my first ever taste of competition. I won this first District preliminary, went to the County stage, won that. By now I had a local singing teacher, Myra Rees, and several months of hard practice later, won the National title, performing *Darluniau* (Pictures). I sing it to this day.

For someone who has suffered from nerves during big moments in my life, I don't remember suffering from any during the first few early rounds. I do remember standing on the stage, with hundreds of eyes looking at me and feeling the trickle of sweat run down from the top of my head to the tip of my toes. However, I took it all in my stride, relished the challenge, and the buzz after finishing the song ... well, I remember it like yesterday.

I also remember the journey home. The winning feeling. The way Roger and I laughed and celebrated in the back of the Saab whilst our parents sat proudly in the front. I felt such certainty there and then. I knew what I wanted to do. I wanted to sing and act. I wanted to perform. I had felt the blood rushing through my veins. I had felt alive on stage. The feeling did not vanish. With the help of another teacher, Jennifer Evans Clarke, I went on to win more competitions. I sang (soprano) in the National Youth Choir of Wales. I also played the viola, violin, piano and harp. I performed with the Welsh Philharmonic Orchestra of Wales. Yes, music was my way ahead.

If those words come out with a certain emphasis on how sure I was about my future back then, I am aware that I am writing this as an ultra runner, not a virtuoso musician.

You see, my happiness back then on my beautiful Gower, in our beloved Saab, with my singing successes and that winning feeling, is not the whole picture.

And here's another thing. It's not easy to put my finger on what precisely it was that disturbed my perfectly happy upbringing. If those long days among the dunes of Rhossili and Llanmadoc – or those moments of pure delight on the way back from Aberavon – were the bright uplands of my youth, I feel it would help if I could say: 'Right then, by way of contrast, here are the gloomy valleys of my other childhood.' Black and white, yin and yang. That would be clear. To run and run, day after day, hints at a certain inclination towards the extremes of the emotional spectrum and it is absolutely true that in the course of doing what I do, I experience highs and lows that are poles apart. But there is only a vague uneasiness when it comes to finding the counterweight, the downside to my early years.

It is there, though. During this period, the girls in my class were, obviously and naturally, advancing toward adolescence, and peer friendships started to become very important in our social and emotional development. I felt it at junior school – a sense of not quite belonging, or at least of not quite fitting into a dominant group. We were a small, close class and I was somehow surplus to the requirements of the girls who gathered to play their games at break-time. One girl I was friendly with didn't worry what the others thought and positively relished not being attached to a girl-gang. In fact, her attitude and sporting skills made her the perfect person to join the boys' cricket and football team and she became their prized player.

I, on the other hand, felt wary about my station in school life. Besides, I had two left feet when it came to football and often ended up at break-time playing Pac-Man on our school's Acorn Electron computer or playing hair design with a boy from our class. He ended up as a successful model. I'd like to think I helped him on his way.

Many of my schoolmates and I are still good friends and we meet up regularly. Despite my doubts, I got on with everyone. But there were two girls in particular who bothered me at junior school. Maybe they simply didn't like me much. But as a nine-year-old, that was hard to accept.

I wasn't alienated, as such, but today we might call their behaviour passive aggressive. To the outside world it wasn't obvious but to me, I noticed and felt it. They didn't bully me physically but they were the pack-leaders; they were more developed, taller, less naive, more mature than me and they built an exclusion zone around their circle. We all went to the same parties but I was always the last to be asked or to be picked for a team. Sounds petty but as a young girl finding her feet in adolescence, these things did hurt. They were clever enough never to be explicitly hostile, but that somehow made their rejection of me all the more troubling – if only because I spent a lot of time asking myself if it wasn't just all inside my head.

I had many things going on in my life – I had friends outside of school too and it didn't bother me on a daily basis so didn't feel the need to tell my parents about it until they discovered a little diary I'd been compiling and hiding in my bedroom. It was written in a code I'd invented and some of the contents were to do with whom I did like and whom I didn't. Mam and Dad coaxed an explanation out of me and said that perhaps they should come to school to discuss my situation, but I asked them not to. I would sort it out. I would face both girls myself.

There was no showdown. No reducing of the two girls to tears, no begging by them for forgiveness. Not that I wanted that. I just wanted them to know that I was stronger than they thought.

I was genuinely building up for my big moment when the two simply left for another school. My disappointment in them remained unspoken.

I remember the girls to this day. I suppose they had a lasting effect on me. I have certainly developed an acute intolerance towards bullying in any shape or form, but I think I have been able to turn what happened to my advantage. Rejection focused my mind and made me stronger. We had avoided a confrontation, but I felt more prepared to face whatever came next.

The next challenge – the next 'whatever' – wasn't far away.

I must return to the subject of nerves. I know I'm supposed to be steering you towards my knee and me, but I have to flush these nerves out of my system. Nowadays, I can embrace nervousness on the start line. I almost crave butterflies in the stomach, as evidence that the race I am about to run is truly going to put me to the test, that it's worth the effort, and that I am ready to take on whatever it is that's about to be thrown at me.

The nerves of my youth, however, were something else. They were unpredictable for a start. I knew they would strike, because they often did, but their effect varied in a more unsettling way. Sometimes, when I was about to sing or play an instrument, I could haul myself through them and soon be transported by the music into a place beyond fear. On other occasions, though, they seized me and would not let go. I'd forget words, or my voice would tremble. Sweat would trickle down my face, my back. On too many stages and before too many people, I could not perform. Stage fright is a terrifying thing. You stand there, with hundreds of eyes looking at you and the words, music or voice fail you and those seconds of complete emptiness, the mind blank, feel like hours.

Such times used to haunt me. As a teenager I would shudder at the memory of each episode. I had worked so hard and all for nothing.

I now live in a world of DNF (Did Not Finish) or DSQ (Disqualified), but they are nothing compared with those times of FTD. Failed To Deliver. And yet, in adulthood the FTDs' edge has grown less jagged. I look back on them and say: 'Yes, you worked hard, and, sure, it was a disappointment. So, we'd better work harder still next time.' My words, not my mother's. I would go home and cry from frustration. But I'd wake up again the following day, or maybe the following week – dependent on how long my dark mood would last – and say, 'OK, let's go again. I'm ready to give it one more go.'

Over the years, I have taught myself to accept those nerves, to see them as a good thing. I know it's said often and by others far more qualified than me, but facing your fears and doing it as publicly as singing on a stage or running a marathon is a fast way to grow in a way you never dreamed possible ... but it also does come with a risk of failing. 'But if we never fail in life, how can we appreciate the sweet taste of success?' is something I wish I had learnt earlier in my life.

Many top athletes tell tales from their youth, of moments when something went badly wrong. And how the failure only gave them extra determination. Failure can be a powerful fuel. But those athletes are defined by their successes, not their failures. Successes stick with you. Failures eventually fall away.

I am no World or Olympic champion but in my case, failure was nothing more than a snag in the warm blanket of my childhood, and I know I used both that experience of being shut out at school and also my later determination to work my way through stage fright to help me become the woman I am today.

The decision to drive myself harder certainly had an effect on me at senior school, Ysgol Gyfun Gŵyr in Gowerton. I had not always excelled when it came to exams – probably those wretched nerves – but I now pushed myself, almost out of sight of my teachers, unrelentingly. I was the plodder on a mission. When I received my GCSE grades (8As and 2Bs), I think my school had a pleasant surprise. I was ecstatic.

When it came to my A levels, hard work was going to conquer all, especially those nerves. I was still going to make a life for myself in musical theatre and I was fortunate to have a great mentor – my godfather, my mother's brother John Rhys Thomas. Uncle John provided inspiration in my early years. In his early professional life, John was a teacher and TV director, and later a headmaster. But his big passion is the theatre and he is still a successful director/producer. When I set my sights on a future in performing on the stage, I was fortunate enough to have Uncle John monitoring my preparations. Music and Drama spoke for themselves and if I could add French to my English and Welsh, well, to be trilingual would be pretty useful, surely. Music, Drama and French, then. In my first year of A levels I was still running, but in the serious matter of what I was going to do in life after school, it was the performing arts all the way. At the age of 17, I was disappointed to have received a low grade for a project. I overheard the teacher talking to another: 'Well, if she wants higher grades, then she needs to work harder.' So I did. I decided to stop racing and concentrate on my course work and singing.

Two A grades and a B later, I was going to Cardiff University to study Music. There, all mapped out. Until, finally, we come to the knee.

CHAPTER 2

THE KNEE

I arrived in Cardiff with a determination to give university life my all, plus some more. I went from stall to stall during Freshers' Week, signing up for the Athletics club, the Ski club, Climbing, Music, Choir, Orchestra. All my passions were there to be pursued and I enrolled in each and every one of them.

I was leaving this bazaar of clubs and societies when I bumped into my good friends Sarah and Bethan, who had been ahead of me at school but whom I knew well from our time together in the national track team. They were playing a different sport now.

'Come and play rugby,' they said.

Now, I knew about rugby as a spectator, having often been taken by my father to watch his beloved Swansea at St Helen's. My brother Roger was a very good player and I'd seen a lot of him in action. I was a runner, though, doing my own thing. I wasn't sure I was cut out for team sport. I had played netball and hockey at school but wasn't very good. All that dependency on others and having to curtail your individual instincts for the good of the collective – it scared me a little.

I waved my collection of fliers and forms at them. 'Look at all this,' I said. 'I'm fully booked.'

'You remember Cerys Matthews?' I nodded. Cerys and I, our siblings, our families all knew each other. 'Well, she's gone off to become a rock star.'

It was true. She had both left and she had made it. Cerys's band Catatonia were to be massive in the 1990s and she is still successfully writing songs and books, making music, presenting on the radio and television. But back in the early season of 1992, her sudden departure left the Cardiff University Women's Rugby Club in the lurch.

'So, we're a winger down. Come on, Lowri. You're a runner … and you'll love it … plus you'll be helping us out … pleeease.'

'No way,' I quickly insisted.

'The social side is brilliant.'

I wavered.

'OK then. One game. Only ONE game,' I promised them. I knew there were subtleties and complex systems to master but they spared me: 'Catch the ball,' said coach Stevie with a smile, 'and run. And if you cross that white line there, put the ball down.'

We played and we won. Away at Aberystwyth. I scored a try.

Coach Stevie RH was well respected and very popular within the university's rugby community. He approached me after the match. 'You're a natural,' he said. 'You're not a winger, mind. We'll put you in the centre next time.'

'Next time?'

'Oh yes.'

And, of course, I was lured back for more. On our way back home to Cardiff, we laughed and sang as we celebrated our victory. The whole experience was such good fun. I knew straight away that these girls would be my friends for the next few years of uni life.

I loved playing the game and belonging. The camaraderie of the rugby club was something I hadn't experienced before. I would turn up to the Music Department, a soprano with a pair of black eyes, and my lovely voice tutor John Hugh Thomas would exclaim in horror: 'What on earth has happened?' Instead of practising for hours in the music room, I was practising my rugby skills on the pitch, but I didn't want to disappoint John Hugh and just could not tell him the truth. 'I walked into a door,' I'd mumble. Sopranos surely weren't supposed to play rugby. But he knew. He always knew.

Five months after being persuaded to start from scratch, I found myself playing for Welsh Universities and Wales Students as a centre. A few had mentioned that if I carried on training hard, there'd be a chance I could make it into the senior side too. Now that would be amazing, I thought.

Around the same time, the 1st XV were ready to face the best university team of that time, Loughborough, and I was picked to play. It was the semi-final of the British Universities Cup. We were 80 minutes away from a grand final.

The game was a few minutes old when I went into a ruck. What happened next remains a little sketchy, but I remember hearing the sound of cardboard being ripped apart. I remember other players hearing it, too; standing up; recoiling. Initially, I didn't know where the noise had come from but I soon realised that it had come from my knee. I remember no pain then, but I know I shouted something like, 'It's me,' as I collapsed. I put both hands over my knee. Compression. Squeeze tight and everything will be all right.

I hobbled off with an apology to my team. 'Sorry but don't worry, girls. Give me five minutes and I'll be back on the pitch. I won't let you down.'

Nobody said anything, but I did wonder why they looked at me in amazement as I stood on the sideline. I was offered a pair of borrowed crutches to watch the remainder of the game. I was advised that perhaps I should have the injury assessed in hospital. 'Oh no,' I said defiantly. 'I'll soon be better with some magic sponge and a few painkillers.'

I ended up that night in Birmingham hospital. I rolled my eyes in the waiting room, frustrated that I was not with my friends and we were wasting the doctors' and nurses' time. Soon after, they were telling me that I should have immediate surgery on my broken bones, my torn anterior cruciate ligament and my cartilage.

Saying I was in a bit of a shock would be an understatement!

These were the days before universal mobile phones. I needed to speak urgently with the medics in my family. I desperately needed to hear their voices, but I couldn't track down my father or my mother. I tried to phone my Dad's sister and my godmother Aunty Helen and her husband Uncle Mike who lived close by. But no answer there. Anybody would do. I had to speak to someone. I couldn't find anyone, not even my brother, who was away at school. 'You need to have an emergency operation,' the consultant said. 'I just want to go home,' kept repeating itself inside my head. 'I just want to go home,' I told the Birmingham doctors.

Eventually my parents rang back. It was arranged that I be transferred to Morriston Hospital in Swansea.

Relief. I'd be fine now. I'd be back playing rugby in no time. I lay in my hospital bed and waved positively to my parents and smiled as I was wheeled down the corridor of my local hospital. I was on my way to theatre for a three-hour operation. 'I'll be OK,' I said. 'Don't worry about me. I'll be up and about in no time.'

When I came to, hours later, my first words to the nurse, who happened to know my family, were: 'Don't tell my parents where I am. They'll be worried sick.' I drew her a little closer to me and in my post-operation drunken state, slurred. 'Don't tell them that I'll be back playing just as soon as I can.'

That was the groggy reawakening. The rude one came with the pain. I had thought that once the joint was cleaned out, everything reset and all the screws in place, I'd quickly be on the mend. Instead, once the anaesthetic disappeared, it was excruciating. Almost as demoralising as the pain was the sight of this bloated (swollen wouldn't begin to describe it) thing sticking out, elevated and useless, before me.

I'd never felt so crushed. My solid bones had been reduced to fragments and now my dreams of moving into the Wales Women's rugby team were going the same way.

I did not allow anyone outside my close family in. I turned icy: 'Don't bother coming to see me. I'll be out soon enough.' They politely kept their distance. I shared a ward with other patients with broken joints and, though I cried when I was on my own and felt no one was watching or listening, I refused to show my frustration and anger in front of others. After a few weeks, I was discharged. In the wheelchair, my mother pushed me a certain distance down the hospital corridors but I soon took over, propelling myself as quickly as I could out of that place.

Looking back, I appreciate everything they did for me at Morriston. Without them, I would not have been able even to contemplate running the absurd distances of later years, but at the time of my release – that was how I saw it – I couldn't leave fast enough.

The weeks and months of spring and summer passed and my mood did not lift. When in the company of friends, I was the entertainer. But in front of family or when on my own, I was woolly of thought, short-tempered and prone to weeping. You can never judge a book by its cover. I was a prime example of that. I hid behind this chatty, full of life personality. But behind closed doors, I was different. My family walked on eggshells around me. And yet, even in these dark days, a sort of process began.

Injuries for an athlete are obviously horrible, but they are equally inevitable. Recovering from them is a test we have to face. First of all, I reconfigured the timescale of this recovery, reluctantly accepting that it was going to be a long-haul business. And because the end was so distant, I set myself smaller goals, destinations I could visualise myself reaching. One day this would manifest itself as 'one step at a time' on a wilderness of frozen tundra, but as I lay at home on Gower with my frustration and bitterness, I had to start even smaller.

'I'm going to get out of this sofa.' It took a few failures – a few more tears and shouts – but after a few weeks, it was a destination reached. Next goal: to be out of the cast. Then I could set the goal of throwing away the crutches.

The removal of the ten-week-old cast was a huge deal in the mind of a goal-setter. This liberation would be a real game changer. Free of my body armour, I told myself I would be able to make literal strides towards a full recovery.

How wrong I was! The trouble was, when the cast was removed, my leg emerged as rigid as it had been when encased. It was a real shock to find I could flex it no more than mere millimetres. I had been so looking forward to getting rid of the cast, but instead it was to be another lesson in accepting the setback, of digging in and being patient and starting all over again with the process of setting goals. It's funny because in my almost obsessional planning of my rehab by tiny steps, I never did lose sight of the end goal: to play rugby again.

The micro and the macro, living together in the mind of a player barely on the road to recovery.

With a view to putting this unbending knee to work, I told the nurse on the day of the cast's removal that I intended to start pool-work immediately and had brought my swimming kit with me. 'Can I start training?' I asked enthusiastically. As in, that very evening. She laughed and told my surgeon, who had come in to see the unveiled joint, 'This one's planning on going swimming tonight.'

Mr Hoddinott, who was the son of the Welsh composer Alun Hoddinott, smiled too. 'Well,' he said, 'if Lowri wants to start training, she can.' He then paused. 'But perhaps I need to let you know that you've suffered a significant injury to your knee, to the extent that you may have to temper your plans to play rugby for Wales. To be frank, there is a possibility that you may never be able to run at full tilt again.'

I reacted with an instruction to my Dad to drive me to the swimming pool. For years, my parents would take me to the local swimming club at 6.30am to train. With all the years of training and racing in the pool, I was a strong swimmer but this time I struggled to even reach the edge of the pool. Once immersed, I thought, the water together with my determination would miraculously make my knee move just a tiny bit.

Again, disappointment. The knee didn't move. And over the many months that followed I began to suspect that Mr Hoddinott's more candid appraisal might be closer to the truth than my hopes. Maybe he was right and I would not be able to run properly again.

As much physio as I did, however punishingly I went about my exercises, the knee remained stubbornly unwilling to bend. I'm not the first athlete to suffer the blues that go with inactivity. The aerobic high of exercise became a faded memory. The overall sense of well-being that accompanies general fitness slid away. I tried to stay away from fellow athletes. Insecurity and introspection took their place. I curled up far too often on the sofa and did nothing.

It wasn't all bleak. I emerged sometimes and proved to be quite the social animal. I was lucky. I had a great gang of close friends, my best friends, who never allowed me to wallow in self-pity for too long. They'd encourage me out to support my peers, male and female, playing rugby and if there weren't lifts in the vicinity, they'd carry me on their backs from one destination to another. There were always fellow students looking for a night out and I found myself downing beer with the same enthusiasm I had once reserved for training. I can't say I'd have stayed in my 'pity party' for long, but it was perhaps just as well that I soon snapped myself out of it. Or rather, I was snapped out of it by something I saw. My light bulb moment.

I'm not sure I was in the full curled-up position on the sofa at home, but it was definitely from there that I watched the London Marathon of 1993. I'd cried a lot of tears for myself and now they flowed again – except they weren't for me, but for the runners. And not so much for these participants in the 26-mile race as they set off cheerily, often in costume, often not very quickly, but for those much later in the run, beyond the 20-mile mark. Here, struggling against that place in a marathon known as The Wall, all their reasons for doing what they were doing touched a nerve – running for a dying loved one, raising funds for somewhere that offered compassion and different charities. Here were runners putting themselves through a personal ordeal for the good of others. Everyone it seemed had their own personal reason for running the marathon. I found it incredibly moving. And incredibly motivating.

If it took a marathon to get me off this sofa, then so be it. A marathon it would be.

CHAPTER 3

STEPPING INTO THE UNKNOWN

I'm going to inject a little pace. Sometimes you start a race and you're not entirely sure how you're going to feel, but once you're into your stride, you say to yourself: 'Well, I may as well push it along a bit. I'm feeling good.'

I worked on my knee with the inner tube of a bicycle tyre. Pull. Flex, knee, flex. Come on. I made my list of goals: I'm going up the stairs today. OK, halfway today. I'm going to make it to the lamp post 200 steps from the house. I'm going to make it to the path 400 paces away. I went from doing half-dips on my crutches to lifting some weights.

I started to run again. Not far, but I was up and about. And the recovery process developed as a metre turned slowly, very slowly into metres and a mile into miles. My speed increased and my times came down. I had one leg slightly shorter than the other now, but it seemed I could compensate.

I think I may have explained this to Mr Hoddinott, my surgeon, as we met one morning on the country lane that runs between his house and my parents'. He was in his car and I was doing a set of 200-metre uphill striders. It wasn't a pretty sight as I struggled all red-faced and gasping for air, but in my mind, I was back on it.

As he drove down the hill, he saw me before I saw him. I'd like to think it was a professionally satisfying moment for him. He had warned me not to build up my hopes, but here I was, picking up my knees (in my head). In reality it was more a shuffle than the stride of an accomplished runner, but I was running and making plans to run a marathon and that made me happy.

'Good morning,' he said in his polite, calm voice as he came to a stop on this country lane. 'I see you're back running?'

I stood there frozen. Was this a question or a statement, I thought. I didn't say a lot. I physically couldn't. I was exhausted from the session but also I couldn't lie and say, No. I was caught in the act. I wasn't supposed to be running. It wasn't in the plan.

'Oh, I'm just going, Mr Hoddinott, for a slow, very slow shuffle.' I was afraid that he'd warn me against returning too quickly to the sport I loved. It had been 20 months since the accident. Far too soon, I thought he'd say. But he didn't. He smiled. 'Glad to see you're back on your feet,' he said, and off he drove.

I can't say that there weren't days when I felt like giving up and, often, I wouldn't achieve what I had in mind. 'Patience', my parents would remind me.

First, I completed my studies at university, where I also went back to playing rugby. I was now moved into the back row and, suddenly, this new move saw me being selected to play for Wales. I was incredibly proud – standing on rugby pitches singing the Welsh national anthem and representing my country. I loved playing the game then and I love watching – and working on – it now.

I still dreamt about becoming a singer but I needed a year out to get together the funds and scholarships required for further voice training at a music and drama college in London.

So, I worked as a sport development officer. I still played rugby, for Swansea Ladies now, but soon my playing days would come to an end. Alun Wyn Bevan was my new boss and a dear friend, a former rugby referee, a commentator in Welsh on the game and simply one of life's great enthusiasts. He was at the time acting as a sports mentor in the Amman Valley, which runs from the Black Mountain (*Y Mynydd Du*) at the western end of the Brecon Beacons National Park down to the River Loughor between Swansea and Llanelli. Within this dramatic valley lay the seams of the finest anthracite, the coal that is the hardest to ignite but, once burning, gives off the most heat and the least smoke. This anthracite was once the pride of the South Wales Coalfield. This 'steam coal' was once the fuel of choice for the ships of the Royal Navy, the White Star Company and Cunard.

Alun Wyn never stopped thinking of new ways to get those that had stumbled in life – or been slapped down by it – back on their feet. He was also a keen marathon runner. Somehow, he had managed to secure a number of competitor places in the November 1995 New York Marathon and since the Amman had not exactly flattened him in a rush for tickets, he had one spare. He offered it to me. I was 21 years old and was going to run my marathon.

If only it were as simple as saying: 'Well, thank you, Alun. I'd be delighted.' I mean, I was. Obviously. But it wasn't as straightforward as saying yes to this chance to complete a mission I had set for myself and settling into the routine of preparing myself physically for the challenge. Again, obviously, I began to do all that and with a fair degree of discipline. I was starting from scratch. I had increased my mileage to three-mile runs and those sessions were not consistent.

Four months before New York, I found a training plan in a running magazine and followed this Guide To Your First Marathon assiduously. It suggested aiming at ten-minute miles, so that's what I did. My sights were set, my Sony Walkman was full of my favourite tunes and safely tucked into my running pouch, and off I went. I had no GPS watch, but ran to a point I'd roughly calculated for distance and did some sort of mathematics on speed when I reached it. Time was not important, speed did not inspire me. It was all about achieving the goal. I'd give myself a time limit instead of distance and would run out for 15 minutes and back in the same time. Slowly but surely, the time would increase until I'd tell my parents on my Sunday long runs, 'See you in three and a half hours!'

The first session of any marathon plan is often the hardest despite being the shortest in distance and with the least amount of pressure with regards to speed. It's being consistent throughout your training that is the toughest thing of all: I didn't need to be good, or fast, or strong; I just had to go and go often ... And, trust me, somehow over time I built in confidence, in strength, in stamina and soon the 5K I struggled to get round four months ago became my recovery run, the one I popped out to do while the dinner was in the oven.

It was during my marathon training that I was introduced to the runner's high. I'd struggle (and still do) with the first few miles of a run but I found something magical around the five-mile mark. Whether I'm running seven, ten, or 38 miles, something kicks in at mile five. I relax, stop thinking (or obsessing) about every little thing going on in my life. I start to feel the rhythm of the run, my heartbeat, shoes on the pavement, and the music or podcast in my ears. I don't believe in 'easy' miles. Every mile is tough, every mile is earned. But after five, something clicks and I enter that happy place. I am enjoying running. It is that euphoric feeling where my mind is all of a sudden significantly clearer. All of my worries and anxieties start to subside and I feel instantly lighter, mentally and physically. It is almost like feeling sluggish, and then hitting a giant reset button. All my problems, fixed (at least until the next run!).

Here, on the matter of completing the mission, complications arose. I was not risk-averse in any way. As I child I had shrugged off the cuts and bruises that went with being out all day, running slightly wild on the sands of Gower. My parents always inspired my brother Roger and I to grab life with both hands. They encouraged us to make the most of our 'green and blue gym' – they took us swimming, surfing, horse riding, rock climbing and canoeing around the UK and France. From an early age we were taught to approach the world with curiosity, to work hard, to take risks and see what we could achieve. And I have I found that I have achieved more than I ever thought myself capable of thanks to them.

As an adult I had jumped from planes and deep-dived too close to sharks. I had discovered in the face of serious injury that I could be patient and determined. I had played rugby. A question nagged at me, though: what if I didn't make the finish? What if my knee gave up before the finish line? What if I failed? It was as if stage fright was back.

I am going to make a small confession. When it comes to preparation, I'm very diligent, but that wasn't always the case. Two nights before the New York Marathon, my very first, due to be run on Sunday 12 November, 1995, I went out with Alun Wyn Bevan's group of Welsh runners to some Irish bars. Alun didn't drink at all.

The others were responsible. I, somehow, drank for all of us. I could offer a lot of excuses here. I got carried away with the excitement of being in New York. I was jet-lagged. I'm a rubbish drinker. I'm sure you've heard the excuses before. I know there's a long tradition of people from Wales – I'm thinking of Dylan Thomas here – arriving in the Big Apple and getting a little carried away. But it sort of goes with being a poet. It's not the sort of antic a novice marathon runner should be proud of. And I'm not. But it happened and the next day I had to get over it. I had to clear my fuzzy mind of guilt and its ache and concentrate exclusively on my maiden voyage as a marathon runner. Instead, I woke up to discover I'd lost my bag containing my passport, purse, cards, money and my marathon registration papers.

'Let's retrace our steps,' somebody suggested. In the excitement of it all, last night was a bit of a blur.

'I have a feeling,' said Alun, ever the optimist, 'that they'll have been handed in.' Not even he sounded convinced by this hunch.

The day after this Friday of misjudgement, we had to go through registration in a large convention centre. I cut a rather morose figure. How could I register for a race when I couldn't prove who I was? And remember, this was in 1995, everything was registered on paper. Welsh is a great language for swear words. I went through the whole list, all aimed at myself. But with self-flagellation came serendipity. The process of wandering around with no ID, a little dry of mouth, feeling guilty, a bit foolish and very annoyed at myself, meant I had too much on my mind to leave me prey to pre-race nerves. I had been sure that by now, I would be stricken by those old, familiar demons. But I wasn't. I wasn't exactly a model of serenity, but at least I wasn't worrying about fluffing my lines or, more pertinently, feeling my legs turn to jelly within the first mile. If anyone had mentioned the benefits of such a compensation, I'd probably have swung a punch at them. I was not nervous but neither, as I say, was I in a good place.

As I went to register, I meekly explained my situation.

'No, it's Lowri not Lousy.' Although I did feel lousy.

'That's L.O.W.R.I. M.O.R.G.A.N.,' I said hovering over this gigantic file full of runners' details, desperately trying to find my name amongst another 26,752 runners. This was painstakingly slow and it was all my fault.

Suddenly, over the public address system, I heard an American voice booming across the convention arena: 'Is there a LORRY Morgan here? Paging LORRY Morgan …'

Like an eager school child, my hand shot up. 'That's me,' I told no one in particular. My bag had been handed in at the British Consulate General by a Mr Barrymore. I didn't know a Mr Barrymore but it was explained to me that he ran a pub that bore his name right next door to our hotel. The Barrymore. We'd been there the night before. I was awash with gratitude and relief. My faith in the kindness of the human spirit was restored. He invited us all over for some pizza and drinks after the marathon. And we, of course, accepted the kind offer.

Misery gave way to good old-fashioned nervousness about Sunday's race. Nervousness, not nerves. This was the fear I needed; this wasn't the fear that was going to choke the notes in my throat. On the big day, I was ready to go.

It was a bitterly cold morning. I stood there (in a black bin bag to keep me warm) with Alun Pugh, another member of our group; we had decided that we were going to run the marathon together. And off we duly went, with 26.2 pure New York miles to go.

The buzz was incredible. Soon I was running as if I had only a mile to run. Alun gave me a few words of advice. Drink water at every station. Don't drink any sports drink you weren't used to. And pace yourself.

I had been warned – by my friends and in my magazine guide – about the dangers of setting off too quickly. I soon deliberately slowed down and didn't push myself too hard, but I had also been told that the whole exotic occasion, from the excitement of the runners to the non-stop encouragement of the crowd along the way, might sweep me along at a pace I wouldn't be able to sustain. I tried to force myself to shut out all the sights of the city and its sounds. This wasn't about impressing anybody. This was for me. I reeled myself back in a little more. But it was impossible to lock myself away. I couldn't divorce myself entirely from everything going on around me. I was loving it. I felt I belonged.

Overconfidence can lead to trouble. I knew about the marathon's wall. The Wall. The invisible thing that can physically stop you in your tracks. The wall that everybody hits. All those months before, I'd watched from that sofa back home as people ran slap-bang into it in London. I had been so moved by their physical torment and their mental determination to keep going that I had resolved to expose myself to such extremes one day. This day. This very day in New York, where there was no avoiding the posters that were almost an exaltation of this legendary barrier that rises up with about a third of the race to go: 'You can't run through it, but you can run around it.'

There was another one, too: 'Twenty miles is only halfway'. I did not know of this other 40-mile race in New York City, I thought, until I realised that the last 6.2 miles felt like the first 20 miles.

I never hit the wall. I didn't even find it. There was nothing around which I had to force myself. I came to the 20-mile marker and felt good. Of course, I felt tired, but I fought against this familiar fatigue by reminding myself why I had signed up for all this. I pitted my courage against my blisters, my aching soles and battered Vaseline-covered toes and found I was in control. Perhaps it was a signpost to the future, to greater distances ahead. I sort of double-checked that my body really was in sufficiently robust shape to respond – and wasn't playing some kind of hangover joke on me – and turned to Alun and said, 'I'm feeling OK. Would you mind if I go on?'

'You go, Lowri,' Alun said. 'You're looking strong.'

So I decided to increase my tempo. I finished in 11,065th position. My time – 4 hours and 7 minutes – didn't make me a champion by any means. But I felt like a champion when I crossed the finish line. On top of the world.

'So how did it feel?' Alun Wyn asked me.

Joyous. Exhilarating. Scary. Exciting. Emotional. Humbling. Tiring. Riveting. Inspirational. All of this and more was my answer.

My meeting with the wall would have to wait.

CHAPTER 4

DO I LOOK LIKE A RUNNER?

A month after New York, I went backpacking. It was rugby that drove me. I had a plan to play in New Zealand and do some work as a sports development officer. It didn't work out. Because I fell back in love with running. Whenever I arrived in a new city, I could not wait to go for a quick run. It allowed me to see parts of the world I would not normally see and through different eyes: the big forest near the city, the mountains that shadowed a village. I'd run the route of a local race, or explore what happened if I just followed the river. I ran every day during my backpacking months – I just went out and ran on feel. And along the way, I realised that my passion for the longer distances and the goal of finishing had been ignited.

In Australia, I sort of changed tack. I found myself doing new activities and almost before I knew I was so deeply involved, I was phoning my parents to tell them not to worry, but I'd just gained the qualifications in two forms of diving: sky and scuba. And somewhere in between the open sky and deep blue sea I'd been doing a lot of skiing too. I don't remember telling them about being bitten by a shark off Fraser Island until weeks later by fax. That would have worried them. It was only a little nip as reef shark-bites go and didn't stop me from doing any of the wonderful things that were filling my time – and that were preventing me from reaching the rugby fields of New Zealand. By the time I did cross the Tasman Sea, running and extreme sports were my new passion.

I returned to Wales and gained a few extra caps for Wales. By now though running was an integral part of my daily life. Pushing distances became a part of training and every time I pushed beyond my limits, I realised they didn't break, they only bent.

I found myself having to choose between rugby and racing on

weekends and soon I was worrying about getting injured during matches which could stop my chances of competing in a race. With the Women's Rugby World Cup looming I felt that I wasn't dedicated enough mentally to be part of the team and was taking the place of someone who deserved it more than me. Looking back, I don't regret a single minute of playing the game; I had a wonderful time representing my country and my clubs and made lifelong friends.

I have, since New York, run a dozen official marathons. I have also competed in two Half Ironman triathlons, which are one-day events that put a half marathon at the end of a 1.2-mile swim, followed by a 56-mile bike ride. You see how I'm going up in distance?

I didn't personally set out to increase the mileage. I was by now a children's TV presenter and my colleagues, knowing of my love for endurance and extreme sports, invited me to participate in different challenges, during which the cameras would follow me. Would I have done these challenges on my own accord? Yes, I think so, but having the added pressure of knowing that failure would have been a very public affair gave me the extra oomph I needed to train harder.

Anyway, as I was saying, in this quest of mine I started to increase the miles travelled in a day. Were they not enough for me? I suppose I have to say they weren't. Ever onward, then, as the saying goes. Ever further. I am edging closer, you may have guessed already, to multi-stage ultra running, where a marathon on one day may become another the next ... and then another. Or maybe more than a marathon. Sometimes a stage of 26.2 miles is the day of light relief. It's odd that distances that were once impossible slowly became the norm.

The first thing about multi-stage ultra running is that you can't run all the way. The terrain does not always allow it and the human body certainly cannot do it. The management of running, walking, resting, drinking, eating, talking, sleeping and going to the toilet is all-important.

The second thing is that I must pause to put something – me, if you will – into context. Stopping to take stock, as I say, is essential. I need to talk about what I do when I'm not spending hours, days, weeks in training or competing, and how what I do in my work life allows me to have such a life in sport. I am not a professional athlete.

I have a job, the beginning of which is a little difficult to pinpoint. A race has a clearly-defined start. My job does not. For a specific moment, may I take you back then to, let's see, it must have been around 1998, some three years after the New York Marathon?

I was combining a few things. I was working as a waitress at the Oxwich Bay Hotel on Gower and was employed on what was called a 'casual' basis by BBC Wales in Cardiff. I was the general factotum (the dogsbody, really) known as the 'runner' on *Pobol y Cwm* (*People of the Valley*), the Welsh-language television drama series that is the longest-running soap opera made, in any language, by the BBC. Made, that is, by BBC Wales and shown on the Welsh-language channel, S4C (Channel 4 Wales).

But I knew I wanted to perform. I wasn't giving up on that dream. Was it through acting, singing? I wasn't sure and yet, while that deep-rooted feeling had never disappeared, my hopes of becoming a professional singer were slowly drifting away.

I started to realise that I didn't have the attributes to become the singer I wanted to be. Yes, I still wanted to head for those bright lights – but maybe the stage was not the destination any more. Still, I enjoyed performing and that same year and with those ambitions swirling vaguely in my head, I applied for a more full-time job as a wrap-around presenter on S4C. Maybe the bright lights of a studio would be my calling?

For my audition I had to do a one-minute piece-to-camera on a subject of my choice. Performing into a television camera lens was – often still is – a daunting business. We had to say some links to the camera, interview a celebrity and then talk for a minute about whatever we wanted. I was advised by a friend in the business to think of something completely different and make it memorable. I stood there and I gave them a minute – more or less to the second – on standing outside in the rain in a nightclub's long queue. I spoke about the people I saw and the scenarios I had witnessed. I'm not sure where it came from, this little monologue of mine, this sixty-second soliloquy. It was more stand-up than children's audition. Perhaps I thought the best way to disguise fear was to perform as if being in discomfort. Luckily, the producers laughed and I landed the job. I was now a television presenter, set to work on the children's series *Planed Plant* (*Children's Planet*).

Now might be a good moment to insert a 'but'. This was of course a dream come true. I was literally going to work in the bright lights. But – there it is – consider these two sentences: 'You've got strong shoulders,' and 'You don't look like an endurance runner.' Now, bear with me again.

Here's an example of how mixed up things were. After New York I'd stopped drinking. Alcohol was not a part of the new confusion. But I had started 'social' smoking. I don't know what it was … perhaps a bit of peer pressure, something to do while they were all drinking, between filming takes. Perhaps it suppressed my appetite. A long-distance runner and a smoker. Weird.

Growing up, I doubted myself. It may not have been obvious to some but my close family and friends could see it. I often thought I was not good enough. I didn't doubt my ability to work hard, but I questioned if I had what was needed to be successful in singing, in my school work and in running.

When it came to running, it wasn't what my body could do, it was how my body looked. Even though I enjoyed running, and was pretty good at it, I doubted if I'd make it on the world stage amongst other talented female athletes, purely because I wasn't tall, or lean, or naturally 'skinny'. And unfortunately, even as a teenager I believed that in order to be fast, I had to fall under at least one, if not all, of those stereotypes.

Throughout my later teenage years, I started to weigh myself. I would get on the scales every day to compare myself to my friends who ran. I really believed that there was a perfect running body shape, and that body shape was not mine. It took me a long time to convince myself that the perfect running body belongs to anybody who runs.

I had also seen myself on camera during the *Planed Plant*

audition and was surprised at how large I looked. For all that you tell yourself that the television camera always adds a few pounds, it doesn't help if you belong firmly in that category of woman that feels societal pressure to conform to a certain look and body shape. I saw in a survey on a sports channel somewhere that out of a wide range of women athletes who responded to a questionnaire, 80% felt that same pressure. And that was among elite athletes. This is a real issue for women and men of all ages and I, at the age of 26 and having just landed a dream job, still had (and, at certain unwelcome moments, find myself believing that I still have) reason to be worried.

I recently found an old food diary of mine, dating back to when I was 17. I didn't consciously realise it at the time, but even then I did not think that I was light enough to be on the starting line for the track races I'd been entered for. Around that same time, I remember wearing a sleeveless dress in a party and a man saying to me. 'Wow, look at those big shoulders.' I was shocked. They were strong shoulders. Shoulders that had helped me become a competitive runner and swimmer. And despite telling myself that I was of a perfectly adequate weight to line up for a track race, I still began to log my calories and changed what I ate. To be faster, I felt I needed to become thinner.

I still get it today. 'You're much smaller than you are on TV,' and 'How is it you can run long distances when you weigh so much more?' and 'You don't look like an endurance athlete?' are questions and comments I was, and am, often confronted with.

Immediately, I began to doubt myself. And I let those comments and doubts interfere with the celebration of my early sporting achievements.

Such teenage angst shouldn't have been worrying me now. I was a woman in her mid-20s, working and running marathons. I was enjoying life. Except for the fact that I still thought I was overweight. Surely this was no frame of mind in which to launch a new career?

A fortnight into this new life, I went down with a kidney infection, lost a lot of weight extremely quickly, went back to work and saw myself again on television. I looked better. Or I thought I looked better. I'd been ill and still felt poorly, but I looked slim on camera. To keep myself in the shape – the only shape, I felt – that might let me make it in television, I slowly succumbed to an eating disorder. Do you succumb to it? Fall prey to it? Anyway, for a while I – like many women, and runners – was bulimic.

The eating disorder didn't start with any particular decision or notion of commitment. There was no bang of a gun: 'Off you go, then. See you in ten pounds' time.' I didn't binge and purge every day. But it took a hold and a quick fix became a habit. Soon I was in a spiral, weight and mind going up and down together. I kept going because I couldn't lose the pounds where I wanted. My face still looked bloated on screen to me. I had this distorted view of myself, a wish to be better, and it was driven by contempt.

I started training for my second marathon. It was the children's programme, *Planed Plant*, which I was presenting that had asked me to run the marathon. That is, to be filmed in all my distorted glory.

At first, things grew only worse.

But just as I could blame nobody but myself for reducing me to this state, I take the credit for raising me back out of it. I alone had the power to change my attitude. I had seen this with my mother, who had a depression around the time of her menopause. She had dealt with it by asking for help, changing her own perception of herself and moving on with positive thinking and gratitude.

So I challenged that doubt and fear.

If television and marathons were to be yin and yang I would have to eat sensibly and intelligently to survive them. And I did. I do not suffer from an eating disorder now but I recognise certain triggers – the sight of other athletes who look so much stronger, better equipped and, yes, slimmer, than me – and know that I have to handle those triggers with extreme care.

But I also know I have become a runner of long, long distances – and to their story I shall return almost immediately – and I finally understand that when I see myself in the mirror I can take me for what I am. In my twenties, I didn't like what I thought I saw. I'm more at ease with the person who looks back at me now.

Because today I realise I don't need to look different to be considered a runner. I am one. I can run. Uphill. Strong. Fast. I am a runner. I was made for it. My soul feels it; my body knows it; my heart longs for it. These are the thoughts I listen to now.

CHAPTER 5

HOW ABOUT A RUN IN BRAZIL?

I'm going to skip through that second long race of mine, the London Marathon that pulled me out of my eating disorder. Not that I did skip through it, of course. Or through any of the ten that followed. My best time for a marathon is 3 hours 8 minutes, which is good but not good enough for a chapter. I shall also push on through my triathlon years when I smoked during my Ironman training; I quit when I realised, frustratingly, how much more I could achieve if I gave up the nicotine. I must force the pace a little here.

I want to linger, however, on the other half of my life in the first years of the twenty-first century. The job in television.

As in all things, including running, the more you do the more confident you become. The better you become. Broadcasting in general is a wonderfully insecure business. I am lucky to have worked with some wonderful colleagues, although I have, like many in the world of media, had some gloriously volatile moments. I have had contracts come and go, have walked in to an office only to be asked to leave again, had my contract end and, an hour later, been asked to front the same live programme the following evening. But I love being a part of the industry, and I came into it with my eyes wide open. It's never nice though, but the more I got knocked down, the stronger I became at building myself back up. I have in fact faced far more testing demons in my life. There are people out there who have faced and are facing far greater challenges than me. I have a choice. Many don't.

I have ended up working in a tough industry which has given me the chance to travel, to meet remarkable people and to have learnt about this incredible world … and myself. And if I had my time again,

I would not change a thing. I am here today because of my past. If I have come to understand that I am compelled to go to extremes in order to discover something about my worth, my resolve, my fears, then television has played its part.

One example. After two years of grafting, in 1999 I moved from presenting the wraparound service *Planed Plant,* made in Cardiff, to another children's programme, *Uned 5 (Unit 5),* made in Caernarfon at the opposite end of Wales. It was a youth/children's magazine show; it had its comparisons with the BBC's *Blue Peter* to name one. I was going through a blonde phase with a black streak. It wasn't what I wanted, but the hairdresser for the show thought it would be great. If you saw the photos now, I don't think you'd agree. Yes, I know what you're thinking and I too ask myself why on earth I agreed to this particular hairstyle. I've never been a trendsetter and in fact this style on me was more trend-ender than trendsetter. But my hair and looks at the time were not my priority.

The commissioner told me I was going onto *Uned 5* for no more than 'four weeks max, Lowri. Promise.'

I drove four hours up from home, turned up to the new office with a car full of belongings and nowhere to stay. Luckily, a new colleague offered a room and we became the best of friends. Four weeks later, I was asked to stay for another four months. Then another year. Before I knew it, I had been living in Caernarfon for over three years. The three and a half years in such spectacular locations – Snowdonia and the sea were always within touching distance – passed very happily. I made lifelong friends, had fantastic opportunities in and outside of after work. I would spend hours and days climbing, bouldering and running in the beautiful Snowdonia mountain ranges, often after work to catch the sunset from Snowdon or Crib Goch.

Because of my love for adrenaline sport, the job gave me the opportunity to try out different adventurous activities; to kite surf, to wreck dive and swim with sharks, to race Ironman competitions, to jump out of planes, to explore. Together, my colleagues and I presented four hours a week of live TV – a great learning curve for me – but in 2003 my contract came to an end and I was preparing to go home. I was a few months away from my 30th birthday and it was time for me to leave children's TV. I was sad to go but knew it was time to move on. Before I did, I was offered 'one last special', as it was put to me.

'Which one this time?' I said, thinking there couldn't be any more outdoor activities or adventures left in Wales, or the world for that matter, that I hadn't been filmed doing. 'And which way?' I'd been up into the sky, over mountains and round and round racetracks.

'Down,' they said. 'To see the Titanic.'

Do you know, embarrassingly, for a short while I wasn't that enthusiastic about going down to the bottom of the Atlantic Ocean. Not because I had lost my sense of adventure, not because I was ungrateful, but because I didn't think I could sit still in the tiny space of a submersible for 12 hours knowing that I was dropping to that depth – 12,500ft (3.8km), down into the abyss. But I agreed and committed to doing some research, and during those nine months of research, the more I found out, the more I was hooked. I read about life onboard; the history of that booming era; I read stories about the people who travelled on this magnificent ship. Researching the ship became an integral part of my life – I read something relevant to the Titanic every day.

As a musician myself, one of the most enduring and poignant of Titanic's stories for me is that of musicians Wallace Hartley, John Clarke, Percy Taylor, Georges Krins, Theodore Brailey (the quintet), and John Hume, Roger Bricoux, and John Woodward (the trio). The quintet typically played in the first and second class reception halls at lunch and dinner, while the trio played outside the à la carte restaurant for first class passengers. Although each had a different reason for accepting the contract to serve on Titanic, all hoped to increase their fortune with passenger tips. To qualify for this job, all had to be excellent musicians with the capability of playing every song in the White Star Line Song Book – some 300 tunes ranging from ragtime to classical to hymns. They also had to be polite and engaging to appeal to their clientele. And yet when they realised their horrible fate, all eight joined together to play – something they never did – to offer comfort to passengers and crew. John 'Jock' Hume, with irrepressible spirit, is reported to have said to Violet Jessop whom he passed on the stairs: 'Just going to give them a tune to cheer things up a bit!'

The more I learnt, the more emotional I got. What they all went through. And soon I was aware of how privileged and honoured I was, to be about to become part of a very small group of people on the planet to have visited the wreck of RMS Titanic ...

There was the little matter of surviving pressure 377 times greater than atmospheric pressure at sea level. This is where the Russians came in. Little Welsh-speaking *Uned 5* were going to sea and into the deep courtesy of Research Vessel Akademik Mstislav Keldysh and the submersibles (to be more precise, the self-propelled Deep Submergence Vehicles – you see, I had, after all, done my research), MIR I and MIR II. From this very same RV Keldysh and its two MIRs, film director James Cameron would shoot the underwater scenes for his Oscar-winning motion picture, *Titanic*. I hasten to add that he wasn't there with us (although we did cross paths literally as his expedition crossed over from ours). There wouldn't have been room for him anyway, not with *Uned 5* on board. Sorry Hollywood, Caernarfon coming through. Well, *Uned 1* really. There were three of us on board (myself, a director and a cameraman) but for our shoot underwater, I would be on my own down there, at the controls of five small cameras. Even so ... maybe not at the same time, but James Cameron and Lowri Morgan, fellow directors of the Titanic, eh?

I was so busy operating those cameras, writing notes and thinking of things to say in my fireproof suit, that I was oblivious to danger. There were so many things that could go wrong at this depth. Snagging on the wreck is one; fire in the cabin is another and of course flooding. The pressure at the wreck site is a tremendous 6,000 pounds per square inch. The only protection we would have is the MIR's thick, nickel steel sphere. If something were to go wrong with the sphere then it's safe to say that things are pretty final.

There weren't any remote controls, no digital controls, no micro action camera, no memory cards as we have today. Instead, I had to check the tapes, change tape after tape in all the four cameras placed around the submersible, label them, and make certain they all had batteries.

It took us two and a half hours to reach the sea bed, travelling at around 100ft a minute but time passed quickly as the MIR was so smooth.

Seeing the sea floor coming up at you is like landing on the surface of the moon, nothing around except the flat sand and the occasional starfish and rocks that disappear into the blackness of the dark ocean. However, I was surprised at the amount of life there was. Over the century, different species of corals, anemones, crabs and fish have colonised the wreck. It was fascinating down in the midnight zone. And something darker. I know it sounds a bit silly – we are constantly teased about turning the flimsiest Welsh connection into the tightest link ever forged between Wales and the world – but among the first things I saw on the sea bed were lumps of coal. Massive rocks of coal. It filled our seven-inch porthole windows. The White Star Company bought its fuel – 6,611 tons of steam coal for the Titanic's ill-fated maiden voyage – from the Lewis Merthyr Consolidated Collieries. Welsh anthracite.

And then I saw her. I turned to the camera and said, 'Nothing I say here, no photo or video I take, can describe the sight of seeing Titanic for the first time with my own eyes.' It was quite simply the most amazing thing I had ever seen. We edged closer to the wreck itself. It was like being on an emotional rollercoaster. On the one hand you couldn't stop being excited as you saw this magnificent ship lying there in front of you, but on the other, you felt a sense of guilt for being excited. This was a graveyard for 1,517 people after all. And I knew it should be treated as such.

It was the details more than the great hulk of the ship that moved me: ceramic tiles, for example. But it was seeing a child's boot and children's toys that really got to me. Porcelain dolls and soft toys – a teddy bear, two and a half miles down in the pitch blackness of the bottom of the ocean – lit up for a moment by the light of a passing Russian mini-sub, captured for Welsh television and left where they had lain for a hundred years. A first class plate lying next to a third class plate. The irony.

It was almost like space opened up. The current had kept the floor clean of build up so you could clearly see the debris on the bed. I was completely overwhelmed. After waiting for so long, I was able to actually be in front of the shipwreck itself. It took us six hours to go around the whole ship, which is gradually being eaten away by micro-organisms. It's slowly disappearing. And after nine hours in the MIR, Titanic disappeared from my eyesight as we made our two-and-a-half-hour journey back up to the Keldysh. It was an experience I shall never forget.

I moved from North Wales back to the south, and into a flat in Caswell, on Gower. I freelanced for a few months: went diving in America for a holiday show, presented a few one-offs (including a documentary following my journey to the Caribbean to find the Welsh buccaneer Sir Henry Morgan's Seventeenth Century ship) and I also worked one day a week as a researcher on a rugby programme. But I soon realised that there was nothing consistent for me to get my teeth into. It dawned on me that if the TV companies didn't come to me, then it was up to me to go to them and to come up with programme ideas.

I wrote a series idea which I felt 'suited' me; a children's series that showcased outdoor activities. I'd go along and try different sporting events with the children – kite surfing, coasteering, surfing, mountain biking, trail running, sea swimming, canoeing, climbing, go karting, etc. I knocked on a few company doors but nobody wanted the idea, until I knocked on a certain executive producer's door. Dafydd Rhys had a TV company called POP 1. He liked the idea and said he'd take it on and offer it to the commissioning editor in S4C. It was rejected. but he offered me a job.

For my new work, I had to go a little further away, off Gower over the River Loughor to Llanelli. And here starts my ultra running story.

When I joined POP 1 TV, I was initially there as a cover for a friend on maternity leave, which meant I didn't take it for granted. But I enjoyed. I did a series based on looking after other people's pets for a week. I worked on a documentary that followed the life of the organist of St Paul's Cathedral. After the rejection of the children's series idea, Dafydd Rhys and I discussed another series based on me taking part in five extreme challenges, including rowing the Atlantic, scaling Mont Blanc, climbing a peak in South America and skiing down it, running this ultra race in Brazil called the Jungle Marathon (which had already been turned down a few years earlier when POP 1 offered it as a series idea) and doing a base jump. S4C liked the idea but it was all too expensive.

We toyed with the idea of recreating some famous film stunts. I'd done a bit of stuntwork on the film *Up 'n Under*, written and directed by John Godber and starring Gary Olsen. It was a rugby film – rugby league, not union. It was set in league heartland up in the North of England. To be precise, it was about a rivalry between two pubs in Hull. I was offered the job and since it was shot in Cardiff, I was readily available. I really enjoyed it, so much so that once I'd had that taste of stuntwork, I wanted to do more – and was asked by the stunt co-ordinator if I had an interest in possibly becoming a full-time stunt performer. One thing I lacked, he felt, was a martial art and my interest in stunts was soon reduced to fiddling around with this idea of recreating a few for Welsh television. Which again, came to nothing.

But as they say, when one door closes, another one, eventually and sometimes slowly, opens.

When my job as maternity cover ended I had something lined up with the same company. *Ralïo* (Rallying) was the Welsh-language series that followed the World Rally Championship, which I went on to cover for nearly twelve years. I was going to be on four wheels, but not before we gave our two-legged endeavour one last blast.

We resurrected the idea of the series of challenges a few years after our first attempt and included another idea of me surfing the Severn Bore. Again, we pitched them to Rhian Gibson, Head of Programmes at S4C. Well, why not? My relationship had recently come to an end and I had plenty of time on my hands. I was almost back full-time on that sofa. I was still running but, goodness, I needed a project. Something to get my teeth into.

'Too expensive,' came the inevitable reply from S4C. 'Far too ambitious,' said Rhian. 'No way can we commission something on such a grand scale. Six is ridiculous. Even three would be out of the question.' No need to rub it in. 'You have to be realistic.' Yes, yes, we got it.

'Let's do one,' she said. We couldn't believe what she'd just said. 'Just the one,' she emphasised. And now came the million-dollar question: which one? 'Mmm, hard, isn't it?' I didn't fancy the Severn Bore surf much. 'Let's see,' said Rhian. Please, not the Bore.

'That thing in the jungle. Let's do that one.'

CHAPTER 6

AMAZON PREP

I set about preparing for the 2009 Jungle Marathon as professionally as I could. I stress this because I repeated it to myself ceaselessly back then, the need to be professional. Preparation and thoroughness would be everything. I needed to be detached and calm and industrious because even 18 months out from the event, there was another part of me that viewed the project with a great deal more scepticism and trepidation. This was the unknown I was stepping into. There was no MIR technology to keep me safe in the Amazonian jungle. There would be a television camera following because that was the whole point of doing it. But that camera's presence somehow would only make it worse. What if I didn't finish? What if I failed to deliver? All captured for posterity.

I tried to concentrate on what I did know. The Jungle Marathon took place in the Tapajós National Forest of Brazil, over a distance of 150 miles (242km) split unevenly into six stages. It was a self-sufficient race, which meant I'd have to carry with me everything I'd need for seven days of running and sleeping. The only outside assistance we had was drinking water.

The race had gained a degree of notoriety and press attention after a television series had been made on it. The second episode had ended with one of the competitors nearly dying from heat exhaustion. You see the runner being stretchered off-camera and then suddenly someone shouts, 'Oh no, I think we've lost him!' And then, smart as they were, the film-makers ended the episode at that point and everyone had to wait another week to see if the poor man had made it or not. He did, thankfully.

To call it tough is an understatement.

The daytime temperatures would be around 37C and would not

drop much below 30C at night (which was quite cold in comparison to the heat of the day). At all times the air would be as humid as just about anywhere on earth and I would have to start each stage with a minimum of 2.5 litres of water increasing my rucksack to 15.5kg. There would be checkpoints and refill stations along the way, but not many.

I should be duly advised that I was to face a personal challenge like no other. And then of course there was the wildlife: the jaguars, piranhas, insects that would sting, the leeches that would suck, the fish that would bite and the anacondas that would wrap themselves around the entire field of runners and suffocate them and swallow them whole for lunch. OK, OK … but it was not difficult to imagine things a little skewed.

So, the best thing to do was be utterly practicable. Do the knowns, and the unknowns might shrink. Be professional. I built a support team. First, there was this great shaven-headed bear of a man, Eurwyn Davies, ex-Royal Marine Commando, Ironman competitor and a paramedic from Cardigan. He would be in the Amazon with me, my support, my rock at the end of every stage, should I reach it, and a shoulder to cry on. He was also Welsh-speaking. I really thought I would not have the strength to muster up links and PTCs (pieces to camera) during and after each stage so having Eurwyn there would mean he'd be able to either interview me on camera or translate the gibberish I'd be speaking throughout the challenge to the viewers at home.

He also had the important role of being the binder of my feet. We discussed what to do with my feet a lot. To tape or not to tape? Eurwyn was of the view that it was better to avoid blisters than treat them. To tape was the Marines' way. I opted to tape. Would it work, Eurwyn's combination of zinc oxide tape with a little Friar's Balsam, a tincture of benzine oil, for adhesion? I have seen big tough men cry when a touch of Friars' Balsam is used to glue blisters back together. Yes, it does sting, ridiculously, but it's a small price to pay for its effect. Each toe was wrapped individually to protect the nail and then the whole foot was taped from just below the toes to the heel. Nobody did it like Eurwyn.

Nigel Thomas, an ex-Royal Marine and ex-Special Air Service, now became my trainer and mentor. He was introduced to me by a mutual friend of my brother. We met in a coffee shop with Dylan Morris and we hit it off straight away. It was as straightforward as that, but what wandering trails we were about to hit and what hours we would spend together on them – sometimes deep in our own thoughts and sometimes talking non-stop. Sometimes I felt I could take no more, that enough was enough; the constant running, the climbing, the pulling of tyres but Nigel never, ever shouted. 'I didn't get through selection for the SAS by shouting,' he said. 'The only person allowed to shout here is you. And only to yourself.' But it was his job to prepare me for the worst. 'Train hard – Race easy,' is what he said. He pushed me because he had to. When I was tired, he was not always entirely sympathetic.

And he was entirely right. If I couldn't complete the training I would not complete the race. It meant he was always lovely Nigel, but sometimes cruel Nigel. When I stopped, he'd give me a few seconds before he'd say, in the politest of tones, 'Off we go.' And he'd always be there; he was in this challenge as much as I was.

We needed someone to explain on camera the psychological games that are played during these long, arduous events. So, I turned at such moments to Dr Ross Hall, ex-Army and now sports psychologist at the University of South Wales. He was brilliant at putting me back together in time for the race. He taught me to break the bigger goals into tinier pieces.

Eurwyn did my toes; Ross did my head.

And then there was Dyfri Owen, my physio, who looked after all the muscles, bones, tendons and ligaments in between.

I had my team. I had back-up. I also had Rhian Jones, who made sure that running remained fun. After all, if you're going to spend 100 miles a week running, you'd better make sure you're having fun along some of the way.

I knew Rhian through Shelter Cymru, the charity for the homeless in Wales. I had done a bit of work for them and Rhian was fully involved. We met again at a friend's party and once I knew she was a runner, we talked a lot about running. I explained that I was about to embark on a new challenge. My weekly miles so far consisted of 30 miles a week. I had just over a year to prepare to get my mind and body ready for running 140 miles in a week and in extreme conditions. I really didn't know how I was going to increase those miles. I mentioned this to Rhian and we decided to work together as a team. She'd help me and I'd help her. Simple.

Rhian was training for a marathon so we agreed on meeting once a week for a 20-plus-miler. I would run to her house which was a few miles away and our weekly long runs soon became a twice-weekly event. We'd go along the beach one week and head into the Brecon Beacons the next, or the range called the Black Mountains on the Beacons' north-eastern flank (not to be confused with the Black Mountain at the western end of the Beacons). It was so much more than the running. Rhian would talk about the homeless and her fight against a general lack of sympathy for them. If we, the public at large, saw the real picture, she said, especially when it came to the sheer number and the heartbreaking individual stories of young people on the streets, then we would see homelessness in a completely different light.

Placing limits on what I think I can accomplish is something I tend not to do. I've heard that people are actually able to cover about twice their imagined limit: if you think you can run only one mile, you can really run two; if you think you can run two, you can run four. You might not be able to cut your 'best' time in half, but you can reduce it by a significant percentage. That has been my experience. And truly, I was surprising myself every week and every month with how my body and mind was adapting to the challenge. Slowly, slowly, I was running more and more. And the more I did, the more of a habit it became. It certainly wasn't becoming easier. In fact it was getting harder, but I was getting stronger and faster and relishing hitting targets and smashing personal goals. I was also a road runner not a trail nor a mountain runner. I needed to spend more time on my feet; the stages out in the Amazon were nothing like running on the road. It would take double the time to cover the same distance in the jungle. A 20km stage could take 4-5 hours to complete and with the penultimate stage of the race 100km in distance, I needed to get used to carrying 15kg (minimum) on my back over very long distances. I also had to get used to running and shuffling slowly for a longer time.

Through Rhian I also met up with Emyr Morris, who was an endurance walker, not a runner. I really didn't realise one could walk that fast before meeting Emyr. I had seen the elite athletes in their walking events fly by, but didn't appreciate how fast Emyr was. I had met him and his twin sister Elid when we were youngsters. We all played violin together in the same orchestra. I had big hands (apparently) and was moved to the viola section (which I loved) and carried on studying it together with voice at uni.

I had been increasing my weekly mileage every month by 10-15% allowing myself an easy week every so often. But now I was struggling mentally. I was running by now 60 miles a week with Rhian but wanted to include a weekly 30-40 mile single session (knowing that one stage in the race would be a 55-miler) into the schedule.

As I expected, not many people put their hands up to join me, but Emyr did. I accepted his invitation to go power-walking with him. Emyr was walking 30-40 miles in a day every week; regardless of weather, he'd be out 9-12 hours every weekend walking and hiking. It was a perfect answer to my problem. Because I'd be carrying my own provisions and equipment in the Jungle Marathon, I joined him with a rucksack on my back, weighing 15kg. I needed my training, as far as possible, to replicate what I would experience in the Amazon.

With Emyr sometimes we talked a lot, he liked to talk just as much as me, but sometimes we would walk in silence. Rhian and other friends would join us as we'd spend days out on the mountains. I was always behind, struggling to keep up with them with my weighted rucksack, but I kept telling myself that this was part of the journey and they, thank goodness, were very patient with me.

I am fortunate that I have met many incredible and inspirational people though running and I am very grateful for that. They have certainly helped me along my running path. I would like to think that I too, have helped them a tiny bit along theirs. I am sure that this is true for many runners out there. I have seen the close friendships formed in training and at races, and have wondered why, when pushing the mind and the body to its limits, that we often form such strong relationships.

For many of us we use running or any exercise as a way to de-stress, a way to declutter what we may be going through in our lives. Even with your training buddy beside you, this can make it a very personal time. This often is the time we may need to have a little rant about something that's annoying us or something that is going on in our own thoughts. Sometimes we may need advice on decisions, we talk and share (and sometimes it is the silence we share) to help us de-stress. Even as an anxious teenager about to face my exams, my father used to say, 'Go for a run, Lowri.' I would drag myself out in a teenage huff, with the weight of the world on my shoulders, but I'd always, regardless of my speed or the distance covered, return with a spring in my step having unloaded many of the stresses and worries I carried with me. I used to go out during my GCSE and A levels listening to my dictated notes playing on my faithful Sony Walkman as I pounded the village's streets learning my lines. I always feel deeply privileged to be part of that space and energy; to be allowed and invited to spend that special time out on the run, either on my own or with friends.

Running is raw and honest. Full stop. There is no glamour (not for me!) and there is no room for pretence on a tough run. We see each other going through all emotions when running, we sometimes see each other at our lowest – the steep hill at mile seven when you are doing an eight-mile training run; the run where you forgot to fuel properly and hit the wall at 18 miles; the run where everything hurts and you just want to cry; the run where you trip over and cut your knees; the run after the night before – and our friends get to see all of this. They get to see the raw version. And they don't judge because they know. We know what it's like because we have been there. It happens, it's part of our sport, it is what makes us stronger.

However, this is where it gets good because even though there may be tough times, our running friends also provide the best support network available. We share our last gel, hand over our last tissue, give away our last drop of water. We provide encouraging words, a smile, a hand over the rocks, a push up the steep hill. We are in it together, and together we motivate and inspire each other.

Of course running can be tough when you are working towards a goal or you are pushing yourself to get a PB, but when it gets tough, remind yourself that the good times will outweigh the bad times. You will smile and giggle at the silly little things, you will share daft jokes, laugh over a love of jelly babies, and remind each other how crazy you are! And you will still be laughing when you sit down together to have a cup of tea at the end of a training run; you will be hugging each other at the end of the training run; you will hug each other when you receive your medals. Those are the memories that you will treasure for years to come and keep you motivated to keep going out there, together.

I had my professionals who became my friends and I had my amateurs who became my friends.

The first person whose help I sought, however, was a doctor. Geraint Jenkins, cardiologist at Morriston Hospital. I have another of those little things that I'm going to have to share with you.

Both my grandparents on Dad's side were excellent golfers and my grandmother was probably a pioneer of the sport for ladies.

Dad's sister Helen was an able all-round sportswoman, but she particularly favoured sailing. Mike, her widower, is a keen sailor, and the two often sailed on the haven in Pembrokeshire from the beautiful Lawrenny to Dale and on into the open sea beyond St Anne's Head. Mark, their son, is following in their footsteps with a passion for extreme sports as well, when his busy job allows.

We spent many a holiday with them on their boat. One summer, when I was eight years old, and sulking because no one else would come to wind-surfing lessons with me, my Aunty Helen enthusiastically volunteered to join me as company. They say my grandmother had the same zest for life. I never met Dad and Helen's mother – my grandmother the golfer, that is. She died at the age of 36 from heart failure.

In 2009, my father himself was having a few issues with his ticker. It wasn't just his knees that were slowing him down. Now, did I share a family condition? Had something been passed down to me? I had had pneumonia as a child and my chest still bears scars of the infection and I wondered, given that I always seemed to go down with a chest infection after an extended period of exercise, if my immune system had been weakened. My standing pulse was 47 beats per minute, but at given moments in my life and for no good reason, I had experienced palpitations. Was I in any sort of condition to take on the toughest challenge of my life?

I was put on a treadmill, coated in sensors and wires. It was a training session in its own right. I had also worn the sensors for 48 hours. The doctors had to see the heart at work at something approaching full stretch. It didn't feel comfortable.

I had just been down to the Royal Marines Commando training camp near Lympstone in Devon. It was a sequence planned with television in mind. We had four programmes to fill – three 30-mins pre-race and one hour-long series-finale on the race itself – and would need lots of footage. There are only so many places a camera can be on a long course and only so many things a runner can say while going about the business of being exactly that, a runner, in a very demanding discipline. I knew the game but insisted that the running came first. I knew that putting me over an assault course would break up the tedium of the long-distance search for a decent line from me when I might not be in a mood for a chat. But it hadn't gone that well.

I had to wear all the gear, (except the rifle), and my feet did not like the hardwearing boots; within minutes of running in them, I could feel blisters developing. I certainly did not want to complain in front of these tough guys. I carried on training – carrying a soldier over my shoulders in a fireman's lift, practising on the ropes. I then moved on to the aerial assault course which had to be completed in 13 minutes. If I'm honest, I relished the challenge, but then I struggled to get over the assault-course wall and felt frustrated and a little inadequate. We moved on to the endurance course (two miles of tunnels, pools, streams, bogs and woods, then a run of four miles back to camp): it was tough but I did quietly enjoy it. Although, typical of me, I still could not shrug off the frustration of that assault course. I also kicked myself for naively going on an eight-mile run earlier in the morning.

A month later, here I was in a consultant's office, wearing a mask and covered in wires on a treadmill, to see if I was likely to drop dead at any moment. This wasn't a bundle of fun either. I wasn't in the best of places, more so because I hadn't performed as well as I had hoped on the VO2 max test. My heart, I was sure was fine and dandy. Yes, it was. I wasn't close to being race ready with only seven months to go, but I didn't have a problem.

'Well,' said Dr Jenkins after he had collated and consulted and come to his conclusions, 'there it is.' My heart was up on a screen, beating away, little bits opening and shutting, the whole thing going at a fair old lick. It was quite disconcerting. 'We've had a good look … It's a very healthy heart to look at.' He paused, which is something a cardiologist might think about not doing. 'There's something going on with your heart's electrical system. We call it a right bundle branch block.'

My heart – the one that didn't work properly – sank. 'You might need a pacemaker in a few years but that's way in the future, and I'm not sure if I can allow you to race.'

I walked out of the hospital with my dad and, for once in my life, was lost for words. I had always been fit. Despite a few years of alcohol and cigarettes, I had lived a healthy life – how could this happen?

I was glad my dad was there. He turned round to me and gave me a big *cwtsh* (the Welsh word for cuddle). 'Better you know now,' he said. 'At least you and others are aware. You really need to listen to your body from now on.' It was just what I needed to hear. The words have always stuck with me and I now do listen to my body, very carefully. I might not be the fastest, but when I do feel myself pushing hard and feel light-headed, or hear my heart shout, I stop or slow down. I no longer innocently believe that I could push through anything.

The big question then, though, was – was I going to tell the TV production team? So much time, effort and money had been invested already in the project. Could I really just tell them, 'Adios. Sorry, you've spent a lot of money on me but now, after months of filming, I can't do it.'

I decided to say nothing. I decided to wait to see what Dr Jenkins had in mind for me.

A few weeks later, Dr Jenkins – also a keen endurance athlete – got back in touch with me and explained that he had gone for a second opinion, as doctors and consultants do. He had gone to speak to a world-renowned specialist in the matter. He looked at my results, heard what Dr Jenkins had in mind, and they both came to the same conclusion: that my heart would be able to cope with the extreme conditions of the Amazon – but I had to listen to my body and be sensible. I had to be on top of my systems: i.e my hydration, calorie intake etc. I had to be prepared.

'You're clear to carry on,' he said.

I'd like to report that once I swept aside doubt, I leapt into action with vigour. And in a way I did, I suppose. I entered the 2009 London Marathon as part of a team – 30 of us intent on breaking the world record for, wait for it, the biggest tied-together team to complete 26.2 miles. Do I need to remind you that the record stood at 24, set by the Metropolitan Police? Roped together all the way, we 30 did it. I am an athlete with a WR to my name … (only for the record to be smashed the following year!)

In general, however, the ultramarathon training was hell. I had to go further than ever before and be prepared to do the same, or more, the next day. There were bad days, but there were also good days. The good days, I decided, far out-weighed the bad.

I had still not completed a 100km race – which would be the distance of Stage 5, the longest in the Jungle Marathon. I wanted to see and feel how covering that distance felt. So Rhian came up with an idea. During one of our runs. She had the idea of walking along the West Wales coast, from the beautiful beach at Mwnt, north of Cardigan, to Talybont in Gwynedd, on the other side of Barmouth, a town that sits on the estuary of the River Mawddach. Barmouth is what Abermawdd in old Welsh (The mouth of the Mawddach) has become, which just goes to show how language can travel. Or how Welsh can be mangled into English. Her brother worked on the Wales Coast Path and he was keen to join in the fun.

We were aiming to do 60 miles in 24 hours. I had by now increased my weekly mileage to 100-mile weeks and I wanted to see if I could go a little bit further … always a little bit further!

I had no idea where I was fitness-wise, endurance-wise. The only thing I had to show for what I had done was my notebook with all my running logs. With work mostly on weekends, I hardly raced and I didn't have a GPS so went by feel – I knew I could run 10 miles comfortably at 8 minutes a mile, and knew that I could walk the mountains on an average of 3.5 miles an hour, so that's how I worked things out. You have surely guessed by now that I am rubbish when it comes to technology and have always preferred using pen and paper. Today I am slowly catching up with modern society and I now have my trusted Suunto GPS watch but back in 2009, it was all pen and paper.

Anyway, back to the 60 miles in 24 hours. Rhian, her brother Alun and I decided that we weren't going to run the distance so I'd decided to take advantage of that and test out my kit and again my 15.5kg weighted rucksack full of food – mostly dates, sweets, water, first aid and spare clothing to be exact. If the weight was too much for me, I would drop the water and share the food out. We left Mwnt and my first words to Rhian were, 'I don't think I'm going to make the whole journey.' A great positive start.

But I carried on, looking at my feet and telling myself it was all about putting one in front of another. And if I did just that, I'd be one foot closer to the finishing line.

It was at sunrise, eleven hours into the challenge, that the camera caught me at a low point. Why, oh why, do cameras always catch you when you're looking at your most bedraggled?! We had been going throughout the night. I had never run nor walked through the night without sleep. It was, at times, wonderful and humbling; I felt we were the only ones on the planet as we quietly made our way along the coastline under starlight, walking on the beautiful beaches and meeting fisherman going out on their journeys into the dark with only the moon and their head torches to show them the way. But there were times when the tunnel vision created by the light of the head torch and the sleep deprivation brought on some low ebbs and a feeling of vertigo. It was the first time I experienced that desperation to sleep; even a muddy, rock-strewn path looked cosy.

The day, when it arrived, served only to highlight how tired I was. In the dark, I was focused on every footstep, every sound, every movement. But under a glorious sunrise, I could relax a bit and, after all that intense concentration, relaxation plunged me into the darkest of moods.

'This isn't fun any more,' I said. And I meant it. So why do it?

Because to confirm the ferocity of your determination you have to confront it at its weakest.

We completed the walk but with six weeks to go, it still didn't make me less nervous.

The last race I did at home before heading off for Brazil was across Wales at its narrowest point, the 45 miles between Clun on the border with Shropshire, England, to Clarach on the middle of the coast that defines Cardigan Bay. Nigel joined me. We were four weeks from the Jungle Marathon and needed to perform well, not just for physical assurance but mental as well. I filled my rucksack until it weighed 15.5kg and set off. There were fell runners at the start but this was a LDWA event (Long Distance Walkers Association) so there were many walkers too.

The route took us over *Pumlumon* (Plynlimon), the highest of the Cambrian Mountains and the source of two of the finest rivers of Wales (and England), the Severn and the Wye. There was more water to come, stored behind the Elan Valley dams in the series of reservoirs whose contents flow, by gravity alone, 118 miles to Birmingham in the Midlands of England. The Elan and Pumlumon are spectacular but no place in which to get lost, which is what happened to us. We had 18 hours to complete the route. Add four extra miles to the proper course, and it came to 49 miles, that it took us 17 hours to complete. We were overjoyed. We had fun. We were last but we were successful. Successful? I don't know what that word means. I was happy. But success, that goes back to what in somebody's eyes success means. For me, success is being the best version of myself on that day. And that day was a good day for me.

Being a part of a LDWA event taught me a very important lesson in ultra running.

There's a common theme in our little world, that you need to be 'pushing yourself to the limit!' and training flat out all the time. It's the same when it comes to racing, too. During my first few attempts at the longer distances, I saw walking as a sign of tiredness, weakness. When I noticed competitors taking it easy and slowing down to a walk, I presumed they were tired and struggling.

'Keep going. Don't give up,' I'd say, feeling empathy for them but quietly relieved that I felt 'strong' as I passed them.

A few hours later, they'd only go and pass me. This time it would be them giving me the words of encouragement.

But now I look back on it, those people who were walking were probably being a lot smarter than I was. Because the thing is, a lot of the time it can be to your advantage to walk certain parts of races. Firstly, you're saving energy for the parts you can actually run effectively, and therefore you can re-overtake a lot of the people who may have overtaken you. Secondly, 95% of us aren't elite athletes. Of course, we still want to do our best but it's also about actually enjoying your race and not getting a DNF. I learnt from listening to the best. Later on in my running career, one of the best ultra runners in the world told me that even she walked the uphills and that there's no place for ego on the trail.

If you feel that you need to power walk that mountain, do it, I tell myself now. There's no shame in that – conserving energy will allow you to make up time on terrain, inclines or declines, that favour you. Respect the distance, and know your strengths and weaknesses because these races can expose even the best.

The elation of finishing that race soon disappeared and I found myself back in the hole of self-doubt. I won't lie. I had struggled with the different challenges I had faced over the months of training. How on earth would I be able to replicate what I had done, and do it back to back, totalling nearly 150 miles in a week, in the extreme conditions of the Amazon?

Dyfri, the physio, tried to cheer me up with an ice bath in a wheelie bin. 'I really don't want to do it,' I said to him. We both knew I meant the Jungle Marathon, not the freezing plunge. Nigel was even more brutal: 'Lowri's struggling. She may not do as well as I expected.'

I was full of fear.

CHAPTER 7

FACING THE FEAR

Eurwyn and I travelled from London Heathrow to São Paulo and from there we flew to Alter do Chão, near Santarém in the state of Pará, where the Tapajós River meets the Amazon. Already the climate and the landscape felt incredibly alien and on a scale that was truly intimidating. We were little ants in this giant steam room and in all directions there seemed to be natural features too vast to go through or climb over. Still to come were twelve hours on a boat up the Tapajós to the start of the race in Itapuama. I was so pleased I had Eurwyn with me. He would take care of me, ease me carefully into all of this. I was going to have a relaxing few days before race day.

'Right,' he said. 'Four days to acclimatise is all we've got. So, turn off the air con in your bedroom and let's go for a run. Six miles this morning and six tonight.'

Mindful of the heat and the humidity, I took more water with me than I ever thought I could consume. Within the first two miles the 2 litres had all gone. It felt like running at high altitude and I could not get enough oxygen into my lungs. The conditions were so oppressive that I was wrenched out of my physical comfort zone as alarmingly as I was struggling to get my head around being in this environment. Fear is a protective force, but it can run out of control. I told myself that facing this fear was exactly why I was here. Your worth is being questioned. What is your answer?

I doubled up on the water the next day. Eurwyn, however, was doubling up, too. 'Let's go out in the midday sun and do twelve miles in one hit,' he said. These acclimatising forays were some of the most important runs of my life. By the time I met up with all the other runners, I found I wasn't taking on as much water and my mind was much more at ease with the heat and the sounds and the thoughts of what lay ahead.

We boarded an Amazonian riverboat, which was a test in itself. It was a vessel big enough to accommodate rows and rows of us in our hammocks, but to board it we had to wobble our way down an unstable plank. Fighting for hammock space on the boat was fierce, but we all managed to settle in for the long journey up the Tapajós River.

Earlier that week, Eurwyn and I had met Ryan Sandes – Salomon runner and one of the race favourites – and spent a few days acclimatising in the same hotel. Not knowing who he was, I had asked Ryan 'if he had run any marathons before?'

He humbly and quietly muttered a few races in his soft South African accent. Little did I know then that he was the South African ultramarathon star who had earned the prestigious honour of winning all four of the 4 Deserts events, was named Running Hero between 2008-12 in his native South Africa, and then went on to win some of the most famous ultras in the world.

I tried to dig myself out of a very deep Amazonian mud hole. But he didn't seem offended and the three of us got on well for the week leading up to the race start.

Back on the boat, Ryan had found a quieter spot away from the noisy engines and had kindly kept a space for me and my hammock there. Eurwyn was on another boat by now – the crew boat. Everybody else on the competitors' boat looked in supreme condition, it seemed to me, from the way they balanced themselves on the gangplank to the ease with which they unslung their hammock and unwound themselves into it. Those hammocks of theirs – they looked very light. I couldn't stop making comparisons: their shape, my shape; their kit, my kit; their food, my food. It was hard to ignore the sound of the engine despite being near the bow of the boat, making it hotter than ever and noisier, but we settled down and headed into the night.

We awoke to find ourselves moored on a sandbank in the middle of the river. We were invited to swim and relax for a few hours. We were told to keep a lookout for the pink dolphins of the Tapajós. They are extremely rare and we didn't see one, but it was a useful break all the same, to walk and talk and absorb the stunning scenery. Back on board, we headed for a village that would be home for two days until the race started. A last slice of calm. We were charmed by the schoolchildren and teachers of the village, who sang us in with a song of welcome. We all cheered and applauded and set up camp in an area on the other side of the handful of houses by the river.

We had a briefing in this camp and the doctors gave us a once-over. I explained my situation and handed in my certificate from Dr Jenkins to say I was fit to run in these conditions. We were given a bit of survival training by the local *bombeiros*, who seemed to be the army, police and firefighters all rolled into one. They told us what wildlife to look out for, what we could eat, what we couldn't, where to find drinkable water, how to make a camp and how to make a fire.

There was a warning at the beach about stingrays. When in the river we had to shuffle in our shoes to ensure that, if you did disturb a ray, you only touched its wing instead of standing directly on the barb. So shuffle we did. The day was full of briefings, including an intense lesson on snake identification, and an 'up close and personal' encounter with a boa constrictor. Their advice was, if you get bitten by a snake, try to identify it and head for the nearest checkpoint to advise the medical staff … if you can make it there in time, I thought to myself. We were also shown how to make fire (just in case); what we'd have to do if we got seriously lost (yes, there is a difference); how to get fresh water; and then, more interestingly, flora and fauna – what we could and could not touch.

It was all very dramatic and possibly just an exercise in taking our minds off the race – at least, that's what I told myself to make myself feel better – for which we were now given our numbers. I was number 73 in a total of 126. If they had been trying to take our minds off the race, they were very much back on it now.

We killed more time by taking a short run around the village and relaxing on the river beach. I ran with a group of Americans, Kevin Bass, David Cermak and Brits Tom Bird, Vicky Johnson and Joe Gale whom I had met earlier that year on a Jungle Marathon weekend course in Dorset. Tom, Vicky, Joe and I had got on well on that weekend. I tried to stick with them but I lagged behind. My heart sank. I was going to struggle. I wondered if all of this was a silly mistake.

We later lazed in the water or swam, until one of the competitors was stung by a stingray. In truth, it was not easy to relax at all. I still couldn't stop myself looking at the other competitors' kit. I had supreme confidence in mine. I had eventually found – not without going round and round in circles trying to locate it – Likeys in Brecon, an Aladdin's cave for outdoor adventurers. The owners, Sue and Martin, had been so helpful. Over many cups of tea and many visits they'd talked me through what I would need and had never let me down. But I was sure now that over there was a hammock that must have been 200 grams lighter than mine. And I was caught now between rucksacks. Should I use the one Martin had adjusted to fit me perfectly, or this other one, that had not been fine-tuned but which felt a little lighter after pulling out the wires and rods that kept its shape.

That night we packed our big bags and took them down to the boats. They would be taken downstream to the finish. All our little luxuries were gone: the iPods and books; the spare clothes and food packs that were now surplus. We were pared down to the minimum. For toiletries I had my toothbrush, that I now cut in half, and a travel-tube of toothpaste. I squeezed out half its contents. Shoelaces and rucksack strings were reduced in length. Anything to save a few grams. I was carrying 21 packs of dehydrated food and removed the outer layer of foil on each one, pierced a tiny hole in each bag and rolled the air out of every one before covering the hole. Tiny details, but by doing that, I was increasing space in my bag. In went the clothes for the next seven days: two pairs of underwear, three pairs of socks, two pair of tights – one for the day and the other a compression pair for the evening – one T-shirt, one merino long sleeve top, one small hat for the night, one pair of gloves (the advice was not to touch tree trunks and plants), first aid kit and light slippers (the type you get in posh hotels) for the evening. It came to 14 kilos, two kilos lighter than I had planned, before I had felt the heat of the jungle. There was nothing I could do to reduce the weight of the 2.5 litres of water I had to carry. I was ready.

Or was I?

CHAPTER 8

INTO THE JUNGLE

The thing to remember about the Jungle Marathon is that it is an endurance event, rather than a long-distance running event. To complete it requires good management skills, rather than just fitness and bloody-mindedness. You need to be able to pace yourself in the heat, and to consume liquid and electrolytes at just the right amounts, and have the right food and the exact amount of calories to sustain yourself for seven days, without weighing yourself down. There's a lot to consider when it comes to preparing for an event of this calibre.

You also need to have all the inoculations against serious illness, and health insurance to evacuate you if need be. You must avoid the constant risk of food poisoning and infection, and adopt sensible precautions against bodily injury. Your feet and toenails have to cope with being continuously hammered and sodden for hours on end. You have to avoid being bitten by something that could bring your life to an end – let alone your race.

I made a catastrophic start. I had chosen to go with the lighter rucksack, the one that hadn't been minutely adjusted to fit. It was lighter than the other because I had pulled out the metal rods that held the front water pouches in place. As a result, both bottles were bouncing too freely in the pouches. Fifty metres into the biggest race of my life I had to stop. I remembered all those reminders to myself to be professional. I had just committed the error of a rank amateur. 'You ... plonker,' I told myself. A mere few minutes into the race, and I was stuck with this wretched rucksack.

'It's not the mistakes you make, but how you fix them.' My dad would say. I started again. This was a short opening stage, only 15km or 9.3 miles long. That was the good news. '*A short, sharp shock to the system,'* was the more sobering next line on the brief. *'There is a very high concentration of elevation. This stage could really wipe you out totally if you don't take it easy. Watch out for dehydration, pain in your quads and the beginnings of trashed feet.1 x swamp crossing and 1 x river crossing.'*

I pulled the bottles out, held one in each hand and carried on. I'd sort it out later, I said to myself, fuming. Get off to a good start, I had set as a first goal. I was 0-1 down.

It disturbed the quiet confidence that had been building. When asked in the general chit-chat of the last night before the race start what my ambitions were, I had said that to reach the end of the first two stages was as far as I could visualise. I said this partly because of the statistics, that showed that most competitors who dropped out did so earlier rather than later – although the drop-off rate never really slackened too much.

Three men, who had won their places as a result of previous standings, spoke of how they were going to jump with joy as they crossed the line. One asked me, 'What are you going to do when you cross that finish line, Lowri?'

'I'm just hoping to complete the first two days,' I shyly replied.

'Come on Lowri,' they all smiled. 'You need to believe in yourself.'

They were right. It takes strength to get to the start line, but it takes belief to get to the end. I wasn't full of confidence but I did quietly trust in my preparations. I had to. I could not have given more in the preparation. Now I just had to have faith in my own ability. Or else I wouldn't make it past the start, let alone the finish line.

The trail was marked by biodegradable blue flags at irregular intervals all along its way. It had to be, for the route was often barely discernible through the vegetation and trees. Eurwyn and I had recced the start and had identified a sharp incline to a ledge not too far in. This was bound to be a bottleneck that would bunch the runners and bring them to a halt. We had laid a plan to reach this first climb early. Straps tightened, I forced my pace a little to meet this first target. It worked. The score in goals was 1-1. I made it up to the ledge and from there up into the jungle, unhindered by a queue. The runs we had done on arrival had worked wonders.

The terrain had to be respected. The trail was a series of really steep ascents and vertiginous descents and it was by no means a clear path. Fallen trees frequently blocked it. Crawling or scrambling broke up any rhythm. The jungle floor was made up of sandy soil and vegetation, only a foot deep, lying on top of clay so thick that many trees couldn't penetrate it with their roots. The trees packed themselves in and, like a squashed crowd, sort of held themselves upright, interlocking at the top with their canopy. In heavy rain, their embrace could weaken, so trees were always coming down.

Besides the big fallen trunks, there were branches everywhere. And creepers and roots and leaves over holes. With every step came a risk of turning an ankle or twisting a knee. I fell frequently and was soon covered in scratches to my legs, arms and hands. One of the many briefings had warned that nicks and cuts in the jungle could quickly turn septic. I had to slow my pace. Concentrating on where my feet were landing was all-important and even if I was distracted by sudden noises in the surrounding jungle I knew I had to keep my wits about me on this short, opening stage. But even while slipping and sliding, it was impossible not to wonder at the flowers, plants and animals all around.

The cameraman caught me. 'How are you feeling?' he shouted. 'Good,' I shouted back. 'But can't stop, sorry. I'm petrified about getting lost so I'm trying to stick with the local runners.' And that's who I kept company with for most of the day.

Much as I had committed to the jungle part of this Jungle Marathon, and much as my eyes and ears were drawn against my better judgement to all its wondrous sights and sounds, it was still a relief to leave it. The trail sometimes emerged on to rough roads. These were wider and less cluttered with debris, but were often made of deep sand. Running here gave way to power-walking. A purposeful stride, I told myself, to accommodate better all the sliding and slipping of the rucksack on my back. It felt heavy too, now. This was turning into a very long 9.3 miles.

Suddenly, out of nowhere, I had company. Two children, about six years old, joined me on the trail. They skipped along beside me. Surely, we couldn't be far from their home. They stayed with me for the last half mile and we crossed the line together to a cheer from the medics and race organisers. I bent down more wearily. I couldn't show it at that precise moment, but I had really enjoyed the companionship brought by those two little children from a local tribe. We didn't have a word in common, but we had shared a moment together.

The runners' camp was down by a river. One river flowed into another, all heading towards the Amazon. All I knew was that we were by a river. Word was going round that four had dropped out from heat exhaustion and were being evacuated out of the jungle. It was like a scene out of a horror movie and people were dropping like flies, but the Jungle Marathon medics did a great job making sure everyone was looked after.

The first finisher of the stage took 2 hours 51 mins and the final stage finisher came in at 9 hours 08 minutes. We all knew that speed was not going to be the most important thing in this race. It was all about completing the goal.

Because the stage was short, there was time to spare. A luxury. I put up my hammock, that perhaps wasn't so overweight after all. I liked my hammock. I suddenly liked my simple life. Everything I needed was with me and once inside, I could lie in any position or wriggle about with no fear of falling out. This was my home for the next week.

I filled a pack of food with hot water and enjoyed my meal. I went down to the river, did some stretching on the shore and then went in to wash. I left my clothes to dry in the 35C heat. It felt so good to be clean(er). Other runners were lying out in the sun, some investigating blisters on their feet. So far, so good for me on that front. I did some emailing and told my family not to worry. I was fine and had survived the first day.

That covered just about everything. Everything, that is, bar the toilet. I was a Morgan, who had spent years in caravans on campsites and tents in fields. Basic, shared facilities were not a problem. I had crept out in storms and 'been' in the most isolated, windiest (as it were) of locations. But this was a camp toilet for 120 runners, a hole in the ground with a waist-high bamboo fence around it. Excitement, nerves and fatigue all played their part and the heat had an even more prominent role. All I'll say is that if ever I needed an added incentive, more urgent even than the desire to touch a higher plane of fulfilment, an extra spur to go faster and keep pushing, it came with the thought that the nearer you were to the top of the leaderboard, the fewer times the toilet had been used by the time you made it to camp. That said, there was no avoiding the fact that this was an odiferous function at all times. You simply had to take a deep breath and go.

Stage 2. A tiddler, only 24 kilometres. 15 miles. Of course, that wasn't the full description. Here was the brief: *'Mud, mud and more mud. Your feet will be soaked most of this stage. Expect to be covered in ticks thanks to the swamp crossings. However hard you try, it's inevitable that you are going in. But there are still some flat parts where you can pick up the pace. 5 x river crossings, 2 x swamp crossings up to 1km in length (1 totally hideous).'*

The temperature had risen and there was not a breath of wind. I set off and was immediately soaking wet, as if I were running through the river, rather than on the sand alongside it. The stories of runners collapsing on the first day had made me think and forced me to listen more carefully than usual to my own body. How was my heart? It was being asked to work in heat it had never experienced before. Any signs of palpitations? Any light-headedness? I felt fine. Wet, but good. I would press ahead down here on the sand and aim to be more judicious on the hills and the trickier sections ahead.

I was even clear-headed enough to plot my crossings of the rivers. I had asked a lot of other competitors and *bombeiros* about this. There was an 'assistance rope' spanning the river. I could grab that and haul myself across, or I could remove my rucksack, put it in a bin liner, attach that pack to my waist with a two-metre cord and swim across. Head-up and haul, or head-down and swim. I decided on the second one and then changed my mind. My clarity of thought was disappearing.

'Stick with the winners,' I heard my mother say. 'And if you can't stick with them, learn from them.' I looked at them. Obviously, they were all doing what I had been going to do all along. Like them, I plunged into the water and began to swim. I had done a lot of competitive swimming in my youth. I had done triathlons and gone on to compete in the Ironman. Swimming had been one of my strong points. I struck out for the opposite bank.

I sank. I was not as buoyant in running gear in fresh water as in the sea in a wetsuit. My rucksack began to drag me down. My elegant front crawl fast turned into a doggy-paddle, my head bobbing in and out of the murky river as I gasped for air. Panic was slowly setting in, but I kept telling myself to calm down and to focus on the bank. On the plus side, at least the murkiness meant I wouldn't see an anaconda. Not until it was right upon me. My crossing lost a little more smoothness as my arms and legs worked with a little more frenzy. I was slightly surprised to find I emerged on the other side with most of the field behind me.

I ran on my own that day. I needed to gauge where I was physically and physiologically in these conditions. Sometimes I prefer running alone, although I had already discovered something about ultra running that made it different from the one-off marathon. There, you are in a race against others. Even if you are not bothered about your finishing position, you probably care about your time. You will know your personal best. You will always have an eye on the clock, on your splits.

In the world of ultra running, it matters less. Much more moving than the competitor who finishes first is the one who finishes last. Simply because they have made it there. Or maybe those that don't finish, the ones that fail by a whisker or who cannot take one more step. There is a spirit of co-operation in ultras that does not exist in races where to win is the be-all. I felt at home in this family of runners in the jungle, even if we were growing smaller by the hour.

I had to readjust my pattern of power-walking and running on this second stage. I ended up not knowing what I had decided to do in the first place. I came in with my feet in agony. When the camera caught up with me, I managed to say: 'I've always had trouble with my feet.' That was about all I had to offer. No deep, meaningful profound link; just 'I've always had trouble with my feet.'

It was a slight comfort to see others finding it tough, too. A few were having a 'hot-shot', when a needle is inserted to drain the blister and then a strong antiseptic like Friar's Balsam is injected between the raised skin of the blister and the raw flesh underneath.

I had gone for the option of blister-avoidance. I had my feet taped up, didn't I? What was causing the pain, then? I asked Eurwyn to have a look at my nails. I was sure they were all coming off. He started to pull on the zinc oxide tape. 'The trouble is,' he said, 'the skin is coming off with the tape.' Eventually, after much peeling and tugging, he announced that my nails were fine, but my feet were swollen and I was slowly developing what looked like trench foot.

It wasn't the most serious medical problem. More runners had dropped out. Two were in a serious condition. One, it seemed, had not taken in enough salts. The other had taken in too many. They were both in intensive care. It was stark reminder of the dangers and the doctors were more worried than anyone. They wanted to make sure we were all aware of the daily perils and insisted that we all sign waivers to absolve them of responsibility should any of us, well, you know, not make it.

There were people even more worried than the doctors. We all carried a tracker on the trail, so that our progress could be monitored. Should we disappear, for example, there was a chance we might be found. But my tracker that day had not worked. When my parents back in Wales tried to find out how I had done on day two, they could not find me on the results page. All they knew was that two unnamed athletes were on their way to the emergency ward of the nearest hospital, six hours away by boat. My mother, there and then, decided she was going to fly to Brazil. She would find me. She had found a way to get to the race via plane, buses and boats. But before pressing ahead, my father suggested that they go through the gallery of photos that accompanied the page of results.

Among the more typical poses of runners on the move, they found a pair of blackened, bloody, swollen feet covered in bits of tape. 'They're Lowri's,' cried my mother in relief. 'I'd know them anywhere.' The feet had made it. The flight plans were put on hold.

Stage 3. 37.63km (23.4 miles). They were starting to crank it up. The brief: *'Combine the horrors of stage one and two and extend the pain. Don't get lulled into a false sense of security by the flatter parts of the trail. There is much more torture to come. 3 x river crossings.'*

If so far there had been very little terrain even enough for an extended run, on this stage there was practically none at all. The destination was a camp deep in the jungle, to be patrolled at night by armed guards, to keep away the jaguars. The least of my worries. Between them and me stood the highest hills we'd meet. And every step before then seemed to hit a trap. I was stumbling through this stage and nothing could be more draining. The switchbacks were so extreme that there was a constant yo-yoing of competitors. Up and down we went, overtaking on this climb, only to be overtaken on the descent. Such progress bred a sort of familiarity, but our conversations tended to be brief. Energy before chit-chat.

Everybody seemed to be finding the going tough on day three. Perhaps a deep-seated fatigue was beginning to spread. Perhaps the excitement was wearing off, the novelty of the setting. We quickly learned that the event lived up to its billing and was incredibly tough. Even the elite runners said it was the 'absolute limit' of what they could endure, and many in the middle of the pack who had done events like the Marathon des Sables before, were disenchanted with the event as they felt it was unnecessarily hard. One bit of the jungle could look a lot like any other. We seemed to be longer under the canopy too, where the air was at its most humid. The downhills offered no opportunity to relax. You slithered your way down and that rule about not touching the trees for support went straight out of the window. Any tree and every vine in the way served to keep us from nose-diving down what looked and felt like almost vertical drops. The trip hazards were serious – not so much in the fall, but in what competitors were falling into. You couldn't see the jungle floor as it was covered in leaf litter, meaning the competitors had to be really vigilant, watching every step as poisonous insects inhabited holes which had been concealed by leaves, and there were fallen trees of varying sizes littering the trail.

About seven kilometres from the finish, I saw several people in a bad way. I didn't feel great either. I had tried to refuel as much as possible but I was drained. I had knocked my foot against a stump at the end of one particular fall and could feel that more than the other bruises. An old stress fracture was nagging away. I reached a checkpoint and sat down to eat a couple of sweets. I felt light-headed. I was certainly short of temper. Eurwyn told me excitedly, 'You're doing so well. You're something like 20th place.'

Did I care?

'That's 20th overall, Lowri.'

So what? A dreaded thought had crept into my head. I didn't have to do this. There was enough in the can already to make a television programme. Heroic failure had a certain appeal, didn't it? The novice that nearly made it. There was no need to put myself through this. I knew it was a serious moment. I could wait awhile and chew on my Haribo sweets and chew on this doubt. What was the rush? Instead, I found myself clambering back to my feet and lumbering off.

How different it was when I reached the end of Stage 3. My brain shook off doubt and took control of my body. Forget the pain. Think of the goal. 'You can do this. You CAN do this.' Words formed short sentences and became the beat to which I could walk. And the walk developed a cadence and became a stride. I positively skipped over the line. I was celebrating. Three stages down, three to go. 'Halfway there!' I proudly exclaimed.

Eurwyn punctured my euphoria. 'Forget the days,' he said. 'Forget the stages. Distance is what counts. And you've got 90 miles to go. You're only a third of the way through.'

The camera was there to capture the moment. My joy vanished. I issued a curt, 'Yeah … well … thank you for that,' and went off to spend time alone, feeling sorry for myself.

CHAPTER 9

THE STING OF THE JUNGLE

Stage 4. 15 miles (24 kilometres)

I came around from my self-pity soon after and apologised to Eurwyn for my curt reply. 'No need,' he said, smiling. As an ultra runner, he had been there himself, but the producer knew what buttons to press and had asked him to remind me of the distance vs stages covered. As a broadcaster, I get that. Sometimes, you have to ask tough hard questions. They don't always get a warm reply.

That night, the monkeys were screeching loudly in the trees. I was used to interrupted sleep by now. I was slowly adapting to sleeping in the hammock, despite the constant toilet visits (I kept drinking throughout the night, hugging my water bottle like a child does a teddy bear), anticipation of what lay ahead, the nocturnal temperatures (about 30C at nightfall), and the constant noise from the jungle wildlife, including local dogs and roosters and the howler monkeys who produced a ghoulish wail far off in the distance shortly after dusk and shortly before dawn. Even ear plugs couldn't drown out that noise.

I was back where I had been the day before, swaying between extremes. On the plus side was the distance of the leg. Even the accompanying notes were not the worst: *Forget wet feet, you are going for a swim. Lots of flat parts to run if your feet will carry you, but watch out for dense vegetation, and abundance of prickly plants and snakes and spiders. 2 x river crossings and 1 x swamp crossing.*

On the down side, my feet were not in a good state. Swimming followed by running meant we were all suffering from trench foot. My skin was softened by so much water, my nails were about to come off and I suspected that, despite my taping, I had a big deep blister forming. My feet were also swollen after the constant pounding and heat and since my trail shoes were pretty robust, there was not much give in them. Feet and shoes formed a pretty painful partnership. It had to be, of course, that the very first test on this stage was a 150-metre swim across a river.

On the other hand, once that was over, I found myself on trails that had largely been cleared of jungle. I found this sad. Seeing the deforestation and its impact on the wildlife was deeply upsetting. I vowed to return home and, in my own small way, do something to help save the rainforests.

The route was flatter and we could run for long sections. There was very little shade, and I knew I was dehydrating. I ran as much as I could to get out of the sun. I concentrated on my drinking routine: one sip from each of the two bottles on the front of my rucksack, the first containing water only, the second with electrolyte. I then took a third, longer pull from the water bladder on my back. Rehydration and the replacing of salts. Every time I approached a checkpoint, which was every 10km, I'd finish off every drop so I knew I'd be drinking three litres of water in every section. I kept reminding myself of those two highly experienced runners who had had to be taken away to hospital. Take in salt; don't overdo it. Take on lots of water, but space it out between checkpoints, where I could replenish my stocks.

There was variety on this stage, a mixture of sandy roads and high-concentration jungle. Once we were through the swamp, we saw more people and we passed through their tiny villages until we came across a larger one. The children had gathered at the school and we heard their commotion before we saw them. Suddenly they were among us, cheering and banging drums, giving us high fives and running with us.

Having run the previous stage with only myself for company, I found myself sharing the trail with not just the children, but with other runners. I ran a long way with an Australian called Gus, who caught up with me and then stayed with me. He was tall, around 6ft 5ins, and I had to run three steps just to keep up with his long stride. This was also his first ultra.

So how did you end up being here – another ultra newbie racing in one of the toughest endurance footraces on the planet? was the basis of our conversation.

'I once ran a half marathon and fancied this.'

His story – similar to mine. He just wanted to see if he could do it, and it was also an interesting way of sightseeing and learning about the world.

I was getting tired and despite three days of running, I felt that my rucksack was not getting any lighter despite the daily rations of food being eaten. Surely it should? In my deranged tired state, I started thinking that somebody was maybe sabotaging my race?!

'What exactly do you mean?' Gus asked.

'Well,' I said, 'you know that Brazilian guy …'

'Which one?'

'The one that's always laughing and joking.'

'Sure, I know the one you mean. Mauro.'

'Well, I think as a joke he's putting stones in my rucksack.' I had noticed that he was the joker in the Brazilian pack. He was the one who seemed to lift their spirits.

'Say that again?' said Gus, raising an eyebrow.

'I think someone's putting extra weight in my rucksack. He's very clever. My bag should be getting lighter but it's not. I stop and check but there's nothing there,' I said, laughing.

'Wow,' said Gus. He didn't seem too spooked. We ran together for about six hours. 'I enjoyed that,' he said as we crossed the finish line.

I'd enjoyed it, too, although the doctors were about to temper my happiness by inspecting my feet and confirming that I now had a deep blister.

Stage 5. And so, we came to it. The monster. 55.5 miles (89.38 kilometres). *'Watch the piranha and caimans on the water crossing,'* explained the organiser, *'and the dense population of jaguars in the vicinity of Checkpoint 4. Face the steepest of climbs and the sharpest of descents, and if you make it out of the forest alive you can enjoy 40km on the community trails. Dark zone at CP4 starts at 15:30 hrs. 6 x river crossings.'* There was more to come. The biggest stage had its own by-laws, its own conditions, its own time zone and dire warnings: *'This stage will either make or break you. If you don't arrive at CP5 by the cut-off at 15:30 you will be caught in the dark zone (where lives a number of jaguars) and have to stay at CP5 until daylight of the next day. 48 hours before cut-off. The pain is worth it.'*

The long day in multi-stage racing is all about getting your strategy right. My plan was to take the first half relatively easy, have a break and then give it my all on the second half.

This stage had its own legs and the first three were similar to the first three stages of the whole race: lots of hills, dense jungle with water crossings and swamps. The very first thing we had to tackle was a 100-metre river crossing. More wet feet at the very outset.

Squelching my way forward, I feared the worst, but found the run to CP1 was comparatively easy, with some gentle slopes and nothing too nasty. I was feeling strong and kept up with the leading group, who had decided to run together. Ryan Sandes, Nikki Kimball, Mike Foote and Tracy Garneau from North Face told me to stick with them. The miles ticked by. We were laughing and joking and really enjoying running together as a pack through this wonderful terrain, until suddenly I tripped at about the 20-mile mark. By the time I had picked myself up, my companions had vanished into the dense forest. They called back to me, saying they'd slow down and let me catch them again. I shouted back. 'Thanks, but no. You go on.' I didn't want to spoil their rhythm. I was well-used to being on my own. I'd find my own pace and hopefully catch up at the next checkpoint.

Five miles later I was in real trouble. Had joining the race's front-runners taken too much out of me? They were the best in the world and I was the first-timer. I made it to the checkpoint but felt really overheated. My legs had turned to jelly, and images were floating before my eyes: every branch was a snake; every rustle in the bushes a stalking jaguar. If I did see what was really there, it came in twos, even threes. I climbed and climbed, and I became more and more frustrated; I was running out of energy and still had over another marathon to go. I literally trudged my way from checkpoint to checkpoint, arriving a little worse for wear, but still moving. I kept pulling myself along the road on my own, feeling dejected, hot and tired. I found a competitor on the side of the road who, ironically, looked in a worse state than me; at least I was walking. He was the competitor who, at the start of the race, had told me to have more belief in myself. 'Well done, Lowri,' he shouted as I neared. 'You're doing well. Keep moving.' I must have looked better than I felt.

I picked him up.

'Need help?'

'No, thanks.'

'You carrying on?' I asked. There are times during a race when you don't need flowery motivation, you just need some straight talking to. He nodded.

'C'mon then. I need the company.' And we continued together until the next checkpoint. We separated later and I was back on my own, back again in the depths of self-pity and self-doubt. I tried to raise my water bottle but almost missed my mouth. And my feet, oh my … I know I have mentioned my feet a lot, but they were so dear to me and I needed them so badly and I was abusing them with every step and they were shouting at me that we couldn't go on like this. By now, my toenails had abandoned ship. Gone. All of them.

I told myself as I dragged myself to my nail-less feet that, ah well, it couldn't get any worse than this. I hadn't, for example, trodden on a wasps' nest. Other competitors' tales of shouting 'Run, run RUUUUUN …' (as if they weren't already) and sprinting for five minutes while swatting away the last of their assailants had kept us entertained around the campfire. Entertained and slightly alarmed.

Now, on my own and on my dodgy toes, it was my turn. I think they are officially wasps, but I call them hornets, because that reminds me of their size. And they stung like hornets. I stepped on their nest and the next thing I knew I was being pursued angrily – understandably so, given my clumsy destruction of their home. I went through the protocol. As I did, I could hear an unusual high pitched scream. Actually, it was more of a screech.

No, no. It wasn't an animal. It was me. I sprinted as fast as I could for as long as I could. With each sting I cried out.

Soon they all disappeared together. Had I just crossed an invisible line which marked the end of their territory? When I could, I stopped. I found raised bumps all over me. They'd flown inside all my clothes and down between my back and rucksack. I tried to count them as I applied cream from the first-aid kit and gave up at thirty. The strange thing was that even as the swellings began to throb, I thought that five minutes earlier I had been struggling to keep going at a slow walk, and yet I had been able to break into a long sprint. Wonderful what the body can do, I told myself. And now that I had pain elsewhere, it would take my mind off my feet.

This spinning of a negative into a positive didn't last long. My tongue started to swell. I couldn't see any blue flags and I convinced myself I had gone off the trail and was now hopelessly lost in the middle of the Amazonian rainforest and if I was off the trail I wouldn't be noticed by the 'sweepers' who followed the runners and picked up those that had fallen, stopped, failed. If I had a rational thought it was of how much I wanted to be in my hammock. Stronger were the wilder, insistent thoughts about giving up. I didn't define them as reasonable, but there was no getting away from their growing, insistent presence in my head.

I fought them. I had to keep going, I told myself. If I halted even for a few seconds, to lean against a tree, or sit on a tree stump, a snake would have me. The sweepers would find little more than a pile of indigestible smelly kit and a half-chewed bib 73, returned by an otherwise sated anaconda. I did not stop. I carried on.

I made it to the next checkpoint and told Eurwyn about being eaten alive by wasps.

Now might be a good excuse to drop out of the race and save face. I could tell people that I didn't give up, I unfortunately got bitten and had an allergic reaction.

I didn't want to look at the camera.

'My tongue … it's swollen. '

'First of all, they don't eat. They sting.'

'But they've stung me so much that I'm having an allergic reaction.'

He looked inside my mouth and without fuss said, 'No, it's not swelling. See you at the next checkpoint.'

So, off I set again. Thinking about my tongue. It wasn't swelling? I was sure it was, but was my mind playing games again? Was my subconscious inventing excuses for me to give up?

I had to think of something to take my mind off, well, the reality that every part of me was hurting. I started to work on a piece to camera for the next checkpoint.

It went along the lines of looking into the lens and saying gravely: 'I've decided that enough is enough. I'm calling it a day. But tomorrow I will rise and give it another go.' That didn't sound right at all. A bit dramatic maybe? Perhaps I should fall to the ground in front of the camera and let the action do the talking? And do an Arnold Schwarzenegger-type 'I'll be back' end link? No, that wouldn't work either. What about reaching out towards the other runners as they went gliding on their way, the kindred spirits that I could no longer keep up with, and watching them all fade into the jungle? I could then lower my head to the jungle floor, so the last shot would be of the wasps' stings on my shaking shoulders.

A set-up, they'd all say. I shouldn't be thinking of doing it specially for the camera, anyway, I said to myself. If I did anything for anyone it'd be for me. And all the while I sort of threw my indignation about and muttered about how I really didn't need any of this in my life right now.

I carried on shuffling. And shuffling. All the way to the next checkpoint. And once I was there, with another two and a half hours under my belt, I thought I might as well spend a similar time going to the next one. There was nothing else to do out here in the middle of this jungle. Despite my moaning, I loved the area. I felt privileged to be there. I'd look around in awe at the wonderful jungle views, the vegetation, the animals. Then, I'd have a good look at my feet. Still, what struck me as a sensible idea at one checkpoint, didn't seem half so clever halfway along the trail to the next. It's hard to describe the sheer tedium and monotony of being in pain and on your own on a long trail without banging on about it endlessly, like toes on the end of swollen feet banging into the front of trail shoes. I recognise there's only so much foot-talk and introspection any reader can take.

From a runner's point of view, I had decided that enough was enough – over half of the competitors had now dropped out and I had gone further than I had expected in my first multi-stage event. As the producer of the show, I wondered if the crew had enough footage to fill an hour's slot. They did. So yes, I was proud of what I had achieved. I had reached my limit and that was good enough. Nothing to be ashamed of.

So, it's probably just as well that my mother joined me out there, repeating the Confucius quote: 'Glory is not by never falling but in the way we rise when we do fall.' I'd just done exactly that – taken another tumble – when I heard her. I was falling mentally, too. As I clambered yet again back to my feet, I kept repeating it over and over in my head. It soon became as numbingly dull as anything else I'd thought that day, except it replaced those thoughts. It was simple really. It doesn't matter how many times you fall, pick yourself back up, wipe the dust off and carry on. That is what is important. And slowly but surely, the pulse of the mind replaced the aches of the body and the steady beat returned and one foot followed the other. And that was all that counted. Each one, a pace nearer the finish line. Even a tiny smile returned to my face.

Not long afterwards – perhaps a few thousand beats later – I came upon two other runners and we joined forces. I had met the Americans, David and Kevin, during the days of preparation in Santarém and we had got along well. Now, we got along even better, a tight-knit trio almost out on their feet but determined to make the cut-off. Not a lot was said. In a trance we pressed ahead, but the factor that counted seemed to be that we were together. We ate together and drank together and gave signs of encouragement together. We made it out of the jungle before darkness fell. I had run, shuffled, walked alone and now I had run, shuffled, walked as part of a team. Both felt good – two elements of what ultra running is all about. The shared experience is part of the individual goal: to find something out about yourself in the company of nobody but yourself sometimes, but also with others around you at other times.

We sat at the checkpoint, unable to string a sentence together. I'd thought about what I might say to the camera for much of the day, but now I could find nothing. People who know me might struggle to believe that I did not talk. It has been said that I am chatty, but these were not normal circumstances. Perhaps it is my way of saying to everyone who knows me that if I was unable to talk it must truly say how tough it was out there in the jungle. Perhaps I was thinking to myself that this was merely a checkpoint on Stage 5. It would be dark soon but there were still nearly 20 miles to go. The marshals did their best to keep us on track. The rest of the way was flat. There was no more jungle.

Out of the blue, my bedroom poster from my teenage years flashed in front of me: 'Face your fear and just do it.' I had nothing left in the tank, but I stood up and told my new friends: 'Sorry guys, I'm going ahead. I have to.'

I heard one of them say, 'You're crazy, Lowri.' I even managed a smile as I waved back. 'See you later,' I said. What would soon have wiped the smile off my face was if I had gone half a mile and found I was in no shape to have taken such a foolhardy decision, but I seemed to have tapped into some reserve. It didn't give me the energy to launch myself like a rocket, but one step at a time I headed into the night. The body and mind were connected. If you're really enjoying what you're doing your body recovers better, and at this moment that could not have been truer. I found a sixth, seventh, eighth gear. I knocked my nail-less feet against the floor. The pain had disappeared.

By now we had broken out from under the jungle canopy for the first time and had a clear view of the road ahead. I felt tears welling up. I hadn't played any music since the start of the race, but now, with the jungle behind me, I did. The song was on the playlist created for me by my fiancé, Siôn. How quickly it had happened, incidentally, that I'd gone from having no boyfriend in the earliest days of the Amazon project, to meeting Siôn Jones, who also worked in sport broadcasting for BBC Wales in Cardiff. I had met him for the first time during a girls' night out (mine not his), and, for the second time, at another party six months later, when I was in full training for the Jungle Ultra. And now we were engaged. It had happened fast, but it just felt right. How had I managed to fit those parties into my schedule? And find the time to meet Siôn, fall in love, and say yes when he proposed? Well, somehow I did and we were happy.

Siôn had organised a surprise party for me a week before leaving for the Amazon. As training intensified during the final few months of preparation, I saw less of my friends. I felt bad for that. So, as a surprise, Siôn organised a meal for 40 of my closest friends together in a Cardiff restaurant. We all enjoyed a wonderful evening but I could not ignore that quiet nervousness in the bottom of my stomach.

Siôn of course knew this so he created a playlist for me on his iPod. Music that would help calm me and motivate me on my jungle adventure. With my ear plugs in, I ran on this newfound high, 'Llawenydd Heb Ddiwedd' ('Endless Joy') by the Welsh language indie band Y Cyrff (The Bodies) filled my ears. The words had a profound and immediate effect on me. And I was smiling again, with tears of joy running down my face. All of a sudden, I could look up without fear of tripping and I felt a surge of energy through my body. So far in the race I'd had to concentrate at all times on my breathing, my gait, my balance, but on this open trail I just let it all go and emptied my mind. Time ceased to matter, except that I knew that it wasn't some flush that came and went in minutes. I had entered a state, a flow, which swept me along for hours.

That moment has stayed with me. I don't know what happened. Was it spiritual? Was it the endorphins? A higher power? I don't know, but something did happen. I am convinced this is where my body gave up ... and my mind took over. I was breaking new personal barriers. I'd been sure I could no longer carry on, but each step proved me wrong. Our greatest weakness lies in giving up. The most certain way to succeed is always to try just one more time.

Here, on Stage 5, I felt it again. It meant I broke away from the team. I think they knew what I was experiencing. I still keep in touch with them and even though our communications amount only to a few words at a time, we know that we have a special bond. I believe we know full well that the challenges we take on will cause pain and suffering and leave bruises and scars, but the bruises and scars will disappear in time and are nothing compared to the glow the adventures leave on the soul.

Since I have crossed a mystical threshold here, I have to tell you that something else happened on Stage 5. I had deliriously told Australian Gus about the Brazilian joker, Mauro – the one I suspected of putting stones in my rucksack – and, lo and behold, here he was alongside me now. If I had run for hours on Stage 1 on this newfound high, by Stage 5 the effects were to be shorter-lived. I had floated off into the night, but the reality was that, still a very long way from the finish, I was landing on feet that were in a gruesome state. I was sliding into a darker hole when Mauro, smiling away, power-walked his way to my side.

He had at most a few dozen words of English; I had maybe six words of Portuguese. Somehow, he managed to tell me that he had competed in many of these races, owned a running shop in Puerto Rico and that he was sure I was going to make it to the end. And if it was fine with me, he would like us to cross Stage 5's finish line together. Of course. It would be my honour, I tried to tell him.

The checkpoints came and went. We hardly stopped at them, partly because I thought that if I took my shoes off for an inspection I'd never get them back on again, and partly because we were in this sort of shared trance.

We had found our pace but were also prepared to stop at any given moment. At one such point, we were so alone that we thought we had gone the wrong way. We were checking for the footprints of competitors who had passed before us, when a snake crossed the path in front of me. Above us and around us, the butterflies were incredible. One, brilliantly coloured and bigger than my hand, landed on my arm. We were mesmerised. It wasn't always on the move that I experienced this rapture.

It was such a beautiful and humbling evening. On one hand I

wanted to get to the end as quickly as possible but on the other hand, I didn't want it to end.

We followed the tunnels of light formed by our head-torches with the cloudless sky and starry night to help us on our way. We could see in the distance the lights of Alter do Chão, the starting point of our time in the Amazon, but we had no idea how near or far the town was. Besides, we had to concentrate on what was immediately in front of us. We were close to the river and baby alligators slid in and out of the water. They were everywhere but we need not have worried. They were just as bemused by us as we were by them as we passed. We, too, had to go in and out of the water at various points. There were obstacles everywhere beneath our feet and reflections of spiders' eyes above us. Frogs the size of small footballs clung to tree trunks.

The quick dips into the river were one thing, but it was a bit more disconcerting to find a 150-metre river crossing towards the end of the stage. We stepped into the pitch-black water, waded and swam as fast as we could to the other side and hauled ourselves on to a sandy beach. It was nearing midnight, we were running along a strand on the edge of the Amazon with a million million stars above us. Wet, wrecked feet carried us along on another wave of rapture. We crossed the finish line together, to big hugs, smiles and repeats of 'obrigado' 'thank you' 'obrigada' and tears. Well, I thought there were. Back home, not long after the race, I began to log and compile all the shots that would go into the final programme – the race itself. I told the editor we should keep a special lookout for the material shot at the end of Stage 5 when I talked about my family and Mauro's constant encouragement. All very emotional and a bit tearful, I said. Always comes in handy, the gulp and weep moment. We found the finish, but for all that we spooled up and down, we could find nothing more than a big hug and a slightly formal farewell. Funny what tricks memory and mind can play.

We had been given two days to complete Stage 5 and we were home in 17 hours. We had avoided going into the second day. As a result, we had an extra day for relaxation. It was like the beginning of a slow awakening. There was a last stage to go, but we could think again of life outside the jungle. I sent some emails and put my aching feet up. Later that morning I went down with Ryan Sandes to watch the other competitors come in. Ryan had the most time to do what he liked. He was in the race lead, but he still wanted to cheer home all those less talented than himself.

One kick-boxer from London had fashioned two walking sticks out of fallen branches. His feet were so swollen he'd cut open the front of his shoes and taped over the toes that now protruded. He was hauling himself forward, swaying back and forth towards the line, where everyone stood to give him a rousing reception. He was going to make it with a couple of hours to go before cut-off and he wasn't the last.

As night fell, competitors – many battered and bruised – were still coming down the sand on the last stretch.

CHAPTER 10

NEARLY THERE

Stage 6. 33km (21 miles). Of the 126 starters who had lined up in Itapuama, six days ago, 60 now stood on the river beach for the run for home. *'Sand, sand and more sand and plenty of sunshine. But the end is in sight and "only" 33km until you reach the finish line at the beautiful resort of Alter do Chão.'*

It was a run along the shore, flat all the way. Of course, I knew my feet were going to hurt and I seemed to have gone down with a chest infection, but after what we'd just been through, well, the one pain was a constant travelling companion and a new little wheeze wasn't going to stop me on this day. In fact, I was out to do this as quickly as possible. I have said before that the normal gauges of accomplishment, such as times and finishing position, are not as all-consuming in ultra running as they are in athletics in general, but I would be lying if I said I did not want to hold on to my position in the top ten.

Having said that, as we milled at the start there was a different buzz. Everybody was wishing each other all the best of luck, shaking hands and hugging. Only with the countdown from ten seconds to the start did the front-runners turn on their race heads. And off they set at a pace unlike anything seen so far. I let the lead-group go off at their alarming speed over the beautiful white sand and I tucked into about tenth place. To get into the top ten exceeded my expectation. Never in a million years did I think I'd be here – top ten! Third lady! Given that this was where I stood overall, it seemed as good a place to claim as any on the last leg. To drop to 11th or 12th would have been disappointing. I didn't want to let my position go.

I joined up with a tall, heavily tattooed German: I asked him what the tattoos meant to him and nearly all of them were reminders of the races he had faced over the years and what he had learnt from the experience.

We talked about endurance running and how he'd already started to make plans for the next one because he needed to fill the void that would come with finishing this one. Just as I'd heard about the marathon's wall, so I'd also caught other competitors talking about these blues. You put yourself through so much for so long that you sort of crash once the ultra is over. The German asked me how many of these multi-stage races I'd done. I'd told him this was my first. My first ultra race.

'What!' he shouted. 'You're not doing too bad considering this is your first. Of all the multi-stage races I've done, this is by far the hardest'. And having read the names of races he had tattooed on his body, I knew he meant it.

'Talk about jumping into the toughest race on Earth,' he laughed. He told me to take care. I said I would.

It was good to run with my head up and my face in the sun. I have to say that I didn't manage to recapture that magical feeling of the day before, though. Perhaps it was this awareness of the need to keep up a good pace on damaged feet that made it a little less than spiritual. Perhaps I'd used up my ration of euphoria. On the other hand, there was no need to reach deep into the well on this occasion. No need to strip this run down to the most basic of actions: put one foot in front of the other. I was going to make it.

I was exhausted but I was still moving. I had lost all technique but I was still fighting with every step. I was also losing patience. With the finish line only a few miles away, I wanted to get to the end as fast as possible but my legs simply did not have that urgency in them. And yet, somehow I felt strong.

My stomach had been jostled so much. I had filled it with food – mostly 'ordinary' food – no gels, no bars, just sweets, dried fruit and nuts as trail mix, my electrolyte tablets and my dehydrated meals of 1000kcal in the morning and in the night.

I was severely sleep-deprived (although I'd soon find out what 'real' sleep deprivation was), and anxious about the finish line – was

I still going to make it? Knowing my luck, a huge anaconda, snake, hornet or something would come and bite me on my backside and I'd be out of the race, just like that! I felt sick just thinking about it. Everything by now was moving in slow motion. I had a film crew in my face, but I couldn't talk to anyone.

It was a strange day, because even as I was judging myself along more conventional athletic lines – holding a position, keeping an eye on the competition, thinking of my cadence, breathing, heart and speed – there was still a lot of emotion in play. Slowly and surely as the hours passed there was an accumulative sense of achievement, a gathering of so many ticks in the daily boxes. A sense of pride. Relief that I had kept going. And enjoyment began to break through. If I began by rather forcing out a smile at the first checkpoints or while passing the groups of people that gathered along the way to cheer us on, I soon found that I was genuinely happy out there. Perhaps I knew that nothing could stop me now. On the last few miles I did not touch that higher plane, but the markers came and went, and as they shrank in number so real pleasure grew. And a fair degree of emotion. I was close to the end. Through gritted teeth, I laughed out loud and felt a tear forming.

Even on that last stage, a few did not make it to the end. Five more dropped out. That must have been tough for them. Or perhaps they had already answered the questions they had asked of themselves and weren't shattered by having to give up so close to home. I knew that for me, the novice, it would have been difficult to take. I had trained with an iron discipline for this event and I did not want that preparation to have been in vain. I could have told myself that so unknown were the conditions awaiting me in Brazil that failure could have been easily excused. Not by me. How far had I been prepared to go? 'Not far enough,' would have wounded me deeply. I would have taken a real plunge. But now that I knew I wasn't going to fail, was I feeling a corresponding reaction the other way? I'd been under my wonderfully weird spell and now, closer to the finish line, I was feeling good. But was I as intoxicated by the prospect of crossing the line as I would have been dismayed by failure? I wasn't sure I was, but I knew that the question would be asked again. No, I would be asking the question of myself again. Until I did, this would have to do. I was excited, proud, exhilarated, but I was also a little sad.

I ran towards the line with a smile on my face and shed a tear. 'I don't know what to say,' I managed for the camera as I crossed the line. 'It's about people finding a strength they didn't know they had,' which was true but didn't quite nail the week. It didn't capture that moment, say, of leaving my new best friends, the Americans, behind at the checkpoint and heading into the darkness to face this incredible rainforest and all its inhabitants and unknowns on my own.

I translated the quote my mother had given me which says that glory is not about never failing but about the way we pick ourselves up and keep going ...

I knew I hadn't given myself or the viewers a full answer. How could I in a minute's piece to camera? But I knew something momentous had happened in my life. Just like my piece to camera after Stage 5. Inside I was crying and I was fighting to hold the tears back as I tried to get my breath back. I can get by in the world with its home comforts, its appliances and its apps. I love my family. My work. I need running, though, to give me perspective. It makes me aware of every fibre which comprises the physical me, which can be flogged so that the mind and soul can be soothed. Not for ever. But for that moment it had suffered and I felt good. My last words to camera in the Amazon were, 'Time to see the family for a *cwtsh*.'

For the record, Ryan Sandes was the overall winner. Nikki Kimball and Tracy Garneau crossed the line together as an equal-first pair of women. They are exceptional athletes – voted Ultra Runners of the Year. Ryan's stand-alone victory was a tribute to his extraordinary athleticism. People who know little about ultra running can be a little sniffy about it because they see people walking. Ryan Sandes took such scepticism and ground it to dust. The women winners stood more for the camaraderie that I had discovered on the long trails through the jungle. We were competitors; we were soulmates.

And as for the novice, I held on to my tenth place overall and was third in the women's race.

I had one last, slightly strange sensation on the last stage of the Jungle Marathon. As I approached the finish I had this craving for a can of Coca-cola. I don't do Coca-cola, full-stop, but I had seen somebody downing a cold can earlier in the race and I became absolutely convinced that this was my key to happiness. I couldn't remove this yearning from my head: head back, chin up and glugging on a can of Coke. When I crossed the line, that's precisely what I did. I don't think the sugar-hit provided a spiritual high, but nor do I feel guilty about guzzling it in two gulps. I do find it odd that such a tiny moment in the midst of so many truly life-changing memories has stuck with me.

On the subject of thoughts on the move, I always had the camera in mind. It couldn't be with me all the way, but I had to be prepared – most times – to deliver a line. Otherwise, what was the point? I had this inner challenge going on, my private struggle, but I was also there to do a job, to be making a series that would be seen by as large an audience as possible. It definitely helped at times to have to think of what I might say – it helped pass the hours. A repetition of 'I'm so tired' would get me only so far. Trying to expand on that theme – to qualify my exhaustion – sort of helped dissipate it. Trying to make pain sound less painful made it exactly that. The job in that respect helped, although there were other times when the thought of going around a bend in the trail to find the crew expectantly waiting for a witty one-liner on the hoof made me want to kick them – except that it would have hurt my toes.

Of course, I would never have kicked the crew. They were my friends. They were as much a part of my journey as all the other mentors, fellow competitors. I sometimes found it hard to muster words for television and I would stand in front of the camera, shrugging my shoulders, frustrated and insisting, 'I've got nothing left to say.' I'd run off and feel bad for not giving them the soundbites they needed but I told myself that they knew me, they knew that I was struggling and that disappointing them was the last thing on my mind.

After I had crossed the line and delivered my slightly flat final words, the crew were not particularly interested in how I was feeling. Despite being pleased and proud that I had exceeded my expectations, they were all a bit subdued. Maybe they were disappointed in my flattish behaviour? What had I said or done to make them so quiet? Had I upset them when I was struggling and frustrated?

The director later explained. They had all gone down with a stomach bug and were feeling very sorry for themselves. They were keeping an arm's length distance as they were worried I would catch whatever bug they had caught.

We were separated anyhow as the competitors were all taken by bus to a hotel in Santarém, where it struck me – and it truly hit me hard – just how smelly we were. We stuck together in the foyer and other people gave us a wide berth. There was a sort of force-field around us. We were stinking. I literally had to stop breathing through my nose.

I couldn't stop drinking now. After my can of Coke, I was back on the water and even when half-asleep I would reach for the bottle. Replenishing was the order of the day. We were all invited to a party that night in a hotel overlooking the Amazon. I was the only one from our Welsh group that turned up. In the confusion of who might still be contagious, it was not clear who was sleeping where. The six TV crew members, worried that they'd picked up a serious infectious tropical disease, decided to take up both bedrooms. Instead of taking up an offer of a spare bed in another South African's TV crew's bedroom, I politely declined and spent the night hours sitting and dozing in the hotel lobby. Was this part of the process of coming down with a bump? Not really. It was more comfortable than the jungle camps. Besides, I had to be ready to leave early the next morning. I could not wait to get back home to see Siôn, my parents and my brother Roger. Plus, I had to be back to work on *Ralïo*. In a few days, I'd be presenting live coverage from the last round of the World Rally Championship so I needed to be compos mentis. I also had a wedding to plan. I was too busy to be feeling low.

It seemed everyone was shipping out sooner rather than later. We didn't smell bad now as we lounged around at the airport, but other travellers still seemed to be avoiding us. Some were in wheelchairs, some had lost what looked like half of their body weight. I, on the other hand, felt OK. The race doctors asked a few of us questions about our general well-being and it seemed that we looked so awful that the rumour had started that we were all victims of some terrible tropical disease. Our feet in particular were proof that we were obviously very sick. The doctors advised us to look cheerful and to remove our feet from public view, or we might not be allowed on the planes. I found I couldn't get mine into my softest, most comfortable boots. My swollen plague-feet remained on display.

Two last things. I ran the Jungle Marathon in 2009 and the four-part television series went out in 2010, making it eligible for the Celtic Film Festival of 2011. We called it *Ras Yn Erbyn Amser* (*Race Against Time*), to reflect not only the event itself but also the fight to preserve the rainforest.

When the invitation to the film festival arrived, not a lot of people at POP 1, the production company making the series for S4C, could go. It was unlike us not to be up for a party, but there was a reason. The festival also went by the name of the Western Isles Festival and it was going to be held in Stornoway on the island of Lewis and Harris in the Outer Hebrides.

'Somebody should go,' said Dafydd Rhys, our boss.

I went. I was on crutches (I'll explain later), so it wasn't the easiest of journeys. But that was the point, somebody said. No point in Lowri going all that way if it wasn't going to hurt. Anyway, much to our surprise, *Ras Yn Erbyn Amser* won the main prize, the highest accolade at the festival – the Spirit of the Festival award.

The second and last thing came in the form of a letter that was delivered long before I went to Stornoway. It was only one short, handwritten note; it complimented the series but it also asked me if I had really done the Jungle Marathon. It was made for television, wasn't it, so it must have been fake, right?

I'm sure I overreacted, but I felt cut to my very core. My very integrity was being questioned. Perhaps this letter was a trigger for delayed post-race blues. For other runners the trough seemed to follow a more conventional and immediate route. For weeks following a peak experience, they struggled to get out of the door. Running, quite simply, had lost its appeal. The elation of the finish line was over, the fatigue had begun to lessen and the endorphins had run their course. The hollowness was filled with a question: what now? For most experienced runners this was entirely normal. I wasn't entirely sure it would be for me.

I was fortunate to enjoy the company of family and friends, who kept the 'running blues' at bay. And kept me buoyant, bouncing along. I often let it all out during my sessions and my poor fellow runners would have to listen to me going on and on about the pain and the impossibility of fitting it all in and the frustration of not feeling in the groove. I'm not sure I can take much more of this. They've heard it many times. At least it passes the time, they say, when we're laughing about it later. I'm not all doom and gloom on our runs – we share full belly laughs too – but they know, I hope, that should the time ever come for them to need to share their worries and fears, I will repay the favour and be here for them.

I have mentioned Ross Hall before. I went to see the sports psychologist at the University of Glamorgan again now. He had been helpful in my preparations for Brazil, specifically in the training of my mind to remain strong in adversity. But he was also wise in many other areas of life. He told me now that challenges come in many different forms, and not all necessarily in the world of running. I, for example, had a wedding to plan. 'If you don't want to race straight away,' he said, 'then you don't have to. When's the wedding? Eight months away?' I nodded. 'Fill any hollowness with that, then. Make your plans for your big day.'

The weeks passed. I very happily married Siôn and we went off on our honeymoon, backpacking around Croatia and island-hopping off its Adriatic coastline. And on the last day, I told him that I thought I'd have to do another multi-stage ultra marathon.

CHAPTER 11

FROZEN STIFF

I'm sure there were many times during the Jungle Marathon when I told myself that I would never, ever be doing anything like this again. I had such a catalogue of injuries old and new, of open wounds and septic cuts and swellings and deep bruises and dull aches that it would have been unimaginable not to reject out of hand the tiniest notion that I might one day be going through all this again. Add in the sleep deprivation, the heat and the humidity, and the sheer overwhelming exhaustion over the six stages and I must have told myself that this was strictly a one-off, never to be repeated. Six weeks after I came home, I could barely squeeze my feet, with their new sets of nails, into my trainers.

And yet, here I was, telling Siôn that I wanted to do another multi-stage self-sufficient ultra run. He took it very well. I think he knew it was coming. He's a good runner in his own right and knows all about the runner's high. He has felt for himself the thrill that comes with pushing yourself towards an almost impossibly distant goal and reaching it. But to train for a multi-stage ultramarathon requires dedication, sacrifice, hours away from home, not just from the athlete but from those closest to you too ... For me, I knew I didn't want the preparation to take over our lives. It had during the Amazon prep as I juggled work, training and family time. Now, I was newly married and so had to try to fit this next race around my other commitments. I might not have wanted it to take over my life and yet I did want to go into the next challenge as ready as I could be.

But which race should I choose? This was a simple question. The tougher one was: right, now that you've put yourself to the test and now that it seems you've passed it, how far do you want to push yourself next time? How far do you want to go?

I finally eased my feet into my trainers and went out for a run. I had no idea where I was in terms of fitness. I had been consistent with my training since the Amazon, although the mileage had dropped to 60 miles a week – I was still keeping a log book of my training. But my racing and training was mostly based on running shorter distances sometimes twice a day. How I ran now might determine how adventurous I might dare to be when it came to selecting the challenge.

It would have to be extreme enough to appeal to the television commissioners, since without that element I would never be able to afford to go, but I had to make sure I wasn't about to bite off more than I could chew. I felt amazing. I ran as if I'd been doing it every day – not through impenetrable jungle, but on a springy carpet of grass and a sea breeze in my face. Those runs are the best – when you realise in a flash that this is all about you. It's not the conscious you, or even the unconscious you talking … somehow it's the higher level version … the place that as humans we so rarely go to … it's reaching out and daring you to be the best version of yourself. For some athletes this moment happens later on in the run or in a race, when they feel like they are flying, like its effortless, like they were born to do this. Some might call this being 'In the Zone', others might call it 'Being in Flow'... I simply call it being 'In the Know' …

I didn't have a time or distance in mind, I just went with the flow. I went from my parents' house all the way around the Gower Peninsula, and 50 floaty kilometres later I suppose I was in a mood to be totally daring. Beware the runner's high when it comes to making sensible decisions.

I researched the most extreme challenge in the world, with the help of Sue and Martin Like, my kit suppliers from Brecon. They were the race organisers, it turned out, of an event in Northern Canada called the 6633 Arctic Ultra. They had made it a point of pride to establish it as the toughest, windiest and most extreme race on the planet. It started at the Eagle Plains Hotel in the Yukon, crossed the Arctic Circle at latitude 66 degrees and 33 minutes North and ended 120 miles later at Fort McPherson – or at least the race that appealed to common sense finished there, the race within my comprehension. Way outside my imagination was the other race, the ludicrously extended option that continued beyond Fort McPherson for another 230 miles, all the way to a dot on the map, called Tuktoyaktuk, on the frozen coast of the Arctic Ocean. It was, that is, either a 120-miler, something in distance akin to what I had run in the jungle, or a 350-miler.

I mean, there was not even a decision to be made. 120 miles in the heat would become 120 miles in the cold. Very neat and tidy as a contrast for a novice on her second outing.

I found myself entering the 2011 Arctic Ultra over the longer distance, of course. 350 miles. Perhaps I should have done more research and found out, for example, that the inaugural 6633 had taken place in 2007, and that over the span of four races a grand total of four runners (one athlete had finished twice) had completed the 350-mile version of the race. In 2008, nobody had made it to the end. I signed the entry form and took the idea to S4C, who commissioned *Ras Yn Erbyn Amser 2*.

There were similarities between series one and two. The first three programmes in the series would concentrate on my preparations over the six months ahead, while the fourth and last would deal with the race itself. It was a bit weird working on the edit of the Jungle Marathon series while preparing for this Arctic race. But not nearly as weird as trying to absorb what I had just signed up for.

Never mind the similarities; far more striking were the differences. This 350 miles was nearly three times longer than the Jungle. No stage racing – the 6633 Ultra was a non-stop race. If you stopped for a rest or a sleep, the clock would still be ticking away. So I divided the race into smaller chunks – eight checkpoints throughout the race which meant I had to cover over 40 miles per day. When I spoke to Martin Like about my plans, he quickly said, 'Wrong plan. You must not break this race into days. With this race, you must think in hours.'

I didn't dare yet think about the weather, except to know that what very little I had worn in the tropics would become layer upon layer of thermal insulation and that instead of one rucksack on my back, I'd have another one, plus a harness attached to a sled on wheels. I was about to be introduced to my pulk and all that it would carry to keep me alive.

I went to see Siwan Davies, Professor of Physical Geography at Swansea University. I needed to know more. I wanted to know more. Greater knowledge might reassure me that I wasn't in the grip of some delayed jungle fever, that I hadn't set myself a goal so far beyond my capabilities that I was about to make a right fool of myself.

I also wanted to learn from this once in a lifetime opportunity. I was going to a wonderful part of the world, which, like the Amazon, had its own specific challenges. Siwan, having spent a long time living and studying in the Arctic told me about the effects of climate change on the area. Even though I was flying out there, I knew, as she had done, that I'd have to repay the world in whichever way I could once I'd returned.

I'd be unlucky if I didn't see the aurora borealis, the northern lights, she said. The Yukon and the neighbouring Northwest Territories would be dry in March. Not that I'd notice because despite being in sunlight for twelve hours a day, I'd be battling to keep myself warm. The temperature would be between -20C and -30C, but the wind chill could take it down to -70C. 'You'll come across Hurricane Alley,' she said, 'with its Katabatic winds.' These were winds that came downhill fast off a high plain, and I'd be walking into them as I went up into the Richardson Mountains.

The race would take us north-east from Eagle Plains to Inuvik on the Dempster Highway and from Inuvik to Tuktoyaktuk on the Ice Road that formed over the Mackenzie River every winter.

The Dempster Highway was named after a Welshman, William John 'Jack' Dempster, who came to Canada as a young man and joined the North-West Mounted Police. He was a 'Mountie' and a famous one, to boot, having played a lead part in the story that has gone down in Canadian folklore as 'The Lost Patrol'. In late 1910, another Mountie, Francis Fitzgerald had set out with three other officers, fifteen dogs and three sleds, on the annual winter patrol. They set out from Fort McPherson but failed to arrive in Dawson City. In early 1911, Dempster and three men formed a search party. In appalling conditions, they refused to give up. Eventually they found the half-eaten remains of some of the dogs. They pressed on and found the bodies of the missing men. The meat of their dogs had not been enough to save them. Three had died of cold and hunger, and the fourth had shot himself. I wasn't sure I wanted to know too much about being lost in a blizzard and ending up half-eaten somewhere near the end of my race's Stage 3.

If I reached Fort McPherson, I would still have a way to go on the Dempster Highway. I would be on the Mackenzie Delta but wouldn't really meet the Mackenzie River in all its winter glory until Inuvik, where the ice that formed a giant seal over its waters would be the race surface for the last 120 miles.

The Mackenzie is one of the unsung rivers of the world. Mention the Amazon and instantly you have an image of rainforest and heat and immensity. The Mackenzie is a little more anonymous. Its main stem flows for a thousand miles from the Great Slave Lake up towards the Beaufort Sea, part of the Arctic Ocean. But … if you go from the headwater of Thutade Lake in British Columbia and add the miles of the Finlay River that joins the Peace River that flows into the Athabasca River that becomes the Slave River until the Great Slave Lake, then the river-system of the Mackenzie extends to 2,635 miles. It's still outdone by the 4,000 miles of the Amazon (which was approximately the total distance I had run in training for the Amazon), but set it against the longest river in Wales and England, the Severn, and it is twelves times longer. The Severn is broad enough where it meets the Bristol Channel and the Atlantic to be known as the Severn Sea in Welsh – *Môr Hafren* – but is only 220 miles long. I'd have to run from South Wales to North Wales and back to cover the same race mileage.

Everything in my ultras seemed to be on an incomprehensibly grander scale. We were running distances that took us to the limits (or what we thought were our limits) of our capabilities and yet they amounted to nothing more than millimetres on the maps, where whole pages had to be devoted to the course, from source to mouth, of the Amazon and the Mackenzie. We were ants.

To survive this challenge, I had to respect my heart. Might I have overdone things in the heat of the jungle? I needed to know how I might function at low temperatures.

I was set to work on a treadmill at Sport Wales in Cardiff where I was given a mannitol test, to see if I might have asthma. The results were encouraging: no asthma; the heart was strong.

I headed to North Wales to get some quality sessions in on the hills and mountains (and to spice up the shots for the camera.) There wasn't a lot I could do to vary the pictures of me running but by putting Rhossili and Worms Head behind me, or by placing me in the old slate quarries around Llanberis in Snowdonia, we could do our bit to show off the splendours of Wales. I had ambassadorial responsibilities on that front, too – not that I was complaining, I love returning to North Wales especially to the mountains. It was no chore to be going up and down the country. I was feeling good, firm of conviction. Exhilarated. My fitness levels had dropped since the Jungle Marathon but slowly I could feel the strength in my legs returning and my head was in a good place. This wasn't a reckless challenge, but a calculated risk. And as for that excuse of a man who'd sent me the letter questioning whether the Jungle run had been faked for television, well, I'd show him. I pushed myself with a vengeance up the steep inclines of the abandoned slate quarries and then repeated. And repeated. I was exhausted, and sometimes when I push myself to exhaustion I can be a little emotional. But not here. I was flying.

The next test came at Bangor University, where Dr Stewart Laing was going to test my reactions in cold conditions and measure my body-fat levels. I was also going to be pushed to the limit again in a VO2 max test, to put a figure on my fitness. I don't quite know what went wrong but I stopped running when, really, I knew in my head that I could have gone on. The researchers seemed a little surprised too with my low score but were surprised with how quickly my heart rate recovered. I, on the other hand, felt down as I went into an ice-cold chamber and began to work again. This was a test of my sweat – as in, I wasn't allowed to perspire. Break into a sweat at -30C with wind chill thrown in for icy measure, and it freezes. And frozen sweat on the skin quickly leads to frostbite. One lady on a past 6633 Ultra had serious frostbite to her nose, so I needed these lessons.

The temperature dropped to -20C. I was clearly sweating. I was amazed at how cold I felt. Not amazed – horrified. Even breathing the cold air was painful. This was after just 90 minutes in the chamber. I was going to be exposed to the Arctic weather for eight days.

'It's all starting to sink in,' I said. 'I'm not very happy.'

The VO2 max results were less than encouraging, too. Twelve months earlier, I had a VO2 max test at Bath University where I trained in a heat chamber for the Jungle Marathon. I left there with a pleasant surprise. I had scored in the mid-60s. But here, a year later, my scores had dropped a lot. My training was all based on time on feet rather than speed work. My miles per minute were slowing, but on the plus side, I found that I could run for longer and longer. The testing team and I agreed that I could have carried on for a little longer. They didn't think it was serious. They didn't ask the question: 'Why did you stop?' I did. I was much more aggrieved. Mind not able to persuade body was anathema. I'd be having words with my head.

My fat was good, though. Fifteen years earlier, I might have struggled with hearing that news, but now I wanted a strong body that could perform and not crumble on the 6633 Ultra. A protective layer was essential, I was told. It was a food reserve. It was scientifically approved.

Even so, with six months to go, I needed to increase my training. By now I allowed myself two back-to-back days of training. Sunday was a long run of 35 miles and so was Monday. I'd leave the house with my husband as he went to work and I'd go for a bimble. My bimble would include running to the mountain ranges of South Wales. We'd arrange to meet back in our house after he returned from work. And then we'd go off again together for a ten-mile run.

Those extra miles alongside someone with a fresh pair of legs were painful mentally and physically, but they really did push my limits.

I would also drive four hours to the bottom of Snowdon and run up and down Wales's highest mountain. Snowdon is often referred to as 'Britain's busiest mountain'. It has its more demanding hiking routes, but you can reach the top by taking one of the narrow-gauge trains of the Snowdon Mountain Railway, with its station in Llanberis. No doubt, my friend the letter-writer would have had me sneaking into a carriage and settling down for a cushy ride up the mountain for a cappuccino in the café at the sunny summit. For the record, I ran up and down twice, returned to the car, took brief refuge there from the wind and the rain and moaned to the camera that I really didn't want to be doing this. Motivation was low so I had to act. Action often comes before motivation. I simply opened the door and jumped out onto the Llanberis path. I don't think the shots of me, head buried deep in my hood, as soaking as if I'd just emerged from the Tapajós river, and with nothing to see of the scenery through the mist, telling myself when I need a good telling off; 'C'mon Morgan, stop your whinging and just get on with it,' would have made the Wales Tourist Board's showreel of the treasures of Wales.

I forced myself out of the car and, leaving a jam sandwich on the dashboard as an enticement to return, off I went again, back up and back down. Thirty miles and 3,300 metres of elevation later, I devoured my deliciously soggy jam sandwich.

With five months to go, I counted up my miles per week: 110. A slow 110 but it was still 110. Two years earlier, I struggled to get out of bed after running 40 miles per week – I was exhausted. Gosh, seventeen years ago I was struggling to walk from one lamp post to another. Now I was running 110 a week. You'd think I'd be delighted, but in fact it had the opposite effect. My target was 350 in eight days. The disparity added to the growing sense of urgency. The race was approaching fast and there was still so much to do. I was getting nervous, really nervous. Was the stage fright of my younger self coming back to haunt me again? Would I just panic and not even show up for this race?

The arrival of my Arctic kit concentrated the mind, too. Enter the pulk. The Incredible Pulk. Or rather, the Pulk Mark 1. This prototype had a single axle and just two wheels in total. I thought it looked sweet, but I hadn't run a yard with it behind me yet. Other vital pieces of equipment included lightweight metal spikes to go on the soles of my running shoes, to give me a firm grip on ice. The Dempster Highway was a road, but it stopped back then in Inuvik. For the last 120 miles of the 350 – it was still a distance that made me gasp every time I thought about it – I would be on the Ice Road all the way to Tuktoyaktuk. So my choice for shoes would be one pair of cushioned road shoes and a pair of cushioned trail shoes for the more rugged terrain. I'd learnt from my mistake in the Amazon. This time, I'd buy UK size 8 trainers and wear three layers of socks. If my feet did swell, then I'd whisk away a sock at a time.

The end destination of Tuk, as it is known, is a settlement originally built by Inuvialuit hunters of caribou and beluga whales. In the Inuvialuit language the place-name means 'resembling a caribou,' and there are rocks in the bay that apparently look like the animals. In March I would not be seeing them. March is the one month of the year when the temperature in Tuk never rises above zero. The thick ice over the Mackenzie River provided winter access to the settlement, the only season when it could be reached by road-going vehicles. When the ice melted, the small collection of houses could be supplied only by air. A project to extend the road had been mooted and since 2017 the Dempster Highway has run all the way to Tuk, but for the race of 2011 I would be needing my spikes for the Ice Road.

I was told that a third of the race depended on your physical strength, a third was down to your mental attitude but the last third was down to your systems – your personal administration. Knowing your kit inside out was going to a key part in surviving this race. So I needed to know how my kit worked, where every screw, water bottle, item of clothing, battery, and safety pin was kept. When you're sleep-deprived, hungry and freezing cold, doing the simplest of things like drinking your water bottle in -30C/-40C would be a massive challenge.

Back at home, I practised with the kit for hours and hours, days and days, months and months, in the comfort of our lounge. Siôn would be there timing me as I packed and unpacked my sleeping system. Initially it took me five minutes to pack the sleeping equipment, but I eventually had it down to 45 seconds. Out came my water bottles, with clear tape wrapped around them to stop my fingers, should they dare expose themselves, from sticking to frozen metal. I unwrapped my bothy bag, a sort of throw-up tent for use in an emergency. There were food packs, to be mixed with water warmed on my little stove. To be able to melt ice and heat it were a must. I was working on the calculation that I would need up to 5,000 calories a day, a figure I would have to revise upwards. Well, I would have to double it.

I hit the trail to burn off some more of these precious calories. I took to my first 40-mile training run at home. It went well. I felt that surge that allowed me to let go inside my head and glide. I really was in this race against time to be ready, but there were days when I felt nothing was beyond me.

I met up with Eurwyn, always a boost to my spirits. He slightly dampened my enthusiasm by putting me in an industrial freezer and making me train for three hours. Far less comfortable was the freezer I went into next. Within ten minutes of cycling on the turbo trainer and running loops around all of the frozen food with all my race gear on in -21C, my banana and cup of water had frozen solid. It was the first time I was afraid of this challenge.

Four months to go. I went to Sweden for a few days with Nigel, and the TV crew that had been so invaluable for the Jungle Marathon and a new team of trainers. A Scandinavian long weekend – it makes it sound like a holiday, an away-break in stunning scenery. But I went with Nigel Thomas – who on one hand was a close friend but on another was also a coach who pushed me to the extreme when it came to training weekends. It was his idea for me to spend the weekend with two Norwegian Special Forces instructors. We headed north to the iron-ore mining town of Kiruna in the far north of Swedish Lapland, where wind chill could drop the temperature to -60C. I took my pulk and Nigel and his colleagues set us – me and my sled – off on a 40-mile run to their base up north. He and the crew followed by car and Ski-doos for the first ten miles. We, my pulk and I, started at two o'clock in the afternoon, with no idea how long it would take.

It was -30C. The winds developed to 30 miles per hour, dropping the temperature to -62C.

It wasn't long before I shouted out: 'I'm panicking a little.' I had started to sweat. We stopped to experiment with the layers of clothing. I was wearing too many, it seemed, for running, but now that I'd stopped I was getting cold very quickly. So, Nigel advised me to warm up in the car. Very appealing, I thought, but no thank you. I remembered the letter, with its intimation that the Jungle Marathon had been a stunt for television. There would be no short cuts, no easy options here. I would warm up by working. Off I set again. As night approached, the temperature dropped to -40C.

I had five layers on. A merino wool long sleeve vest, a thick fleece jumper, a hybrid thin down jacket, a down jacket vest and a windstopper on top. In my bag I had my thick down jacket for when it got REALLY cold.

Just before starting the 40-miler, I had failed to fully shut one of the zips of my underlayers. With three pairs of mittens on and my nervousness, I could not properly close it. I decided that the zip not fully closed was good enough and that the outer layers would do their job of keeping me warm.

How wrong was I! That's all I could focus on for hours was the draft coming through the tiny hole which I hadn't closed properly. Lesson 1. Do not cut corners when it comes to dressing properly. It was something I had learnt in the Amazon. No matter how powerful, experienced, fast, strong, intelligent you are (which I am not!) you will never win a battle against Mother Nature. She is far greater than us. You have to respect her. There's no room for arrogance or even complacency in these conditions.

The pulk was a problem. Not so incredible after all. It was attached to my harness securely, and it rolled along on its wheels smoothly enough, but the tubular poles that went from the sled to the harness had a sort of bouncing motion that did not seem to co-ordinate with my running gait and height. They were too long so the pulk was being dragged along the floor and was pulling me back. It took me 14 hours to do the 40 miles. My legs carried me for the first 20 miles and my head had to persuade me to do the last 20 … I was doing 2-3 miles per hour and yet I was pushing as hard as I could even at that slow pace.

It was demoralising. How was I going to survive 350 miles in one week? The initial plan was 20 hours on the move with 4 hours off during the 6633 Ultra. That idea went out of the window. How on earth was I going to make it?

I really did not know.

But there was more to come. There was one little thing to do before I went to sleep.

I now had to repair my pulk's puncture, over and over and over again – blindfolded.

I smiled. I reeled my feelings off, did my pieces to camera, slowly repaired my tyre, muttered a few expletives under my breath, but I still smiled. Inside I was angry. Not with anyone else, but with myself. Why, oh why, did I put my name to this race?

'Lowri's done well,' said Nigel to the camera, 'but she's had a shock.'

You could say that again, Nigel, I thought, grinning through gritted teeth as I stood beside him. Fine for him to say, as he went inside his hut for a good night's sleep after all that driving with the heater on.

'Where am I sleeping?' I asked as politely as I could, trying not to disclose my frustration as I saw him join the TV crew and the other soldiers in the hut.

I, it transpired, was to prepare for a night outside in the snow and ice, separated from it only by my bivouac sack – my bivvy bag, a lightweight, waterproof loose cover – and my sleeping bag inside it.

In the same way I was experimenting with layers of clothing, so I also needed to work out how to sleep. Should I use the tent or the bivvy bag? I was veering towards the bivvy. Should I pull the zip to the very end and encase myself inside it and risk condensation, or should I leave a tiny gap that might let some freezing air in?

Despite leaving a tiny hole, it was claustrophobic. I was panicking. I could feel my heart rate rising and the rhythm of my breathing quicken. I hated it but kept telling myself to breathe deeply and calmly. It was only a bivvy bag. I wasn't trapped inside it, I said to myself. It wasn't as if I couldn't get out. But with the temperature way below -60C, I felt I was trapped. I lay there thinking of options. If it got too bad, I'd jump out and run around in circles to keep myself warm until the crew in the warm comfy hut got up. For a brief moment, I felt like going to the hut to ask to be let in. I was desperate to do the latter but, whether it was out of stubbornness or pride, I decided against it.

I lay in the bivvy bag on the hard, icy ground and tried to calm myself. Eventually I managed to sleep for about two hours, but I was awake when Nigel emerged from his hut with his usual smile and encouragement and put me to work on the stove. I had to be able to put it together, dismantle it, and master its functions in the darkest, coldest conditions. With my eyes shut, I had to be able to generate heat.

We then left by Ski-doo and headed at speed deeper into the land of the Sámi people. We were aiming for Sweden's highest mountain, the 6,700ft Kebnekaise in search of lower temperatures. Going up in feet in order to come down in degrees. Once up there in the true cold of his dreams, Nigel set me off on a couple of hours run-walk slog on tired legs. When that was over, he made me light a fire – not the stove, but a real fire from wood shavings set alight by a spark from a fire-steel. Only then did we go back to the stove, to assemble it yet again. And dismantle it. Prepare for sleep. Into my sleeping bag. And back out of my bivvy. And build the stove again. And dismantle it, blindfolded. Now back into the sleeping bag. And out again. Because when your fingers are frozen, you're wearing a few pairs of mittens, you're sleep-deprived, and you're hungry, doing the simplest of things like putting your cooker together, melting ice in a stove, or pulling the zip up in your sleeping bag is an absolute nightmare. I had to be able to do these things automatically – like doing our shoelaces or brushing our teeth with our eyes closed.

The soldiers told me that they could see physically and mentally I was strong, but they worried about how I could survive these conditions. They taught me how to light a fire on snow. They said, 'People are obsessed with creating these big fires when actually all you need is a small fire.' They were right of course. Even the tiniest of fires was enough to boost our spirits.

We were joined by two members of the Swedish Special Forces. One of them, Goran, introduced himself by taking off his jacket and hat and walking around for 15 minutes with his face exposed. He showed me a patch (in a shape of an elephant) on his cheek, where his skin had turned white. 'Frost-nip,' he said. 'Early signs of frostbite.' Nigel took his shoes and socks off and ran around for thirty seconds in his bare feet. He sat down opposite Goran and stuck them under the Swedish soldier's outer layers and up in to the warmest part of his body, his armpits. 'Nothing prepares you for these extreme conditions,' said Goran, pressing his large, warm arms to his sides and down on Nigel's freezing feet. Time and time again, they talked of hypothermia and recognising the first signs.

These men were tough. But they were humble and I admired them a great deal. Just like when I was with the Royal Marines, they never made me feel out of place or belittled in any way. They treated me as if I was one of them and I was grateful for that.

Perhaps they talked me into a frozen daze. During another long training run into the Swedish mountains, I began to hallucinate, though I didn't realise it at the time. It was not a swirling, drifting, misty kind of hallucination. Out of nowhere came a clear vision. I saw a little hut with a curl of wood-smoke rising from its chimney. Skis were placed upright in a row outside the door. A cup of something warm would go down a treat, I thought. But when I approached the door, the hut and the skis and the smoke all melted away.

I should have laughed, but the weekend in Sweden troubled me. 'I think I've lost some of my self-confidence,' I admitted to Nigel. And now, back in Wales, things were growing only worse. Three days after returning I had to make an admission: 'Fear has taken a hold.'

I stopped running for weeks. And when I did return, I was laboured with my breathing and I felt increasingly prone to panic. I reluctantly did a piece to camera: 'I'm really struggling now. I had such a shock in Sweden.' I couldn't stop myself from delivering a final line – 'I don't want to do it any more.' – as the tears ran down my face.

CHAPTER 12

NEVER BEGIN A RACE
UNTIL IT'S FINISHED ON PAPER

I quite like making lists. Here, for example, is what I jotted down after the Swedish ordeal. I could do my bivvy routine in my sleep – as quick as this:

1. *Floor mattress out.*
2. *Bivvy (with sleeping bag and another mat inside) out.*
3. *Cooker (with food sachet) out.*
4. *Left shoe off.*
5. *Left foot into bag.*
6. *Right shoe off.*
7. *Right foot in bag.*
8. *Sit in bag.*
9. *Boil water.*
10. *Empty into water bottle (use as hot water bottle).*
11. *Boil rehydrated food / Eat.*
12. *Close zip (leaving a breathing hole the size of a pound coin).*
13. *Check race schedule/timings.*
14. *Alarm set for 20 or 40 mins.*
15. *Sleep.*

Yes, I love a list: jobs for today, chores for the week, goals set with nine months to go. Eight months, seven months. A list is a little line of targets. Or it can be a summary of a lot more abstract stuff. Why do I do what I do? What are the processes along the way? What are the risks? I have made several lists of the stages, emotional and physical, I go through when I'm running. Most of them have been incorporated into the story so far, like the planning, the excitement of the start, the slight sense of fear, the pain, the quest for the mystical rush that might sweep me along. Yes, I think most have been de-listed and rearranged in the story, but I was looking at one such compilation of mine and, as I find myself here, three months before the start of the 6633 Arctic Ultra and in a worryingly vulnerable place, I thought I might resurrect Points 10 and 11 in their original format. So, please, imagine that these have just been torn from a notebook:

10. *Point of No Return. Most non-elite runners have a bit of built-in 'safety valve' which allows them to contemplate the (hopefully remote) chance of quitting if things get too rough.*

11. *The Pain Cave. There will come a point where everything just hurts. You'll be annoyed at the course and race directors for making you climb that stupid hill. Your shoes will be the wrong choice. Nothing tastes good. Your stomach feels wrong. And every damn step hurts. Welcome to the pain cave …*

Training was as important as the race itself and involved exactly the same processes as the event towards which they were aiming. If anything, the phases (the numbered points on the list) were more keenly felt because the preparation stretched out over a full year. The 6633 would last only eight days but it would feel like eight weeks. The point was that, with the race now only twelve weeks away, I was supposedly past the point of no return, but I was definitely reaching for the safety valve, the get-out clause. I invented excuses and imagined turning up to the office and saying, 'I would have loved to have done this race, but my dog ate my pulk and I just can't do it.' I didn't want to go on because I was so far into the pain cave that I saw no daylight. I was at the bottom of the Atlantic and the MIR's lights had just gone out. I was feeling low.

Here's the next point on the list:

1. *Realisation. I won't go as far as calling it 'enlightenment,' but usually, somewhere in the darkness of the pain cave, you will discover some really amazing things about yourself. Maybe day will have turned into night and the stars are twinkling.*

You may be alone on the trail, and a mountain view will
simply take your breath away. You'll understand your place
on the planet, and in the universe, just a little better. And
you'll know. This is why you run ultras.

I badly needed a Point 12 to enter my life. The omens were not good. After Sweden I somehow managed to increase my weekly mileage to 125 miles a week, but it was done almost listlessly. I found out that the Incredible Pulk had been wrongly assembled and it was sent back for repairs. At least it might explain why it had been so bouncy. The Mark II of my pulk would surely be an improvement on the horrible dragging feel and noise of the pulk in Sweden, which, over 14 hours, had been frustrating and mentally torturous.

There's a saying – nobody plans to fail, they just fail to plan. I hoped that this was my way of planning NOT to fail.

I had nevertheless entered the Beacons Ultra. This race would start in Talybont-on-Usk, that was also Talybont on the Monmouthshire and Brecon Canal. This old artery of industrial Wales is now devoted to gentle tourism and cuts through the northern half of the Brecon Beacons National Park: a playground for many ultra runners – Welsh and from further afield. The canal was always peaceful here in Breconshire, certainly when compared to its use on the second phase of its journey in the early 1800s through Monmouthshire. In Brecon the canal took water from the River Usk and channelled it all the way to Newport. That was the clean bit. In Monmouthshire, barges filled up with pig iron and coal at wharfs, like Gilwern, Govilon, Llanfoist and Goytre. These wharfs were also served by steep tramroads that came down the escarpment, from the coal and iron towns of Brynmawr and Blaenavon among others at the heads of the South Wales Valleys. The barges were horse-drawn to the large industrial town of Pontypool and further down, through a series of locks, to Newport. While Cardiff was still insignificant, Newport was shipping the heavy produce of South Wales to the world.

These pieces of history do fascinate me. I run in many places and I often do some research or imagine what life would have been like years and centuries ago. It seems to help me drift off into a dream during races, to disappear from the pain cave of the moment. I can let my imagination run away with pictures of a past era.

My race was in the altogether less industrial setting of the Brecon Beacons. We would leave the village of Talybont-on-Usk and go on a loop around the peaks of the second-highest range in Wales after Snowdonia, all the way back to Talybont. And then, like an order from Nigel, repeat. That is, it was a race over two 23-mile laps. Just for good measure, as if thrown in with a bit of devil-may-care abandon, I then planned to run home to Gowerton. So, 46 miles in the Beacons, plus 58 miles to home. I was going to run 104 miles.

Why?

Quite simply to see if I could do it. I wanted to see if I could run 100 miles in one go. I wanted to see if I could run through the night without sleeping.

In general, I was in a deflated mood. I had had a busy week of travelling up and down the country, working long hours on live TV. I had no time to taper, to rest before the big one. And specifically, the day before the race somebody had let me down on a personal matter and I was in even less of a mind to run 104 miles.

My mind wanted to be elsewhere not on the start line.

The camera, of course, had to be there, didn't it? It was my job, but sometimes I hated the sight of that bloody camera. Merely thirty minutes into the race, I turned to it and snarled: 'I don't want to do this race. I'm not in the right frame of mind.' Two hours later I repeated the message: 'I have only negative thoughts in my head.' I was feeling every footstep.

And then, bless it, a Point 12 came over the hill. I have been helped at moments of crisis by the voice of my mother, and now I can add Point 12 to my list of saviours. For three hours I toiled along in my misery and then, out of nowhere, found my rhythm, found my flow.

I had tried incorporating running loops into my training. I once ran for 24 hours, with the pulk, around a three-mile loop of a park in Cardiff; passing my car on every loop was hard. But if I could build my mental strength this way, then I'd be able to cope with the lows that came during the 6633 Ultra. So this race around the Brecon Beacons – two loops of 24 miles – was perfect. As I approached halfway, I could see my car parked at what earlier was the start line and in another 23 miles would be the finish line. I could see the marshals. The pull of my car was so strong. I yearned to be back in it on my way back to Siôn. 'Why dont you stop now, Lowri? You could be on your sofa with Siôn in less than an hour,' said the voice in my head.

As I approached the checkpoint/finish line, I said to Sue Like, 'What am I doing here? I should be home shopping for mulled wine and Christmas food, but no ... Lowri has decided to spend a day in the pouring rain and howling wind, hauling my sorry self around the mountains.' I don't know when I started to speak about myself in the third person. But I ignored the voice and as I passed the car park, I picked up speed, thinking that this would help with ignoring the temptation to quit.

Sue caught up with me a mile further along the canal. I was about to leave the trail for the mountains for the second time.

'How are you feeling now?' she asked meaningfully.

'Blooming brilliant,' I said. And I meant it.

The flow came a bit too late for me to storm to the front and claim the unlikeliest of victories. In fact, the organisers kept telling me to slow down and think of the long term goal. I was going to be running another 50 plus miles after this race so I needed to pace myself, but I finished in sixth place in the women's race in a time of 9 hours 20 minutes. Not a bad day's work, all things considered.

It was, of course, only the warm-up for the run for home. The night shift was about to begin. I knew two toenails were coming off – something my body and definitely my feet became quite used to – and I felt a blister (Point 11) and I might have toyed with the notion of reaching for the safety valve of Point 10. 'You've done an ultra today. Stop now. Nobody will think any less of you.' I would, though. I got back on the road.

I was soon assailed by a different type of discomfort, an overwhelming urge to sleep. I didn't have a watch on me. I had no idea of pace nor distance. I knew the route home and just concentrated on putting one foot in front of another. But I remember turning to Nigel – who was my support crew, driving patiently behind – and shouting, 'I bet it's midnight' And lo and behold, it was. If I just lay down for ten minutes … and closed my eyes.

Well, it wasn't going to happen to me in Ystradgynlais, the town where my father was brought up. I carried on.

In those moments, it's all there to play for: there is no one forcing or motivating you to keep going, and no one stopping you either. It's a battle between you and yourself. It's a decision as to how hard you want to fight. It comes down to how much you want it, how far you are willing to go to discover who you really are and how hard you can push to be the person you believe you can be. It's very hard to understand in the beginning that the whole idea is not to beat the other competitors. Eventually you learn that the competition is against the little voice inside you that wants to quit. And I'm proud that I didn't listen to that voice.

After a total time of just over 20 hours, I could look the camera in the lens and say, 'I didn't feel confident earlier, but I think I'm going to make it.' I had five miles to go.

After 21 hours and 15 minutes, and 104 miles, I rang the doorbell at my parents' house at just before 5am. They weren't in. Of course. I knew that. Luckily, my brother Roger was staying over. I rang again. He eventually opened it, bleary-eyed.

'You're back early,?' he said.

'Yes'

'Oh,' he said, half asleep. 'Well done. Glad you're back safe.' And went back to bed.

It didn't come with a flash of light, but perhaps, like a pulk on Mount Kebnekaise, Point 12 moves in mysterious ways.

My first 100-miler was a training run. Not a race. I wanted to see if I had it in me. It was a journey of peaks and troughs, of highs and lows. There was no fanfare, no huge applause, just a smile and a pat on my back from Nigel. And that's exactly how I wanted it. I did not run 104 miles for any other reason other than for me. And I went to bed at 5.30am having proven to myself that I could do it.

There are so many cheesy, overused metaphors which can be used to draw parallels between marathon running and life, taking things one step at a time, pacing yourself (it's a marathon not a sprint after all), be the tortoise and not the hare … but until you've actually run one of these monsters, whatever the distance, you don't really understand the power of it at all.

Mentally I felt great – I had ticked a box that had been empty for a while. However, I was in a bit of a physical state after the 104-miler. I went to see Dyfri, my physio. I made a list for him:

1. *Ankles x 2*
2. *Knees (1 x so-so, 1 x grim)*
3. *Base of spine*
4. *Neck*
5. *Feet (goes without saying)*

He inserted his acupuncture needles and did his best to soothe me. Given the miles I had had to do in training, I was never going to be in optimal condition, but he declared me fit to go. I went on a seven-hour run not long afterwards … and hated it. I went to see Ross Hall and he told me not to worry about these last few flaws in my domestic performances. The Arctic was all that mattered now.

'Don't think of it as a 350-mile race,' he said. 'You've just completed a 100-miler, so break the race into 3 x100 miles and a 50-miler at the end. If you can't mentally cope with that thought, then break it into smaller chunks again.'

A few days before Christmas, when the temperature dropped to -6C (almost balmy), and it snowed heavily in the UK, I took my chance and turned it into a training few days. I slept outside and went through the list and the routine again and again and hated every blasted pull of the bivvy's zip. At least it had one, though. There was no zip in my running.

As I'd lay there in my sleeping bag in the garden, listening to carol singers going round our streets, I looked up to the bedroom window and saw Siôn smiling through the window, giving me a thumbs up. I smiled back.

There was one last piece to slot in before departure for Canada. The pulk was back, except now it was the Incredible Pulk Mark 2, a twin-axle sled that I had trialled and much preferred. I was a pulk pioneer. The Morgan four-wheeler has become the pulk of choice in icy ultras, offering a much more even ride than the earlier model.

CHAPTER 13

FAST FORWARD TO 2019

An update from near today. I know I'm about to leave, for a little while, the 6633 Ultra in the past. No Eurwyn, by the way, this time – he had to stay home in Wales. The camera crew would have to double up as my and the athletes' support team. That was the deal with the race organisers. If they were coming out, they'd have to double up as support crew. Our little cast was: Emyr Penlan, the director, and Joe Davies the cameraman. Alun Morris Jones was also with us but he would be too busy editing the pictures as we went along to scrape up the presenter should anything befall her. Although he did a good job during the first 24 hours over Wright Pass. More on that later. Numbers were strictly limited in this ultra, which should have served as another warning.

Sorry, I'm losing track, which is a cardinal sin in ultra running. But I just want to fast forward eight years from there, the eve of the 6633 of 2011, to here, the Dragon's Back Race of 2019, because one race has always led to another and this chain has its connections.

So, here I am in 2019, quite a long way down the line (spoiler alert, and still alive), getting ready for this next race. And all has been going well. I began stretching out the miles on the 26 December 2018. I had accepted a place to race the infamous Dragon's Back Race, with a view to peaking in Conwy, North Wales in late May. I had actually presented a documentary on the race in 2012 and was invited to race in 2015 but I had politely turned it down as I was pregnant with Gwilym and he would have been only a few weeks old at the start of the race. So, out of the blue, in 2018 an offer came to race the 2019 edition.

I must admit, I was a bit scared as I read the invite. I had heard so much about this incredibly tough race and I had never raced a

114

multi-stage mountain race before. I thought hard about it and discussed with Siôn how we'd fit the training and racing around our family and work, but I still accepted the challenge straight away.

Yes, all was going well. For four months I was back in the flow. My mojo was back. I had plenty of motivation. I had a new coach who gave me daily goals so I never thought of the bigger goal, and the days, weeks and months flew by. I was getting into the habit of getting up at 5am and getting the miles in early – sometimes 30 miles before taking Gwilym to nursery or going to work – and then if I had time and needed to do more, going out again for the second time, sometimes with Gwilym in the pram, sometimes just Nel the dog and me.

And then my knee, my dear old rugby knee in the middle of my slightly shorter right leg, started to swell after training for this race – one of the toughest in the world – and refused to go down. It remained stiff and sore for days. As runners we get these niggles. Things hurt. The legs are heavy and tired and you're carrying a niggle that you're worried could become more serious. Maybe you are actually injured, maybe you just need a rest. I'm sure many runners can relate. But when do you know the difference? This time, I put it off, I just needed to rest. I was used to having this knee swell or ache and it always disappeared within two days of resting. No problem I thought – I'll be fine in a day or two.

But it did not improve.

At the very time I should have been increasing my mileage, I had to reduce it. Something wasn't right.

I took it to Mr David Pemberton, who probably knows as much about knees and what can go wrong with them, especially on the rugby field, as anybody in the world. I say this because not only does he mend knees at elite level, as an honorary orthopaedic surgeon to the Welsh Rugby Union and the Cardiff Devils Ice Hockey team, but he's also still playing veterans' rugby.

Mr Pemberton spent quite a lot of time on my knee. 'Well, Lowri,' he announced when he saw it, 'this knee of yours.' He gave it another stern look. 'May I ask when you had your original injury?'

'Twenty-six years ago.'

'Twenty-six years ago, eh? Let me see … and where did you have the surgery?'

'Morriston Hospital.'

'Morriston. I see … And who was your consultant?'

'Mr Hoddinott.'

'Well, goodness me. Huw Ceri Hoddinott. Do you know, as the saying goes, I was there. I'd just joined Mr Hoddinott's team. It was his very first operation as a consultant.' He gave it a prod. 'We used to chat about this knee,' he continued. 'A lot. We knew all about your exploits. You have amazed us.'

'Well, thank you,' I said. 'For making it possible.'

'You're welcome. It's done ever so well, hasn't it?' He paused. 'But now?'

'Well, I'm due to run the Dragon's Back Race in a month's time. But on my birthday, that's just been, I went to do a recce of some of the sections.'

It had been an idyllic start to the day – I spent the morning with my family, and then went off to the mountains while Siôn was in work and Gwilym at nursery. The plan for the evening was dinner with my family. But once I started the run, I really struggled. I took my sticks but still my knees suffered on the trails and I ended up hobbling along, grimacing with every step, holding everyone else up. It was also mentally exhausting. 'I am thinking of pulling out of this race,' I frustratedly told Siôn that evening. 'How am I going to complete this?'

'You've got to go and see someone about your knee and then you have to decide …' said Siôn. 'Do the race and risk DNF and further injury or pull out now and get yourself better and come back stronger later in the year.' I agreed to the latter.

Holding back the tears, I carried on explaining to Mr Pemberton, 'Two days after the recce I couldn't get out of bed. When I did, I had to use a walking stick to keep up with my son.'

'And now?'

116

'It has eased, but I haven't run on it properly for a whole month. The race is in two weeks.'

'Right. I think we'd better get an MRI scan done. It could be cartilage; it could be arthritis. Or it could be a pre-stress fracture.'

'That doesn't sound too bad.'

'Well, if it's a pre-stress fracture, then you're out of the race. No arguments. That's it. If it's a cartilage, well, we'll see after the scan.'

'So, I could do it? The Dragon's Back.'

'If it is the better-case-scenario … then I can't stop you.' A last prod. 'But this will.' He said pointing at the knee. 'Maybe not this time. But soon. That's another conversation. Yes, you've amazed us, but the truth is, this knee will eventually bring your ultra running days to an end.' I must have appeared a little down. 'It doesn't mean you have to stop everything. Use your endurance for another sport. I recommend cycling next. I'll introduce you to one of our physios who's in the next room – she's a British cyclist.'

I have a future, it seems, but in a different sport. I am not destroyed by the news. I have cycled quite a lot in triathlons and Ironman races. I am not a strong cyclist but I am willing to learn and work hard. I shall have to pick up where I left off. It does mean, however, that just as I am about to take you back to Canada and the start of the most demanding test of mind, soul, heart, lungs, fingers, feet and knees, I am on the brink of announcing my retirement from the world of ultra running. Well, after the Dragon's Back, that is. One more race. But I shall have to be careful. I am going to be relying almost entirely on my bedrock of fitness. I am not a pessimist by nature, not by a long chalk, but I have to be realistic.

My coach for the last five months, Damian Hall, one of the world's best endurance runners and Mr Nice Guy, has managed to build my endurance and speed and strength up for this race and I am really enjoying my training these days – Damian has introduced variation. I am no longer motivated by distance per week. I've dropped down to about 50-60 miles, but my climbing has increased. I'm now motivated by vert per week, I am winning local races, I am feeling strong, so this setback has come as a massive disappointment. I have worked so hard for this. No chance now of getting to the start line as strong as possible; now the goal is to arrive in Conwy as healthy as possible because these races, if you go into them with a niggle, they will find it and bite. This may not end in a ticker-tape parade.

Dave Pemberton asked me one last question. 'Say it's arthritis,' he said. 'It may be quite debilitating. If it is … do you think you'll have any regrets about putting your knee through everything you've done?'

'I'll have no regrets,' I said firmly. 'No, not one.'

'Thought so,' he said with a genuine and proud smile.

He understood me.

CHAPTER 14

ARCTIC

So back to the 6633 Ultra.

It is named '6633' because these are the latitude coordinates in minutes and degrees of the Arctic Circle. It is tough. I mean really tough. No seriously, I really do mean it. Many of the racers who participated in the first four editions of the race had previously competed in other winter races both in the Yukon, Alaska and North America, but without exception they all found this to be by far and away the toughest event they had taken part in.

We gathered outside the Eagle Plains Hotel on the Dempster Highway in March 2011. I was competitor 203, which might suggest there were many more starters here in the Yukon than for the Jungle Marathon of 2009. It would be a totally false suggestion. There were twelve of us, shuffling around in the snow, banging our arms against our bodies. This was a race with such a high casualty-rate that it attracted far fewer entries. One world-famous ultra runner had apparently enquired for this year's race but with the DNF rate so high, he decided against it. Besides, the logistics and organisation were so difficult that the race could cater only for small numbers in the first place. And the temperatures were so low that it was of strictly limited appeal. A dozen was a full-house in the 6633.

Everything about it was different. We had worked our pre-race way north and in comfort from Whitehorse to Dawson City on the banks of the Yukon River. This was a place inseparably linked with the Klondike Gold Rush of the late nineteenth century. Between 1896 and 1899 an estimated 100,000 prospectors made their way to the Klondike region of the Yukon to seek their fortune. Most made nothing. Dawson City now was home to fewer than 1,500 citizens but something of the older, wilder days lived on. Like the quaint ritual of downing a cocktail called the Sour-toe. The ingredients of this local delicacy and race tradition were simple: the shrivelled remains of a frost-bitten human toe in a shot of fire water. I really didn't fancy drinking a shot of liquor with someone's frostbitten toe in it. I really didn't want to.

I did though … everyone else did, and I did it. The dramatic moment and my retching certainly made it onto the screen. Again, as I previously mentioned, I was actually inspired by the stories I read about the people who travelled to Dawson's City in search of wealth. They, just like me, had to endure days of walking and surviving in extreme conditions. Surely, my circumstances were easier? I had better equipment, proper food, I had trained … If they could do it with nothing but the clothes they had on, surely there was a chance I could take a bit of inspiration from them?

From Dawson City we went ever upwards into a Canada that grew ever colder, to this hotel in Eagles Plain on the side of the Dempster Highway. If anybody was happy to be here, you couldn't tell. Everybody was wrapped up tight: hat, hood, mask, buff. No skin to be seen. Some things, though, were the same. Those nerves on the start line; those constant words of comfort to myself: 'You've done the training. Believe in yourself.'

The contrasts of ultra running – warm words of comfort against the perishing cold of the air and ground. It was a bit like the contrasting parting words of my parents. They had been a bit worried about this 6633 Ultra: 'Just do your best. But remember, don't push yourself. Remember about your heart. Rest if you must, but try not to quit. But if you want to quit, that's OK too.'

I stood on the start line, battling a sensation I know only too well by now. It is like no sensation I will ever feel otherwise – deep inside your stomach. As I spoke to the camera, you could hear the fear in my trembling voice.

It doesn't matter how many marathons I run, the fear remains. It doesn't matter how well my training has gone … I still experience the single most terrifying prospect – that I won't achieve the goal I have worked so hard for. And it never gets any easier; in fact I think my fear increases each time, because I know what is to come now.

But on this race, I had no idea.

The starters – six for the 120-miler and six for the 350-miler – gave each other a padded slap and hug and waited for the off. When you stand at the start line of any long distance race there is a moment when the nerves subside, you stop laughing and joking with the people around you and your mind focuses for just a short time at the task which lies ahead.

I couldn't believe I was here. At last.

When the race started, it was with a weak sun shining on us and without great ceremony. There was a shout of 'Yahoo,' and a small cheer from the staff of the hotel. They immediately hurried back inside and we set off up the Dempster Highway. A gun went off a couple of seconds later. This wasn't a race to be decided by a photo-finish or by margins measured in decimal points

Ten men and two women. From all around the world. Yet we all had something in common. We were all there to battle not against each other but against our own demons and the harsh conditions of the Arctic. There were professional athletes, SAS soldiers and Royal Marines. Diane Van Deren was a hugely experienced Arctic runner and was aiming to set a new record for the 120-mile course. She gave me a few last reminders: be patient over the first 24 hours; don't go out too hard; read the route ahead and then make my decisions, about when and where to stop, or to keep going.

I wanted to pull my jacket off – I was getting warm. I was panicking about frostbite. 'I need to change my layering system,' I said.

'No,' she said quickly. 'Read the road ahead. Look, we're dropping down into the valley soon. Don't waste your reserves and time by changing only to stop again in 30 minutes to put that jacket back on.'

One runner, who held a few world records, had shot off at the start. 'Look at him,' I exclaimed. 'He's going to finish the race in record time.' He did indeed mention his plans of a race record a few times during the lead up to the race.

'Ah.' Diane shrugged my words off. 'He won't make it past mile 90.'

I saw him at mile 87 sitting on his pulk waiting for the support vehicle, having thrown in the towel. Diane, knew these arctic races only too well.

Everybody else settled into their own pace: a run, shuffle or power-walk that could become on this flattish opening section an extended stride. We'd get the chance to stretch out the legs for a run on downhills and flat parts of the road, which was quite refreshing. It was nice to change the rhythm from the continuous and constant rhythm of our power-walks to a jog. The air was clear and the views of the Richardson Mountains were spectacular. Light winds occasionally blew ice particles across the road surface, on which the 20kg-pulks rolled along and our walking poles clicked. The clickety-click of the poles was to be a soundtrack that might drive us mad.

Diane remained beside me for a while before increasing her pace and leaving me behind. The temperature was dropping towards -30C, but I was having a familiar problem with my layers. Soon I knew what she meant. When I did stop a few hours later to change my layers, it was painful. It felt like hundreds of needles being prodded all over my body as the freezing winds gnawed at my bones.

I was too hot. I stopped to remove two layers (to put the outer one back on), but was instantly too cold. I made a basic error by removing a mitten and immediately felt the sharp sting of the Arctic cold. I hurried to rearrange my clothing. I took a chance on being a little under-layered, checked my face in the mirrored compass (a present from my friends in the Swedish special forces) to make sure everything there was under wraps and set off at a run to warm up again. To remain alert to the signals of the body was vital. The slightest change in core temperature had to trigger a counter-measure, be it a change of layers or an increase in work. The slightest sign of discomfort through friction had to be eradicated. Chafing could be a race-ender.

I was beyond empty, beyond broken. Tears started filling my eyes but as they fell onto my cheeks, they froze. 'No point crying,' I told myself. Nobody could hear me and nobody could see me. I was on my own.

Giving up was not an option.

It hurt like hell. But this was supposed to hurt.

'Rest if you must, but do not quit,' is what my parents had told me, and their words and voices kept resounding inside my head repeating in my head until I shouted, 'DO NOT QUIT. YOU WILL NOT QUIT,' whilst digging my poles even harder into the ice with the hope that it would propel me closer to the finish line.

I had not even reached Checkpoint 1.

I must have looked deranged but I really didn't care. Nobody was listening, only me, myself and I. For the time being I was alone. Resting however would not have eased the pain I was going through. I just had to put one foot in front of another and keep going, hoping that I would eventually find that white, quiet space in my head where pain and worries disappear.

My best time for a marathon is 3 hours 8 minutes. I knew there was no chance of replicating that here, but I had done my homework. I had created a lanyard with a list of the checkpoints and the estimated time it would take me to reach each one. I was aiming to reach the end of the first checkpoint at Arctic Circle, 23 miles from the start, in five and a quarter hours. It took me 6 hours 39 minutes. It came as a real shock. This wasn't even a difficult section. This section was all about getting used to the conditions and your systems. Knowing you could run the section twice as fast was quite heartbreaking. And that was when I had to draw from the lessons I had learnt earlier in my running career. Have patience, Lowri. This is going to take a week. But what is a week in a lifetime?

I didn't realise then that a week could actually feel like a lifetime.

As soon as I reached the Arctic Circle CP, I rushed to find a medic. I could feel something wet and very cold against my back. First the layers, now this, whatever it was. 'Is it sweat?' I asked in a panic. The medics are trained to spot the first signs of stress and anxiety that can rapidly turn into panic. Mine very calmly slipped a hand between my rucksack and my back. I had two layers over my skin, then came the rucksack, then more layers. The rucksack was covered to protect the hydration pack inside. Those outer layers, plus my body temperature, were supposed to counteract the outside temperature. The water had frozen solid. That ice was what I could feel against my back. Another systems failure.

I did a quick calculation. Taking on water was as important as ever, but this was not the jungle. +30C was now -30C. I had four litres in the water flasks in the pulk. I could always use my stove to melt snow if I needed more.

'You're not sweating,' said the medic calmly.

'Here,' I said to him, pulling my extra water container out of my rucksack. And giving it to him. 'A little present.'

After its gentle start, the Dempster Highway had climbed gradually towards Arctic Circle. Nobody stopped at the end of this first stage. The next checkpoint was 45 miles away at James Creek, but there was an opportunity at the Rock River checkpoint to stop and rest. Or even sleep. After Rock River came the climb up to Wright Pass, the start of Hurricane Alley, where the vicious Katabatic winds blew. The general wisdom was to stop at Rock River in order to regather strength for the most gruelling section.

I reached Rock River eight hours later. It was dark by now. I arrived to be met by Diane. She was going the other way, in the back of a car. She had aggravated an old ankle injury and was out of the race. She sat huddled and crestfallen in her support vehicle. It meant I was the only woman left in the race. I couldn't help feeling sad – for her. Diane said goodbye and left. It was a sharp reminder of the need to take care and make wise decisions. I wondered what to do. I'd been walking for nearly fifteen hours.

I like to think that at that moment Point 12 came into play. When I was thinking of doing the 104 miles of the Brecon Ultra and the run for home, I had sought out Martin Like, my kit supplier and the race organiser of the 6633. 'Can I do it?' I had asked him.

'You can do whatever you like, Lowri,' he replied. 'Thinking about it, I reckon it might prove invaluable. You'll learn a lot about yourself on that road. Lessons that may serve you well in the Arctic.'

Well, here I was, in that very place and, for some reason, in that special zone. Four people had arrived ahead of me at Rock River.

Three of them were wriggling around in their sleeping bags and Diane was out of the race. This was the moment. I wasn't going to benefit from any sleep here. It would have been a waste of my time. From researching the route and chatting to previous competitors, I knew I had a big challenge ahead of me on this leg – Wrights Pass comprises of ten miles of climbing, anywhere between 6% and 16% gradient. Ten miles of climbing meant quite a few hours of digging in and just keeping the momentum going. With winds of 70 miles per hour gusting through the valley, the temperature had dropped to -72C so I had to ask myself the question – would I prefer to stay here for a few hours 'rest' and face the mountains in daylight in 'warmer' temperatures with less winds? Or would I prefer to not see the huge climbs of the mountain range and face the severe winds?

I decided to press on into the night, to take on Wright Pass and Hurricane Alley in the dark.

I stopped long enough to change a base layer and put on my warmest down jacket. I put on extra mittens with hand warmers inside, but I couldn't claim to be fully warm. Should I eat a meal? If I took all my gloves off to work the stove, even indoors, I'd never get them back up to a bearable temperature. I quickly tried to suck up some frozen chocolate granola. I gave up on that, left the others in their sleeping bags and took to the highway.

I was taking a huge risk. I had never ventured longer than 21 hours and 15 mins without stopping. But I had to believe in myself. I had to.

It was like learning to breathe from scratch. You couldn't look straight ahead and take in air normally. I had to twist my head to one side, bury my chin into my collarbone and let the side of my hood take the full blast of the wind. I had to catch some air as it whistled past my nose and mouth. I pulled the pulk uphill into this blasting, blasted wind for five hours. The highest peaks of the Richardson Mountains, at 4,000 feet, are only slightly higher than Snowdon, but they felt like Everest. I had no idea of the altitude of the Wright Pass. I couldn't see it at the time. I couldn't stop to lie down in my bivvy. I'd have been blown back down to the bottom. I had to walk on, up, over and out of the Yukon, down to James Creek in Northwest Territories, with its one-hour time difference. Which way did the clocks go? Who knew? Who cared?

James Creek. If the name had a certain charm to it, its full name was the James Creek Highways Maintenance Camp. It was a storage area for snow-clearance vehicles. But it was a sight to behold for my sore eyes. My sore everything. I had walked all through the night, a total of 24 hours and 30 minutes. I had to eat.

I couldn't have done more research on the subject of food if I'd spent the last year studying Nutrition at the University of Eating. If water replenishment and maintaining salt levels in my body had been priorities in the jungle, here it was solids. Sweat had poured off me in my first ultra. Here, perspiration was not an option. To sweat was to die. Drinking was important, but eating was more so. I had consulted scientists and specialists and soldiers, sought the advice of other runners – some that had made it and others that had failed. What had worked for you? Why had you not reached the end? The successful runners said the same thing. When it comes to food in the Arctic you have to think big. You have to eat big: 10,000 calories a day.

Rich food. One runner told me he had packed his pulk with 'sweet stuff, then salami, cheese, porridge. All sorts of things.' I went down the line of 'all sorts of things' of my own: chocolate bars were broken into tiny pieces so that when frozen I could throw them into my mouth; I had nuts, dried fruit, sweets, chunks of frozen cheese, all thrown into a water bottle. I would 'drink' from that bottle and the food would tumble into my mouth. With three layers of mitts, I could not pick food from my front pouch. If I had poured the food onto my hand, I would not have controlled the calories, and my constant movement and the windy conditions meant that it was tricky to eat on the go, hence the water bottles. For me, this system worked. On my front I had two water bottles within easy reach – to be filled and drunk before the water froze. But I had other bottles on either side of the front of my rucksack for food – one that kept my nuts and chocolate. And then there was the bottle reserved for the particular recommendation of my parents.

Not long before the 6633 Arctic Ultra, they had decided to see for themselves the conditions I would be facing. They travelled into the Arctic Circle in Norway and struck up a conversation, as they did, with a local soldier. He told them the Norwegian food of choice in extreme conditions, when his platoon was out on manoeuvres, was dried fish.

If it was good enough for the Norwegian Arctic patrol, it was good enough for me. So, I had my stock of dried fish. On the barren wastes of Northern Canada, I used to wonder what the smell was. I thought it was some sort of hallucination until I realised it could only be me. I had inadvertently created a novel kind of make-up. I applied Vaseline around my face to help prevent the cold and wind from extracting every last drop of moisture from my skin, but this generous application of jelly also collected flakes of fish when the wind blew some from the bottle. With the Vaseline working like glue, that smell stayed with me for a long, long time. Accuracy in the hand-to-mouth operation on the move was not always guaranteed and vanity was on hold. I used a mirror only to check for frost-nip. Since I had only myself for company for hours on end and nothing was visible anyway, I wasn't particularly concerned about appearances. I just hoped a distant, hungry polar bear didn't catch my aroma on the wind.

I now made myself a hot, non-fish dehydrated meal at James Creek and lay down next to a snowplough to sleep. I had four hours on my schedule but two and a half hours later I was awake. I woke the camera crew up, told them my plans and soon after that, I was back on the road, on the next 47-mile stage to Fort McPherson. I was not lonely. The camera crew caught up with me again and I said as much to them. Even when they had gone, I felt the same. I was feeling good. However, I could not ignore the message from the organisers – that most people DNF before CP3.

Hiraeth is a Welsh word for a specific feeling, that is hard to translate. It's one of my favourite words. It's more than being homesick. It's a yearning, a tug on your soul, a sense of loss at being absent from home. I have felt it many times over the years and on my way to completing the 120 miles to Fort McPherson in 45 hours and on two and a half hours of interrupted sleep, I was a prime candidate to fall prey to it again. But I felt so lucky to be here, in this unique, beautiful place, which has a majesty all of its own. It was such a privilege.

When the negative thoughts crept in, I reminded myself of the reasons why I was doing it. For charity. For my family. For friends – new and old. But I was also doing it for me. I was doing it because adventure is my passion. I lived for the challenge, for putting myself in the place where I feel I've got nothing left, where I feel beyond broken, but find a way to keep going. What happens in that place feels magical. Because I love looking behind me at the road I've run, and getting that sense of 'Wow, I can't believe how far I've come'.

That high couldn't last, not with 17 hours to go to the end of the 'short' 120-mile race. I walked all through the afternoon and all through the night. While I can, may I share a practical detail with you? It's that age-old business of going to the toilet. Remember the lavatorial smell in the jungle? Well, out here on the tundra the only smell was from my Norwegian diet of cod. There was no need to find a tree for privacy. There was nobody else out here. The only pressure was time. Thirty seconds max. Go before you're nipped by the frost.

There, it's done. I include the detail here because it was about to be my last contact with normal functioning. By now I was extremely tired and that is an understatement. I was OK with sleeping in the bivvy in a snow hole; after all I had prepared for it. But I had not prepared for the hallucinations I was seeing. You must think that was quite entertaining, something that could take my mind off the continuous walking and pounding, especially in the sleep-deprived state I was in.

At some point on the road to Fort McPherson I began to have company. I wasn't lonely now because there were cartoon characters on the road. But not the type of cartoon characters that have most probably just jumped into your mind. These were not figures of fun.

They stood with their hands on their hips, staring at me. One witch in particular was especially menacing. When they moved, I saw they were armed with machetes. Of course, I knew they weren't there. But the bodies along the sides of the highway were. Weren't they? Ice that had been cleared from the road lay in chunks, forming a gauntlet of naked bodies I had to pass through. I put my hands to the side of my head so I couldn't see the visions. That was when I realised that my nose was bleeding. I had been warned about nose bleeds in extreme cold conditions. Luckily, I had researched this and was not alarmed. I found a tampon and stuck it up my nostril.

I had pain to keep me awake. Bruised heels, that allowed me to push the images away. Shooting pains up my legs. Doubts began to surface. Fort McPherson was 120 miles from the start. That meant I had 230 miles to go to the finish. These weren't just seeds of doubt, but pangs as disturbing as my physical suffering. The wind picked up. I grew colder.

I was the first to reach Fort McPherson in 45 hours 15 minutes. For half of the field of 12 that had set out from Eagle Plains, this was as far as they'd ever intended to go. Diane hadn't made it. Mike Buss didn't manage to complete his final section between James Creek and Fort McPherson. Four did make it: David Smale, Tim Garrett, Steve Saffin and Hugh Morris. Their race was done, with David declared the winner.

Of the six starters on the 350-miler, Andy Topham, like Mike, had had to stop between James Creek and Fort McPherson. David Jorgensen and Paddy Craig made it to here, the end of Stage 3, but withdrew on arrival. That meant there were three left: myself, Tony Kelly and Matt Davies, all of us from Wales.

We had crossed the start line at Eagle Plains Hotel on Friday morning and now it was Sunday afternoon. Although I had, by now, lost track of the days. I had been at Fort McPherson for ten hours, warming up, eating and above all, despite some heavy snoring from someone who shall remain nameless, sleeping for as long as I ever would in the Arctic – six hours. Tony had come in four and a half hours behind me and Matt had just arrived when Tony and I, at four o'clock, set off on the 38-mile stage to Tsiigehtchic. At half past one in the morning, Matt would set out after us, but would not make it to the next checkpoint. That would leave just the two of us.

It was so good to have company. On my own, I would have struggled. We had been warned in a weak joke that the principle feature of the next stages was a lack of features. The Northwest Territories and the Mackenzie Delta stretched out before us, flat and unwelcoming. The few gentle climbs and downhills didn't break up the monotony of the landscape, or bring the horizon any closer. The trouble with such a flat route through a vast expanse was that we never seemed to be making any progress. We would walk for hours and pass nothing, it seemed. Any hill in the far distance remained where it was, out of reach. We had been warned that the next checkpoint was over 100 miles away on a straight road. In the dark, with little air pollution, we would see the light of the village as clear as anything. The village looked as if it was only a few miles away, not 100 miles. This part of the race was brutally and mentally awful.

Tony was from Abergavenny and had a lovely dry sense of humour. Laughter was a point on one of my lists, something to help you through the pain cave. The last time I had seen him, briefly, was at Arctic Circle, where the medics thought he might be showing the first signs of hypothermia. I thought he'd be pulling out but amazingly he bounced back and had caught up with me. He'd warmed up and recovered and here we were, trudging on, not talking all the time, but chuckling away, stopping to eat and drink and planning where we would repeat the operation next. I wasn't sure how long we would be able to stay together. Tony was far more upbeat than me and had this impressive sleep pattern of taking micro-naps and carrying on. I was never going to have a full eight hours of slumber, but at the time, I needed more than a Tony micro. For the moment, though, the painter from Abergavenny and the television presenter from Gowerton shared the highway.

As always happened on a challenge that was supposed to extract positives from deep within me – but that was fast turning into an ordeal, a nightmare with its cartoon witches and piles of roadside bodies – it couldn't last. The sheer, wretched monotony and the damn cold got to us both. To me in particular. Five hours into the stage, the futility of it all struck me. For the next nine hours, I stayed in this dark place until, having walked through Sunday night and the early hours of Monday morning, we reached Tsiigehtchic at just after six o'clock. I was glad Tony was with me for company.

On Monday afternoon, we set off again. Another long, flat slog of 51 soul-destroying miles, this stage, to Caribou Creek. I couldn't stop doing the sums. We weren't even halfway to the finish yet. More than 175 miles still to go. The camera caught up with us. It laid a trap. I knew they knew that I was in a hole and I knew they thought this would make good television. As the producer of the series, I'd probably have agreed with them. If I'd been thinking straight. But in the depths of my gnawed soul, that truly, truly wanted to be anywhere but in this godforsaken wilderness, what I knew more than anything was that I didn't want to be doing a piece to camera. When Emyr started to record and asked how I was, I couldn't say a word. For a long time, I just stared at the floor and clicked one of walking poles into the ice. Faster and faster it went. It was more a tic, a spasm, than a calculated beat. I think it may sum up perfectly where I was in that minute. I knew if I stopped it, I would cry. So this was the next best thing to letting it all out, or a scream. But I didn't have a voice. The cold air had robbed me of that.

Eventually I cracked and started to cry. 'I can't think. I can't speak.' The one stick continued to hit the ice. 'I have to pull myself together. The monotony is playing havoc with my mind.'

I repeated to camera what Tony and I had spoken about a few minutes earlier. We were both amazed that we were the only two left in the race. He and I. Tony was so excited we had crossed the halfway mark. I didn't share his optimism. For me, I saw it as another 175 miles to go. Demoralising.

The tyres on our pulks were not large. Tony's had two and mine had four. The road surface was windswept and pockmarked with holes. It wasn't a smooth ride for the pulk, but the way was hardly strewn with nails or thorns. At some point, though, on its endless track north-eastwards, the Dempster Highway managed – conspired – to puncture one of Tony's tyres. He dragged his pulk for seven miles on one good tyre. By the time help arrived in form of a support crew, he was limping with an injury. The repair job involved taking his gloves off. What felt like an hour after we completed the task, he needed to rest. I happily agreed to stop.

We remembered the cardinal rule of sleeping between checkpoints – to indicate clearly, either with your poles or your pulk, which way was ahead. I had heard the story of the runner who lay down to sleep, woke and set off, only to meet, five hours later, a runner he knew was behind him. He had set off in the wrong direction. With Tony and I being the only two left, the last thing we wanted was to make the same mistake and walk all the way back to Tsiighehtchic. The first part, then, we got right. The second golden rule was to think carefully about where you put your tent or bivvy. We were so tired, we just lay down and pulled our zips tight and fell asleep.

When I woke up forty minutes later, I found we were almost in the middle of the road. We weren't even close to the ice bank which, in the dark, we thought we were on. The Dempster Highway was hardly choked with traffic but when the occasional massive truck went by it did so at a fair old speed. And drivers, like runners, might easily be mesmerised by the monotony of the landscape and not fully alert to the possibility of coming across campers on the road they might justifiably think they had to themselves. This place of mesmerisation, I knew it well.

I panicked. We had lost a lot of time over the night and in my sleep-deprived state I could not work out my timings on my card. I didn't think we were going to make the end of the race within the cut-off. We had to go.

By now, I was feeling refreshed – well, less worn out – and suggested we press on. Tony said he needed to rest a little longer. We had already discussed that this might be the case. Plan B was that I'd carry on, being the fastest on foot, and Tony, who needed less sleep, would eventually catch up with me at the next checkpoint. So I left with a 'See you later, Tony.'

A few hours later I met up with the TV crew. By now I was growing weary of the featureless landscape and its interminable flat whiteness. 'How do you feel?' asked Emyr, my director/support team.

'I don't know,' I said flatly.

'Well, what about that cargo ship?' he said.

'What cargo ship? I haven't seen a ship.'

'The giant ship, almost completely raised out of the ice over the huge lake. The one you've had to walk around.'

I had literally just walked past this massive ship bedded in the ice. I had not seen it. Sometimes the flat whiteness blanked everything out. When the programme was finished, I'd look at it and say: 'Of course. *That* cargo ship …'

I had, incidentally, a strange relationship with passing traffic. When my rhythm was good, I'd look forward to being overtaken by, or meeting, a fellow road-user. It was a brief moment of company, a flash of human contact. A hand raised, a wave. When I was suffering, I deeply resented the drivers in their shirt-sleeves and their high cabs with their flask of coffee by their side.

Having kept Tony's company for so long, I wondered if I could cope on my own. But I imagined that I would not be on my own for long, because Tony would catch up soon.

I entered one of those welcome periods, when I seemed to glide over the road. I arrived at the luxurious (seriously) tiny lakeside cabin in Caribou Creek to be met by a few of the 120-mile runners, who had finished and leap-frogged ahead in their support vehicles. David Smale was there. With the prospect of some warmth at the checkpoint, I dared to take off my socks and shoes, and even cooled my feet in the snow outside. David inspected them and I allowed him to drain a few blisters on my toes. In went the needle and out came a flow of clear-ish liquid.

I took a four-hour stop at Caribou Creek. It was during this downtime that David told me that Tony was out of the race. My companion had lain down where I'd left him at the side of the road and hadn't been able to get back up. He'd hurt his foot. His thigh was bothering him too. Perhaps he had just reached the limit. He was safe but unfortunately out of the race.

I was disappointed for him. He had trained so hard for this race. We had kept each other company for only a few days but it felt like months. Distance running is often looked at as a lonely pursuit, where the closest thing to conversation is the bleeping of a smartwatch. But it's often not like that. Even in these testing moments, there's the sense you're in it together. Perhaps it's a result of the preposterously long distance, or the fact that PBs are of little concern, but the atmosphere here was one of friendliness and support.

What should I do now? Tony had said to me that since I was making a television programme of the race, he'd drop back at the end of 350 miles and let me cross the line first. I said he'd do no such thing. We'd cross the line together. And now we wouldn't. Tony was gone. I was the only runner left. And four hours of rest were giving me too much time to weigh up my options. By going one pace further than Tony and the others, I had already won. What was the point of going on?

I'm sure it was a hallucination but I saw myself back home, telling people I had won the race. I was the last person standing, I told them. I had made myself proud. I could give up now and still hold my head up high. It was so real that I even experienced the regret of not crossing the finish line.

Here I was wondering if this experience was really worth the pain and emotional torture? I had given so much to this venture, had sacrificed so much, had dedicated years to this challenge and had received so much support leading up to the event ... could I return home with my head held high knowing that I had given up?

Yes, I could. I was the only one left. I didn't fear failure. I've done enough, I thought. I've loved it. I know who I am. This race won't define me. I don't need to prove anything to anyone else. It's been awesome, but I am done.

At that moment in the Arctic, I had proven enough, and no, I didn't fear failure. What I did fear was setting my aim too low.

I've mentioned the cardinal rules of bivvying on the go. Well, there's an even simpler pair of rules about running ultra races.

1. *Get to the start line.*
2. *Get to the finish line.*

I hadn't yet finished. The daunting reality was that there were 150 miles ahead, 30 miles longer than the entire Jungle Marathon. I'd done five checkpoints and now had three to go, the next, to Inuvik, being the last on the Dempster Highway. From Inuvik to Swimming Point and from there to Tuktoyaktuk, the race followed the Ice Road over the Mackenzie River. Tuk, I thought. Tuck it away. Never think too far ahead. Get to Inuvik first. That was about as deep-reaching as my analysis went. As I left the cabin at Caribou Creek, four hours after reaching the checkpoint, I passed Tony's pulk, parked up, empty of everything bar his race number, 55. I felt a little pang. It was another reminder that I was on my own now.

Hours passed and nothing seemed to change. All I could see was a white tunnel. By now I was getting tunnel vision. I felt as if I was the only one left on the planet. I was walking up a never-ending hill. Was I walking on the curvature of the Earth?

All of a sudden a woman in a summer dress appeared on the trail. I smiled. I rubbed my eyes and she was still standing there. Looking straight at me.

'Why is she here? She must be cold,' I thought. She was as real as you are. Behind her, I saw more people, staring at me. But as I approached her, it turned out to be a small sapling covered in snow. I shook my eyes as if to shrug the woman out of my mind and carried on.

My feet had swollen so much, they were far too big for my shoes. I was down to my last layer of socks. I didn't have the luxury of another bigger pair. The pain in my feet was indescribable, it was worse than excruciating. With every footstep the pain shot up from my feet throughout my whole body. I knew I had fractured my feet. I knew I had more blisters developing under my toenails.

But I had to carry on. I just had to.

Once you reach the ultimate limit of your endurance, how do you go further? Belief perhaps? Thinking positive? I prefer to think of it as simply ignoring the fact that you can't go further. Ignore the things that we all 'know' and go out and learn these truths for yourself.

The Dempster Highway did not go out in grand style. There was no memorable mountain pass or river crossing on its last leg. It said goodbye without drama. More endless but incredible miles. Mile after mile after mile. But it wasn't true I'd be on my own. Fifteen miles outside Inuvik, I met David Smale and he kept me company all the way to the checkpoint. He didn't have to come out to support me. He could have easily kept on sleeping in his warm comfy bed. But no, he was here. His kindness made me cry (again). 'I can't stop crying,' I said (again). 'People are so kind. It's so humbling. I'm so grateful to them.'

I looked up to the sky, maybe searching for more inspiration, and in front of me was the most glorious display of the northern lights I had ever seen. When earlier in the week I dreaded walking into the magnificent sunsets, dreading the cold, the loneliness, the sleep deprivation, now I looked forward to those dark nights because I knew the aurora borealis would come out to entertain me. It felt as if I had my own private natural firework display to keep me going. And the closer I got to the finishing line, the clearer and longer the displays lasted.

Now that was motivation. Nature at its best.

CHAPTER 15

HUMBLED

I was on the Ice Road. Deep blues and greens and yellows swirled beneath the surface, which was criss-crossed with cracks but strong enough to support trucks. I had by now got used to the banging and cracking noises from the ice as I moved across it. There were bore holes along the way, where the thickness was checked. I saw no checks being made in March, the one month when the mercury never rose above freezing point. I repeat it because I felt it. 'Put me back in the Amazon any day,' I said to the camera along the way.

It was a long stretch of 70 miles to the next check point, with plenty of scope for mood swings both ways. I wasn't down for the entire duration by any means. I soon picked up my pace and spirit. There was an urgency to my progress now, the need to complete this race in the time limit. I knew it was rash to think too far ahead, but after so many hours, I kept recalculating time and distance. I had 117 miles to go in 72 hours. Whether that pressure concentrated my mind and gave it clarity, I couldn't say. I did know that it felt good to be alive. I was living a stripped-down life, out in the freezing air with everything I needed to survive, reduced to 50lbs on my little old pulk. And I loved it.

For most of us, our world today is so physically soft, and at the same time so terribly demanding and stressful that it can be hard to keep up with everything we feel we need to do in a day. For me, running helps regain a healthy balance between my mind, my body and my soul. I love single-mindedly pursuing a goal. I find having a singular goal is quite purifying because there's so much going on in my life in terms of commitments and expectations and I have to find a way to balance it all. But when I go to a race, I leave all that behind and I just focus on the trail.

Soon, night fell and the temperature inexorably dropped to -36C. I was halfway to Inuvik. I was staggering all over the place. At some point, I experimented with sleeping while walking. I convinced myself with the absolute clear-headedness of a drunk that I was quite capable of taking a Tony micro-nap between strides. It didn't work. I was all over the Ice Road. If somebody could see me and not know my situation, they would have kept well away. I looked like a mad woman, eyes bulging as I tried to keep them open, muttering to myself, smelling of fish flakes and zigzagging across the road. Common sense prevailed and I stopped to sleep on a snowbank. I somehow remembered the protocols this time, slept for 40 minutes without being run over and set off again in the right direction.

This was the night of haziness. Of misty memories, punctured – like a blister – by a piercing beam. I knew I was tired, but I knew I wasn't hallucinating. I knew what cartoon characters with machetes looked like and what naked bodies lying dead on the side of the road looked like. I knew what it felt like when a log cabin with skis outside and a curl of smoke from its chimney melted before my eyes. This was different. This was a beam of light … a pair of beams. It was a pick-up truck. And it slewed to a stop in front of me. I held up my hands against the glare. It must have been one of the support vans, catching up with me to check if I was OK. But I didn't know the men who jumped out of the vehicle and started shouting, jeering and circling me. The circle around me got smaller and smaller as they came closer. I could see beer cans in their hands.

It was all happening so fast that I had no time to wonder if I was in danger. What might be about to happen to me? I heard the acceleration of another van come up behind me and then another man running towards me. It was Emyr – he had jumped out of the car and Joe was speeding up from behind. Emyr shouted at the circling men and they shied away, slinking back to their car with a growl. They drove off in the direction of distant Tuk. Emyr offered me a seat in his car. I said no. There were to be no shortcuts. No easy options. Not even here at a moment of peril. I don't think I expressed my gratitude very well. I suspect I may have grunted a thank you and carried on, following the lights of the other men's car. It was only afterwards that reality sunk in. It wasn't a dream. It wasn't a hallucination. What had happened was real. It was only then that I started to cry.

I have a list concerning what seems to go hand in hand – or in my case, foot in foot – with endurance running. It's a sort of side-tunnel off the pain cave:

1. *Embrace the pain.*
2. *Look forward to it.*
3. *Learn to love it.*
4. *It will make you a stronger runner.*
5. *It will make you a stronger person.*

It was all very well having bullet-points telling me to embrace the pain and love it, but my feet needed something a little more connected to what they were being asked to do.

The last checkpoint before the finish line was a SUV parked at Swimming Point. Here I decided to do a bit more surgery on my blister. I had no David this time and knew that I was at risk of the toe turning septic, but in went the point of my safety-pin anyway. I then took out my Swiss Army knife. In for a penny, I thought. I studied what remained of my toenails and slid in the blade. Not to cut but to raise. One nail at a time. I didn't pull them off completely; just prised them upwards. Raised them to the sky by a millimetre.

Hallelujah. I can't tell you how good it felt. It was instant relief, maybe for long-term pain, not gain. I didn't care. There is the spiritual rush that comes with being in the jungle under a billion stars, or out here on the tundra with the northern lights swirling, swaying, dancing their narcotic ballet, but there is sometimes a physical reward, too. Not that glorious feeling that comes with recovery after exertion. Not here, anyway. Here it came with a toenail, a penknife and a slightly trembling hand. I lifted a few of my toenails off their battered beds to be free for even just five minutes of the throb, the stab and the shooting pains that had been my constant companions across Canada. The relief. I added to the pain list:

6. *If points 1-3 are beyond your reach, always have a Swiss Army knife at the ready. Point 4 still applies.*

My spirits, like my toenails, were further lifted when Tony opened the door. He was on his way to the finish by car. It was so good to see him again. I had a little gulp when he wished me good luck and left me to finish the race on my own.

I went through all the emotions on the final section from Swimming Point to the finish at Tuktoyaktuk. The last leg to Tuk. I set off on the eighth checkpoint on the seventh day, Thursday afternoon at five o'clock. There remained 50 miles, more than enough for the pain-relief to wear off. My travelling companions were back.

So far, the rules had come in pairs (I'm never afraid of repeating a list):

Rule 1: Get to the start line
Rule 2: Get to the finish line.
Rule 3: When you bivvy out, make a sign pointing forward.
Rule 4: Don't sleep where a truck might run you over.

I wrote a new rule. No, not a rule, but Lowri's law: *one step at a time.* It comes before all other rules. It is the Law. *One Step At A Time.*

The Law had carried me through Hurricane Alley and up to Wright Pass. The Law had carried me down to the Mackenzie Delta and through the barrier that rose before me with its banner: 'You're not even a third of the way there.' The Law was forward motion on those endless miles of the Dempster Highway, when I never seemed to be getting anywhere. And it applied now on the last leg. Mind over the matter of my feet. Dig deep one last time.

In fact, I didn't have to stretch down to the very bottom of my reserves. I realised I was going to make it. For the first time I began to visualise crossing the finish line. I allowed myself a smile – a private one in this most remote of places, and one hidden away beneath my layers. When I arrived in Canada and introduced myself to the other competitors, I told them I was a television presenter. Now, they would have known that everyone entering the race had to have a portfolio of previous ultras. This was not a place for learner endurance runners. But my fellow competitors were ex-soldiers, ex-marines and highly trained specialist athletes. And I worked in front of a camera. Please don't get me wrong … I was welcomed with open arms by the others, but part of the process of getting to know strangers in strange places is through humour. Banter. 'Where's your make-up artist? Packed your hair drier?' If there had been a sweepstake for the first one to drop out of the 6633 Ultra, I bet somebody would have been delighted to pick my name. So, yes, I admit it, I allowed myself a little smile now.

The race had stripped me bare, which sounds ridiculous since I spent so much time putting on warm clothes. But it had – had taken me apart layer by layer and asked that question: can you still do this? And now I was rebuilding from my inner core outwards, from my soul upwards. I was going to make it to the end. What was more, I was going to make it in good time. I stopped to watch the sun go down for the last time and felt sad, not because it meant the temperature was going to drop, but because this would be my last sunset on the trail.

I told myself to put sentimentality to one side. I put my producer's hat on. She needed a good end-sequence and having her presenter crossing the line in darkness might not be the grand finale she was after. I walked on just to eat up a few more miles and hours, then scraped out one last snow-hole with my little shovel. I laid out my sleeping bag inside the bivvy. I went through the list, the routine that I could do on the very brink of falling asleep. In I slipped, leaving a slightly larger breathing hole this time. The pound coin opening became a two-pound viewing aperture. One last chance to stare at the night sky. The aurora borealis had been with me every night. Well, perhaps not in Hurricane Alley, where I had kept my head bowed and tilted against the wind, my eyes squeezed into the tiniest slits, through which I looked only at the place on the ground, illuminated by my head-torch, where I would put my foot next. One step at a time.

Darkness arrived and I questioned whether I should keep going and finish in the darkness of the early morning – not great for the camera. Or would it be better for me to sleep one last time under the stars, and arrive in day light for the cameras? Also, I wasn't going for a record time, I was here for the adventure, the journey. This will not happen again, I told myself, so let's make the most of it and enjoy the moment.

Now though, I lay in my bivvy and stared at the skies. By day, I had the Ice Road with its swirls of river colours beneath the cracked glass. At night, I could see the lights of Tuk, but had learned not to be fooled by their faint glow on the horizon. I had first seen it from 90 miles away and it hadn't come any closer or grown any brighter. The only lights I could trust were from my head-torch and in the sky. To appreciate the celestial, I turned off my little light. Once again, the northern lights worked their hypnotic, soothing magic on me, their green plumes sliding in slow motion down to the horizon, only to bounce gracefully back and weave their patterns in full view.

I lay there in my white snow-hole and watched this green light show and relaxed. I had melted some ice on my stove and poured into my water bottle; tomorrow's drinking water now acted as my warm-water radiator. I held it tight against me in my sleeping bag and drifted off, only to be shocked into consciousness by that most feared combination of cold and wet. I had failed to secure the top of the bottle properly and water had poured all over me. I felt the water freeze within seconds around my feet. In my panic, I knocked my head-torch off and in the pitch black of the bivvy I couldn't find my spare clothes or the dry towel which lay at the bottom of the sleeping bag.

I eventually managed to calm down and restore order to my tight space. I put on dry clothes, but it was a sharp dig in the ribs, one last warning that I couldn't afford to relax for a second. Nothing could be taken for granted. The end was so close but it was still only relative. In the context of 350 miles, this was a short haul, but that finish was still a full day's march away.

Tiredness and pain would still have plenty of opportunity to leave their mark. As the daylight hours of the next day, my second Friday on the trail, passed, I went through all the stages of agony and elation, fast and slow, uphill and downhill until simple weariness consumed all others. In the course of seven nights I reckoned, give or take the odd half-hour of fitful semi-consciousness, I'd slept for a maximum of 16 hours. Fatigue hauled me into a state of delirium and I began to meander again over the road.

And then, like all the phases, it passed. The end truly was in sight. Tuk was just over the brow, just around the corner. I'd been thinking of stopping one last time to collect my thoughts, work out a line or two for the camera on arrival and muse on life in general and this adventure in particular. Siôn had written me a letter and put it in an envelope, on which he'd written: 'To be opened only if you really need to.' I needed to open it, not because I was in distress, but because I needed to embrace the moment when I could begin to think of home. I needed my Siôn. And where better to stop and feel a little love than the park bench, not far ahead on the Ice Road? I would remove myself from the pulk, take off my rucksack and just stretch out on that bench. I looked down to see what I was doing. When I looked back up, the bench had gone. Delirium still had me in its grip.

As if I'd just walked into a lamp post on the high street, I looked around to see who might have witnessed my foolishness. There was nobody there. Thank goodness. I brushed the ice off. I re-tightened all my straps and set off again.

And then there were five miles to go. Tuk was truly almost in sight. I could have broken into a canter and positively roared into town. Me and the pulk, sprinting for home. Instead, I took that break. I was aware that the line would be crossed and there'd be an end to it, but I was pretty sure it wouldn't be a moment of ecstasy. I was pretty sure the earth wasn't going to move. I was too tired. I smelled of dried fish. Everything in endurance-running is so elongated, so stretched-out that all the extremes tend to be flattened too. Pain shrinks, kept by the mind within a limit that can be borne. And so too does elation. You daren't let rip with delight because with your next step you might slip on the wretched ice. Joy was always tempered by the schedule, which demanded the same again tomorrow, plus some more. This race wouldn't end with a moment of elation because the elation was happening right now.

No, I wasn't going to run whooping and a-hollering into Tuk. But I was going to stop while I still had nothing but my own company, and let it sink in. I was ready now to go home. But I would miss this place, this magnificent wilderness with all its splendours and all its dangers. It had put me to a test beyond my imagination. I had entered without honestly believing it could be any tougher than the Jungle Marathon, but it had been. And I had survived. I was only the fifth person in five races to complete the 350-mile course. I had more than survived. I had won. You may well recall me saying that winning is far from everything in endurance sport. The longer you go, the smaller the imperative to be victorious. Finishing is the goal. If you finish in the front, middle or back of the pack, there is great satisfaction in saying 'I have finished'. Proving something to yourself is more important than proving yourself faster, stronger and more resilient than other people. But here, taking my private five, I allowed myself to say it: 'Private five; high five.'

I had grown to love this place. I went into a sort of reverse *hiraeth*. Instead of feeling the pull of home, I wanted all those whom I loved and missed to come here and see it for themselves. To listen to its absolute nothingness and respect it. As silly as it may sound, I looked down at my feet and said '*Diolch* / Thank you feet for carrying me over 350 miles. Thank you.'

Once you tackle something bigger than you've done before, you break down boundaries and that's so powerful. After coming back from surgeries, meeting world class athletes, this challenge showed me something important: that I was an adventure athlete. That I shouldn't define myself by the things I had not done or didn't think I could do. And that was a damn good reason to race the 6633 Ultra.

A couple of miles from Tuk, a microphone appeared before me. It was real. I did an interview for a Canadian radio station. I don't know which one or what I said. I crossed the finish line 174 hours and 8 minutes after setting out from the Eagles Plains Hotel. As

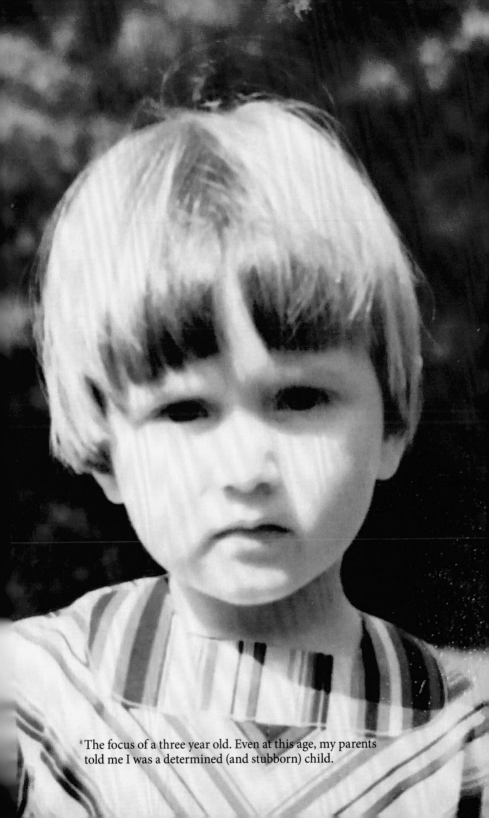

The focus of a three year old. Even at this age, my parents told me I was a determined (and stubborn) child.

My brother and I went to the local Sunday School run by Mrs Gwen Jones and my mother. We were a small but loyal group.

Dad, Roger, Mam (behind the camera) and me on holiday in France. Our parents always ensured that we had quality family time together, especially over the summer.

Having endless fun learning to boogie board and surf with my cousin Lalage on Rhossili in Gower.

Al fresco dining with the family on one of our many caravanning holidays. Mam could always transform the simplest of meals into a wonderful feast (unlike me).

Proudly wearing Wales'
National costume on
St David's Day.

Mam, Roger and me (with Dad behind the lens) on a PGL adventure holiday. Every year we'd have a chance to try and learn different outdoor activities and skills.

The summer of 1984 was spent learning to sail. At the end of every holiday, our parents wanted our feet dirty, our hair messy and our eyes sparkling.

The most valuable practice aid is patience. I didn't always sound good on the piano, violin, viola, harp or singing, but when I did, it was because I had practised.

A delighted and surprised 16 year old having just won the highest accolade in the National Eisteddfod's folk singing category.

I first tried skiing at the age of 7. I was hooked. The attire may have changed but still love the feeling of weightlessness, the rhythm, the camaraderie, the beautiful scenery and the opportunity skiing has given me to travel and explore.

Playing rugby for my country was one of my sporting highlights.
Wales v England 1995.

Competing in my first triathlon in London in 2003. I loved it. I told myself to run the first two-thirds of the race with my head and the last third with my heart.

My first presenting job on *Planed Plant* (Children's Planet) for S4C, the Welsh TV channel, in 1996 with Catrin, Elen, Martyn, Bedwyr (and puppet Wcw). Good times and good friends.

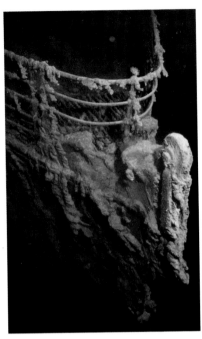

Searching for an 18th Century shipwreck off the Welsh coast for a television documentary.

2003 Titanic Expedition: The bow of the RMS Titanic, nearly 4,000 metres below the surface of the North Atlantic, south of Newfoundland.

On the science research vessel Akademik Mstislav Keldysh and standing in front of the MIR submersible with Russian MIR pilot Nescheta and Expedition Coordinator Belinda Sawyer.

Tough training with the Royal Marines in Lympstone.

The Jungle Marathon in the Amazon. Bitten by hornets, toenails lost, and exhausted. Here I'm telling myself that I wasn't competing against other runners, but against that little voice in the back of my mind telling me to give up.

One thing I like about multi-stage races, and what makes them different from other races, is the camp life. Here I'm comparing toenails with the legendary American ultra runner Nikki Kimball.

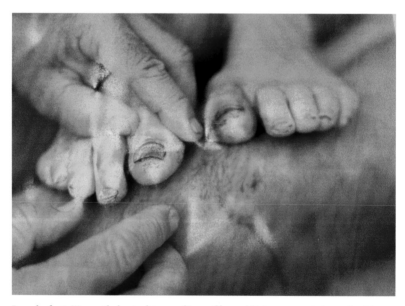

Jungle feet: Toenails lost, skin peeling off, my blisters were injected with tincture benzoin (which hurt). I would not have recognised my own battered feet, but my mother did from the other side of the world. And when she did, she put her travel plans to Brazil on hold.

Crossing the Jungle Marathon's finishing line with nothing left in the tank. The pride of knowing I could not have done any better left me feeling very emotional.

With Eurwyn at the end of the Jungle Marathon. It didn't matter to me how many miles I had run or how fast or slow I had gone - what mattered most was that I had finished what I had started.

All alone on the frozen MacKenzie River. Perseverance has always been something that was in me and a tool that came in handy during the last 100 miles of the 6633 Ultra.

The aurora borealis from my bivvy bag. The view of the northern lights moving in great swathes of colour across the sky like a living organism was Nature at its best. This is why I choose adventure.

After 46 hours on the 6633 Ultra it was all about relentless forward motion. I wasn't thinking about what could happen in a month or a year, I just focussed on what was in front of me and did what I could to get closer to where I wanted to be.

Humbled, grateful and privileged to have been awarded an Honorary Fellowship and Master's Degree from Swansea University in 2012 having been nominated by Mr Howard Morgan, one of the University's longest serving members.

Delighted when the second series of *Ras yn Erbyn Amser* (A Race Against Time) won two BAFTAs for Best Presenter and Best Documentary in 2012. A great night of celebration, especially as my husband also won a BAFTA that evening.

Nearing the end of the Gower Ultra 2016. My parents and Nel came to meet me at half way. She was allowed to join me, and put a smile on my face. Some days you just need to run with your friend.

On the start line of a road race. Sometimes the biggest source of motivation comes from the smallest fan.

Filming with the Himba tribes of Namibia. In a rapidly changing world they continue to live lives of beautiful simplicity. I feel privileged to have spent a month with them.

Peru 2016. I was humbled by the incredible welcome and kindness of the people of the Andean mountains. To document their resilience and their survival in harsh, challenging and extreme conditions was a truly unforgettable experience.

Finishing the 105 mile run around Anglesey in 2016. We started off as a group of four, but Stephen (pictured left) fell ill and Alan (on crutches) got injured. Phil and I continued to the end but it was great to finish it with all four together.

With some of my closest University friends. Still having fun but now together with all our children.

Line Honours for Team Aparito on the Three Peaks Yacht Race. I loved racing with these incredible ladies. (From left to right: Nikki Curwen, me, Pip Hare, Jo Jackson and Elin Haf Davies.)

Broadcasting live from the Cardiff Half Marathon. Interviewing Jamie Simms from Blackwood.

Deep in thought on Cader Idris. 60 miles
into the 150 mile 333 Challenge.

ortpicturesCymru

Emma and I fitting in long training runs around our family and work commitments during the pre-dawn hours. Here we are about to start our 60 mile mountain run home at 9pm with the aim of arriving back in time to take our boys to school in the morning.

Sometimes it's worth waking up early. Pre-dawn on the Brecon Beacons. On a clear day, there's very little noise especially on the mountains – just the birdsong and the sound of your own breathing. The views turn to gold as the sun rises.

The best view comes after the hardest climb. Increasing training mileage and getting to spend the day on the mountains with my family.

Multi-tasking - the reality of life, especially with children. Getting the workout done, Gwilym seeing the ducks and Nel enjoying chasing squirrels.

Smiles and miles. The last few weeks of Dragon's Back training were spent hiking due to injury.

The second day of the Dragon's Back Race. Knee heavily taped up and needing the poles on the descents.

The final miles of the Dragon's Back Race. By Day 5, I was comfortable being uncomfortable. The smile did not disappear all day long.

Crib Goch in Snowdonia. Going fast enough to get to the end of the first day, but slow enough to see the incredible views.

Finishing the Dragon's Back Race. Having Gwilym with me as I crossed the finish line made it one of the best feelings of my racing career.

With the best team I could ever have. Precious time on holiday with Siôn and Gwilym.

many of the starters who were in a fit state to do so, welcomed me home. We did big hugs.

'I've had an unforgettable experience,' I said. 'I am a stronger, better person because of it. It tore my soul to bits and put it back together.' Considering I was feeling a little bit empty, I could have done far worse.

We all slept that night in Tuk Village Hall. I had a hot shower, which was a warm trickle but the best I'd ever had.

Me, myself and I. We'd got on OK. There were times when we quarrelled but mostly we were mates. Now that I had company, I was talking a lot, which I do when I'm not feeling great. Nervous talk. All right, I talk a lot at the best of times, but I talked even more now I was caving in to fatigue. When I fell asleep – on the hall floor rather than in a bed, with my feet raised onto a chair – apparently my legs carried on walking. I didn't get up and prowl the dormitory, but my legs, to general amusement, were moving and twitching all night. The next day, I slept all the way back to Eagle Plains. Perhaps I couldn't bear to watch the Ice Road and the Dempster Highway, that I'd just spent my 174 hours on, shooting by under the tyres of our car.

There was a presentation ceremony at the hotel by the start. It was a very brief affair. I was given a prize, an Inuit figure made of rock. Afterwards, again, I preferred to sleep on the floor, rather than in my bed. One of the SAS runners asked me how I had done it. Had I been thinking ahead all the time, to the day like today when it was all over? Not at all, I told him. Little goals. Tiny goals.

In adversity, I had shrunk my targets. When I was really struggling, my entire concentration went on the next pace. One step at a time. I told him that I had put asterisks by a few points on one of my many lists. It was to do with escaping the pain cave:

1. *Don't let pain set the rhythm.*
2. *Set a rhythm the pain can accommodate.*
3. *The mind controls the body.*
4. *Embrace it.*

When I came home, I seemed to take to the sofa. The first three programmes of *Ras Yn Erbyn Amser 2,* the ones showing the year-long preparations for Canada, had started to go out on S4C during the race. I should have gone straight to work on the final show, but I stepped away from the edit, handing responsibility over to Emyr. Unlike the first series where I sat with the editor to put the series together, this time I could not choose which bits, all the highs and lows from 174 hours, to put in one hour-long programme. I was too close to this edit so I stepped aside and put the television on at home and watched other stuff. I had said I didn't want a fuss. I just wanted to slip back into life quietly but POP 1 said they were going to take me out to lunch. It turned out to be a big surprise party.

Despite saying that I didn't want a fuss, it was great to see the wonderful friends and strangers who had now become friends – people who had helped me to cross the finish line. Everyone there had had a bit part to play in me crossing that line. I turned up on crutches; I had deep bruising and stress fractures on both feet. I had told myself towards the end of the race that I was going to give them TLC. That was one of the things that did take me by surprise. The hardness of the terrain. I think I was just giving them (my feet) some time off. They had done well. I felt I managed to show that I was in pretty good spirits.

And that was the end of that for the time being. After the pain cave comes the hollow cave. The waiting cave.

Once I returned home, I felt lost. I tried to fill the void left by not training, but couldn't seem to find any motivation in what I was doing, whether it was in the gym or in my writing. I suffered through painful workouts when I should have been resting.

Not only had my training regimen dictated almost every day of my life for years, but my brain and body were used to meeting regular goals, navigating training challenges, and mentally preparing for a big event. Once that routine and goal is gone, feeling a little lost can be pretty standard. Also, how could I top running 350 miles in the Arctic? It wasn't 'depression'. I prefer the term 'post-race low' instead, but having spoken to other friends and athletes, it's totally normal for athletes to feel a certain way after a big event is over.

When you're training for a race, you wake up every day and have something to shoot for, and you're going to have positive feelings and energy that go along with that. So the difference between normal sadness and that feeling athletes experience right after a big race is really a loss of energy and motivation. Luckily for me, I was enjoying spending more time with my husband, family and friends, and that void was slowly being filled with other commitments.

There were two spin-offs from the Arctic Ultra. The final programme of the series was nominated for three categories in the BAFTA Cymru awards of 2012. It won in both the Best Documentary series and Best Presenter. Soon after, I received a letter in the post, with Buckingham Palace on the envelope. I was kindly invited to an audience with the Queen. How could she ever have heard of me? It was apparently in recognition of my services to Adventure and Exploration in the centenary year of Captain Robert Falcon Scott's ill-fated expedition – his race against Roald Amundsen – to the South Pole. Scott of the Antarctic and Lowri Morgan. Goodness. I can't believe the names I seem to have been bracketed with along the way.

I couldn't believe who else was in the room. Sir Chris Bonington, Bear Grylls, explorers, mountaineers and adventurers on the grandest of scales. I sat quietly in the corner in awe and looked on until they sort of drew me into their company and we talked about what we had done. It seemed I was unhesitatingly included in their group: people who are naturally drawn to taking themselves – ourselves, for I immediately felt the connection – to extremes.

Because I was very nervous about meeting Her Majesty the Queen, I had made a list.

1. *Bow or curtsy (don't forget to practise).*
2. *The Queen may want to shake hands, but (v important) wait for her to make the first move.*
3. *Make eye contact and then extend hand (for swift shake, but not too swift).*
4. *The Queen speaks first.*
5. *Address her as 'Your Majesty' once ...*

6. *... and after that as 'Ma'am'.*
7. *You can say 'How do you do?' ...*
8. *And you're pleased to meet her ...*
9. *But ask no personal questions about her or the Royal Family.*

I began well. 'Your Majesty ...' But then I stuck out my hand. The Queen looked at me; the seconds felt like hours. Was I going to pull my hand back slowly? Surely nobody would notice. Or should I keep it up there? Thankfully, Her Majesty shook it and from then on, it was ... well, it was unforgettable. I handed her a tiny polystyrene cup (with Titanic Expedition Sept 2003 written on it) that had been taken down to the Titanic. The pressure at 2.5 miles beneath the ocean had pushed it into a thimble-sized cup. She looked at it for what felt like a while and a big smile emerged. She was fascinated. It can only have been for five minutes but we chatted about the Titanic, the Jungle and the Arctic and she put me completely at my ease. During my time there, I met a few adventurers, icons in the world of adventure and a few members of the Royal Family. One was Princess Michael of Kent. She came up to me, admiring my red dress. She asked why I was there. I was slightly overawed and explained my story. She was fascinated and delighted that I had been the only finisher of the 6633 Ultra. 'You beat all the men! How inspirational,' she said. 'Yes, but I didn't think of it like that. It was about beating that tiny voice in my head telling me to quit,' I said. She clapped her hands in delight. 'You must meet my husband. You must!' and she held my hand and ushered me to her husband, who was talking to Sir Ranulph Fiennes. 'Tell them, Lowri, tell them of your adventures.' And that's what I tried to do. For once in my life, I was speechless. It was a wonderful evening; an evening I shall never forget.

For me, no sense of accomplishment can be delivered by watching or reading about other people doing amazing things. Captivating as a film may be and totally successful in making everybody fill up with tears (I'm no exception), it cannot be your long-lasting reality. Only through our own endeavours do we generate an enduring pride in ourselves, an inner sense of worth. Imagine handing a fisherman a prize catch. You may think you're doing him a favour and saving him the trouble, but you are robbing him of his pleasure. A fisherman wants to catch his own fish.

CHAPTER 16

AND A NEW ADVENTURE BEGINS

I talked with Siôn after the 6633 Arctic Ultra and we discussed putting my career before my running now. I don't think I had grand plans to become some high-powered woman in my chosen industry, but perhaps I needed a pause to muse on what it was precisely that I did want to do from now on. I was not feeling any stress. Far from it. The questions I had asked of myself in the jungle and the Arctic had been so penetrating and finding the answers had been so revealing that their effect was not going to wear off too soon, I hoped. The hollowness that had followed me back to Wales from Canada had been filled by a contentment, a satisfaction with my lot. Of course, I was still tempted to run. I was being offered more work – exciting work that took me away from home for weeks on end. I had invitations from all over the world to race and I had to admit that many happened to be in places I longed to visit.

I was travelling more with work too so for my next multi-stage race, I chose not to go exotic (or deep-frozen) this time, but to Anglesey off the north coast of Wales. *Ynys Môn* is not a huge island, but the Ring of Fire (quoting the song by Johnny Cash) Ultra still amounted to 135 miles over three days, taking a full tour around the coast, beginning and ending in Holyhead. I finished in 12th place overall and second in the women's race. It kept me moving, while presenting and producing for television kept me working.

One thing not mentioned as I drew towards my 40s was starting a family. My friends had always joked that I was too busy for children. I used to shrug my shoulders and tell myself it was true. I told myself it didn't make me mean or selfish or less of a woman. It just made me honest.

Out of the blue, I was offered a job. It was my first for Green Bay, a production company in Cardiff, that has since sent me to China, the Atlas Mountains in Morocco, to Mexico to cover The Festival of The Dead, and to the Andes in Peru. I wouldn't always have to run long-distance to see the world. For this inaugural project, they wanted me to go to Namibia to present a series about living a nomadic life in remote places. Nomads, remoteness – I felt I had something to offer.

The documentary was about the Himba and the Herero peoples. The Himba roamed over vast areas of south-western Africa but their way of life was threatened by the loss of tracts of land to mines, farms and to Westernisation in general. Even more destructive was the almost constant warring in nearby Angola. The Herero tribe lived on the strikingly beautiful, but almost entirely barren, Skeleton Coast. The five weeks in Namibia would change my life.

I camped out first with the Himba in the northwest region of Kunene, also referred to as Kaokoland in Namibia. This region had a population density of just one person per two square kilometres. Thanks to their isolation and secluded lifestyle, their culture and traditions had remained unaltered. Initiation into Himba adulthood, for example. It was the same as it had ever been. To us, it seemed a harsh ritual. At the age of 15, both males and females had their four bottom-front teeth not so much removed as knocked clean out. It was a rite of passage, a mark that would allow the Himba to recognise each other wherever they roamed. Puberty for girls marked the end of bathing or any kind of cleansing with water. Smoke-baths with sweet smelling incense and leaves thereafter sufficed.

I knew it was rude to stare, but I couldn't help it. I was transfixed by the wonderful Himba women who greeted us with their ochre-covered hair. I had never seen anything like it. Then a girl took my hand and proceeded to demonstrate how the women cover themselves with *otjize*, a mixture of butter fat and ochre, that left their skin so smooth it was flawless. They had a smell that was strong, but not of sweat or the mustiness of unwashed bodies. It was more like smoked earth and butter, an aroma unlike any other but not unpleasant at all. The *otijize* gave the skin a reddish tinge, the colour of the earth and of blood, symbolising life and applied as an expression of female beauty.

They were joyous company, who welcomed me into their midst. I joined in their ritual dances, although they burst into laughter when they saw my efforts. I spent days with them going out of the village to find wood and collect water. I walked miles with them to find the medics on their rounds across an enormous territory. There were some unsettling moments here. Because I was white and with a television crew, it was assumed I would be given automatic access to the front of the long queue. Mothers desperately pushed their children towards me. I said sorry in a language they could not understand. I hugged the children and played with them to give their mothers a short break, but I had no power to jump with them to the front of the line.

Back in their homes, the women I knew would ask each of us in the crew how old we were, if we were married and if we had children. They shook their heads in disbelief when I said I was 38 and didn't have any. The Himba marry young and have children early.

Several years previously, a wealthy white man with a lot of land had been travelling through the bush when he came upon a group of Himba, whose queen was very ill with cancer. The man took her back with him to the city for treatment. Eventually the queen was in remission and thanked the man. He asked her if there was anything more he could do for her people. Being a wise woman, a visionary with no children of her own and no chance of giving birth, the queen thought long and hard. She asked the man to let her put some of his land to her people's use, namely a new Himba orphanage. HIV had left a lot of children without parents. Not wishing them to feel abandoned, she and her partner brought in other Himba to care for them. They built a school. And this is where we came to next, this village that had grown up around an orphanage and small school. Many of the parents were the original orphans and were now bringing their children up in the same place.

As I tried to film my links in and out of the story of the orphans, they would clamber all over me. I laughed so much, I found it impossible to deliver my lines. Yes, something happened in the Namib Desert.

I'd had a few early miscarriages in the past. Some doctors had intimated that my age and my high weekly mileage were not helping my chances of becoming a mother. When I returned to Wales from Namibia, I quietly decreased the miles and carried on with life in the media.

In the summer of 2014, in the evening after coming third in a 15-mile trail race – I said I'd cut down, not stop – I found out that I was pregnant. I did stop running then. Well, for the first three months, anyway. Once we passed the twelve-week stage, I put my trainers back on – with the consultant's blessing – and took to the trails close to home. If the mother was happy, then the baby would be, too, he told me.

I changed my routine. This was a fresh start. It may not appear too radical, but it was for me. I took off my GPS watch. I ran free. When I took up running in the mid 1980s, there was no such thing as a GPS watch. There were no pace calculators. Only when we did workouts at the running club did we care about our specific pace per mile. The team took to the track and ran intervals at varying paces. That's where I learned to appreciate how and when feelings morphed at different paces.

Now, I love my GPS watch but there's something undeniably liberating about running without constantly monitoring my progress. When I rebooted my running, instead of glancing down at my wrist every couple of minutes, I tuned into my pregnant body and for six daily, easy-paced miles immersed myself in the new 'us' and everything around us. Everyone has their own running story. For some, the aim is to lose weight or raise money for charities, to inspire someone or to remember someone. For others, it's a lust for competition. I think that sometimes I run to escape the man-made world but this time I was running for a different reason.

In March 2015, Gwilym was born. The experts were slightly surprised to hear that I'd been keeping up my 35-odd miles per week until week 39. True, I slowed down a bit and stayed closer to home, confining myself to laps of the park next door in the later stages, but I loved running while pregnant. It kept my energy levels high; Nel the dog loved it. Running for two was good for me.

My pregnancy had its drama but we were lucky and Gwilym was born healthy. When the contractions were painful, I visualised myself running up a mountain. I could cope because I knew a downhill would come soon.

After four days, the three of us went home. I was given permission to start running again when Gwilym was two weeks old. I felt ready. I was suddenly enjoying motherhood and had a strong family support system in place.

As soon as I could, I was lacing up my trainers and heading out. However, on my first outing, my excitement suddenly turned to shock. I knew I'd be slow, but it was as if I hadn't been running for a year, not three weeks. I couldn't go a mile without stopping. I was devastated. I had kept myself healthy and had been running for most of my pregnancy – surely I couldn't have lost all of that fitness? So I reverted to running for five minutes and walking for five; slowly the running time would increase and the walking would decrease.

A few people told me that once I was a mother, my adventures would be a thing of the past. Were they right? Maybe my body had changed too much to go back to where I was before? Were my motivation and drive gone for good? But I had to have faith in myself. If there was a will, there'd be a way. I had been here before, twenty-four years ago with the dodgy knee. I had come back from that.

Running after having Gwilym was far from easy. I realised my body was still going through a recovery phase. Strip those targets down, I ordered myself. Start again. Even with such cold logic, it took me a long time to be fully back in my stride. I had to be patient, which had always been a challenge. I simply had to accept the fact that the day hadn't grown any longer because our Gwilym was now in the world. My 24 hours were the same as everybody else's. If I was to run, I would have to be even more prepared than ever. I had a ready-made excuse, right there, gurgling and burbling in front of me, not to run. But my lovely boy would not be my excuse to stop.

I run now because of my son. He has given me a greater purpose to get up every morning than any job could. I want him to learn the importance of having ambitions – a goal that will take him out of his comfort zone, because by stretching for that goal, he will find talents and abilities he never knew he had. I run for him and I hope soon I will run with him.

I soon rediscovered my love of endurance running, despite the fact that it meant I had to learn to love early-morning starts on just four hours of sleep, and I had to sort out my breast-feeding routines. It took a little time, but I managed to run a 50-mile race three months after having Gwilym. It had its moments. Stopping to express milk at some of the feed stations was a first for some of the marshals. I didn't make the leaderboard, I have to say, but I was back on the racing circuit and I was running.

Gwilym came with me to my races and he came with me to work. When he was four weeks old he popped up on location. On a rally. I would go to film and he'd be there behind the camera waiting for me. Two weeks later he came with me again. This time we were filming a show called *Ar y Dibyn* (*On the Edge*) – in the style of *The Apprentice* – whose aim was to find the next great adventurer. I had been contracted to work on it. The winner would go on to win a year's work as an outdoor instructor, plus kit and an expedition. A great prize if you enjoyed adventure. When I was offered the contract, I told them that Gwilym would be a few weeks old when filming started. The company kindly said that they'd support my decision and if I was willing to accept the challenge that they'd help in making it possible. I asked Siôn and my parents, who were by now retired, if they'd be willing to support me. They agreed and I, full of gratitude, went ahead with the filming. It was set in the beautiful mountains of Snowdonia.

I was the judge together with Dilwyn Sanderson-Jones, an ex RAF soldier, now outdoor instructor, and an expert who often works alongside Bear Grylls on his TV adventures. We'd set contestants a challenge and off they'd go. We had to do the challenge, too. So, when I could, I'd try to take part. I'd climb the mountains we'd chosen, sit to express milk (the other contestants were not expected to do this) at the summit behind a rock surrounded by sheep, then I'd abseil down to hand the bottles over to my parents, who proceeded to give Gwilym his lunch. Nobody batted an eyelid, least of all the sheep.

I never thought I'd be able to juggle it all – not that I'm a good juggler but I'm trying and I'm learning with patience. If you had told me a few weeks earlier of how we'd manage with this schedule of feeding Gwilym, I wouldn't have thought I'd be able to do it. But it is amazing what one can do, especially when you have the support from family and work. I know I'm not alone.

There were many occasions when I found it hard to fit it all in. Not only was there not enough time in the day, but my progress as a runner was heavy-going. I told myself to keep going and fend off negative thoughts. If I was happy and healthy, surely that would be passed on to my child. Running was good for the energy-levels I needed to run my life: do all my errands; work; clean my house; and, of course, look after my son. As soon as I could, I bought a running buggy for Gwilym – then I was a runner and a mother, setting out on an adventure, both of us laughing our way around Cardiff's parks. I suppose I could just have invested in a treadmill, but with the buggy came liberation. Fresh air and freedom. I'm not really a treadmill person.

When I was pregnant I was worried about losing that momentum having run a lot previously, but I think being able to exercise during pregnancy helped me to bounce back quicker. It was always going to be hard, so I lowered my expectations then worked on it consistently. I re-adjusted my mindset. I was doing what I could do, building on the fitness I realistically could, based on other priorities. I wasn't going to beat myself up about it. Instead, I was enjoying the fact I was doing what I could do. If I could lose fitness, I could get it back. And the fitness and endurance did come back. Within a year, I was back racing competitively, even stronger and faster than before.

One of the things that changed was that I was not so governed by the GPS. Often, I would just go out with my buddies (dog and son!) and enjoy it. Fitting in the training around my son was my priority.

Sometimes it turned into an interval session. We would stop to see the ducks, 800m sprint, rest and then go again. Or maybe if he fell asleep I'd keep going as long as I could. Buggy running is difficult, but I found it the best all over body workout; arms, core and legs. Mentally it was so good for me to get out; I could run and be a good mother.

I have to say also that running with the buggy was a lot harder than I'd thought. Pushing gorgeous Gwilym was a lot more testing than pulling the Incredible Pulk. With the resistance it offered, I didn't have to go to the gym for weights – not that I had any plans to do such a thing. In the great scheme of combining work, home and running, well, the gym rarely got a look-in. Running with the buggy it was then, making each mile count, because real time was always against us.

We didn't always meet our targets. Running to a tight schedule proved a little harder than I'd planned. But at least I was doing it, even if sometimes it was only for a mile. And of course it wasn't just Gwilym and me along for the ride now that we had our four-legged member of the family. Nel was more than a mongrel. She was a cocktail of a dog, guaranteed to put a bit of fizz into our lives. She definitely had a bit of Parson Russell Terrier in her and we reckoned that her speed and stamina came from the leggier properties of a whippet. We found her at the Many Tears Animal Rescue centre at Fforestfach, Swansea. She was the smallest of a litter of four, found in a cardboard box abandoned on the side of the M4. Her mother was a springer spaniel but she didn't make it, sadly. She was such a runt and in such poor condition that when we saw her, she was not expected to survive the night. If she did, Siôn and I decided, we would have her. She had made it to the next day and into our lives, and now she set the course on our runs. She never got lost. (I should have introduced her to Nigel earlier). I remember one occasion when I was following her over a new series of tracks and trails and I had to speak to her a little firmly: 'This is all very well, Nel, but we really need to get back to the car now.' We ran on to a fork in the track. I went right. Nel stopped and cocked her head to one side as if to say: 'In that case, I think you'd better follow me this way.' Even on days when I'm fighting the urge to not go for a run, she'll give me a nudge or she'll look at me in a certain way, and despite having no motivation, I'll quickly change into my kit and go out with her. When running with Nel and Gwilym, I soon find the fun in exercising.

Nel was not only a font of wisdom on our runs. She also wrote things for me. Well, I translated what she told me inside my head. Nel's nine life-rules went something like this:

1. *Live in the moment.*
2. *Don't hold grudges (the occasional growl is allowed).*
3. *Play every day.*
4. *Jump for joy when happy.*
5. *Accept yourself.*
6. *Enjoy the journey (I call it the Walk).*
7. *Drink plenty of water.*
8. *Love unconditionally.*
9. *Be loyal and dependable.*

On our outings, people would stop and offer words of encouragement. 'Try to keep up,' they'd say. They weren't talking to Nel.

We made it on to social media: 'Just seen this woman running, pushing a buggy, with a dog running alongside #thiswomancan. #multitasking'

A friend replied: 'That can only be @_lowrimorgan!'

CHAPTER 17

SLOWLY DOES IT ON THE COMEBACK

I found myself going a little overboard in 2016. It was the Welsh Government's Year of Adventure and I was one of the ambassadors. I decided to embrace the concept. I freely admit it, I entered ultra-overload.

I ran the Vale Ultra, a one-day 32-miler along the entire length of the coastal path of the Vale of Glamorgan, from Penarth to Ogmore-by-Sea. Penarth is a leafy seaside town, just around the corner from Cardiff Bay. We set off from the end of its pier (back towards land, I hasten to add), safely above the pebble beach and on to the Esplanade, where we turned left, not towards the nearby capital, but westward, towards Barry.

Barry Island was once best known for its Butlin's holiday camp and its funfair, and Barry itself, more recently, for being the hometown of the Stacey half of the television comedy drama series, *Gavin and Stacey*. A few miles later we'd run pass Aberthaw. Here the race's route became more scenic and remote along the Wales Coast Path. At the far end of the course was Ogmore-by-Sea, a lot more exposed to the sea than Penarth. This was my first long competitive race after having Gwilym. He had just celebrated his first birthday.

The gun went and off I went.

I felt good. I was enjoying it and was keen to get to the finish line as fast as possible to see my son, husband and family. I now had a new motivation to finish races and the thought of seeing them made me run stronger and happier.

Soon after the finish line, the adrenalin disappeared. I was spent. My stomach wasn't great. For the following few hours I lay down in a foetal position as I held onto my stomach. The pain eventually disappeared and I was able to join my family in the local pub to celebrate my brother-in-law's birthday. Looking back at that race, I was surprisingly pleased to note that all the consistent training, all the pushing of the buggy and being pulled by Nel seemed to have done the trick. I finished in fourth place overall and was the winner of the women's race. My friend who I spoke to at the start line was surprised when I spoke to him at the end. 'Fourth', he said. Trying to look pleased for me … 'Great result, but what happened? You were first lady when I saw you.'

'Oh, yes, I was first lady,' I said. 'I was fourth overall.'

My mind experienced an instant thrill. It was good to be back. However, my body took somewhat longer to appreciate the return to action.

The years had rolled by since I had played rugby and felt the glow of being part of a team. It was long ago that I had injured my knee – well over twenty years – and in that time I had always opted for solo running. I was an individual participant, although I was far from being a loner in my sport. I loved the camaraderie that went with the ultra world, all the support and encouragement from fellow athletes and race organisers, all the bits of advice that were given so naturally and enthusiastically. I loved the stories and the humour and the teasing that flowed back and forth in camps before and during races. Even on the trail there was still plenty of opportunity to chat and make new friends, but when it came to the serious business of participating and surviving and finishing there was no getting away from the reality that it was essentially down to just the single person. Me. That was the test and that was the underlying thrill.

Now, though, I signed up for a team. My friend Elin had contacted me. 'I know you've recently had a baby,' she said at the end of 2015, 'but do you fancy joining me on an adventure?'

I have always been in awe of Elin as a person, a professional, and an adventurer. So before knowing what the challenge was – I accepted without batting an eyelid.

I was going to be one fifth of an all-women combination of three sailors and two runners for the Three Peaks Yacht Race. This is an ultra by sea, road and mountain, going from Barmouth to Fort William via Caernarfon and Whitehaven, and including going up and down Snowdon, Scafell Pike and Ben Nevis, the three highest peaks in Wales, England and Scotland. In total we would sail for 389 miles and run for 72, with 11,000 feet of elevation. And just in case swapping sea-legs for mountain-legs wasn't testing enough, there was a cycling section of 36 miles, too, from Whitehaven Lock to the base of Scafell Pike. Elin Haf Davies, Nikki Curwen and Pip Hare were the sailors, while Jo Jackson and I were the runners (and cyclists). I had heard about the race from fellow adventurers, including my cousin Mark, who had raced in it a few years previously. I was told that it is one of the oldest and most remarkable multi-sport endurance races in the world – combining some hardcore distance running with sailing and navigating around some of the most challenging coasts of the UK.

It would be a slight exaggeration to say we had spent months and months training together for the adventure. We certainly planned, spoke on conference calls, and bounced emails back and forth for months trying to raise money and sponsorship for this race. But we had only met up face to face as a team for the first time in Barmouth on the day before the start of the race. My running partner, Jo, had just flown in from Australia. Our one factor in common was that we all knew Elin, who had played rugby for Wales, competed in the Marathon des Sables and became a rower. But not a rower so much of river regattas as whole oceans. She had a triple-crown to her name, having been part of teams that in the past decade had crossed the Atlantic, Indian and North Pacific.

The name of our yacht was Nunatak, an Inuit word for an outcrop of bare rock rising out of an ice-field and enough to bring back shivery memories. We were known in the race, however, as Team Aparito – or, in full, Team Aparito Digital Health, named after the company Elin had founded. This was about monitoring certain illnesses through a wrist-watch monitor and raising awareness among patient groups and promoting collaboration all the way through the system. Part of our mission was to make, as usual, a television programme for Channel 4 and S4C, and part was to raise money for the Find a Cure charity.

This charity element to my adventures was important. I had raised money for Shelter Cymru by way of the Amazon and Arctic ultras. Later in this year of adventure, I would run for Cerebra, which raises money for children with brain conditions. When I was in labour with Gwilym, the umbilical cord had wrapped around his neck and for a moment we feared the worst. Being an older mother at 41, I was reminded that there'd be more complications. But we were lucky. All had turned out fine, but a good reason for competing in races, and especially the televised ones, was to do my bit on the charity front.

There were certain complications to the Three Peaks Yacht Race, almost all of them to do with the sailing part of the bargain. When in port we could use the onboard motor, but only after we'd passed strictly-defined 'Engine On' markers. There could be no overtaking when we were in such a mode. Similarly, there were 'Engine Off' protocols to observe when we were heading for the open sea. The power of the wind was sacredly respected, but if it didn't blow, we still couldn't revert to the engine. We were allowed to take to our oars. Woman power could be added to wind power.

There was also the matter of the International Racing Certificate handicap system, being applied to the race for the first time. Ever since it was first run in 1977, the winner of the Three Peaks race had been the first past the post. Now in 2016 we had a rating system and our seven-tonne yacht would be judged differently from lighter boats. So, there were two main prizes: The Daily Telegraph Cup, for the winner of the 'line honours', the first yacht, that is, to finish the race; and the Barmouth Publicity Cup, for the winners of the IRC, the first yacht to finish under handicap.

I had been taught to sail by my Aunty Helen and Uncle Mike. My parents also took my brother and I to classes over the summer holidays in Gower and further afield, but there was a balance to be struck between recuperating after a run and being a member of the crew on the ocean wave. I was not going to call myself a sailor in front of the ladies I'd be sharing the boat with. They were proper sailors. Hardcore sailors. Just amazing ladies. And there were some things I left to the experts. When it came to the IRC, I think they alone understood the system. For large parts of the sea-stages, I remained stowed away in the cabin. Although Jo (who had competed in several Ironman events and had also rowed the ocean with Elin) and I tried to help with the sailing, the other three would pack us back into the cabin. Our job was to run and cycle, they'd say. The boat was our opportunity to rest the legs. We didn't have that much time to recover before running the next mountain, so recovery was important. Pip had raced before and won and it was something she had noticed on past events. It was vital that the sailing crew were left to sailing and the runners to the running. If they needed help, they promised that they'd ask.

However, I'm not very good at doing nothing. Once I had woken up from a couple of hours sleep, I'd constantly be popping my head up from the cabin. 'Can I help? Anything I can do?' They called Jo and I the 'Meerkats' because of the way we'd pop our heads through the hatch to see how the sailors were doing.

It turned out I needed every minute of rest. When Jo and I jumped off the yacht on the lower platform of the pierhead at Caernarfon and set off on our first run, up Snowdon, it soon became clear that my partner was in trouble. Her back in particular was giving her grief and in a more general sense, Jo was unable to find a good rhythm. We had not run together but had discussed our speeds on different terrain and we were quite similar so it came as a surprise to us both when Jo was struggling early on in the race; I knew something wasn't right. A few weeks after the race, we would find out there was a perfectly good reason for her lack of energy. She was pregnant.

I had been so used to racing on my own, I wasn't sure how to address this situation. We had to stick within eyesight of each other, but did Jo want me to run alongside her helping her along the way, or did she prefer me being ahead of her so she could get lost in her own thoughts? I have been in similar situations and although it does vary, I tend to prefer being left alone when I am in a dark place. But, as the best team builders will tell you, to succeed in adventure as a team you must suffer equally.

'Run ahead of me,' she said. 'Don't worry about me, I'll keep going.' And I knew she would. On the road, I could see Jo behind because of her head torch, but on the mountain and in the fog, I couldn't see her. On Snowdon at 1am, I could still see Jo's torch and we could speak to each other but distance became hard to read. I thought she was right behind me. Was I close to breaking the race rules and was there a chance I could get the team disqualified because we weren't running as a pair? But we were ahead, and I didn't want to lose the advantage, and others were catching us up.

I soon realised that we weren't going to get anywhere close to the finish line if I continued like this. So, on the mountain in the middle of the night, I told Jo, 'Give me your rucksack', leaving her free of weight and to concentrate on her running. I'd take care of navigation.

'Are you sure?' she said. 'Look, every one else is carrying their own kit.'

'With your heart rate going at 160, for example, and mine at 120, doesn't it make sense for both of us to move forward at 140?' I said. 'We'll go a lot faster and for longer without anyone falling apart if we suffer equally. Anyway, I'll be needing your help when I'm struggling on the bike on Scafell Pike.'

Jo agreed with me to carry her backpack and insisted I stay in front and set the pace. I took great care to adjust it to suit her, not me. It was a bit strange but I loved every minute of the whole team thing with Jo. And as a result, we were strong together – our confidence grew and our pace increased

Once back on the boat, we set off in seventh position overall and calculated that the leaders were about two miles ahead of us. From Caernarfon we immediately entered the Menai Strait, with all the mysteries peculiar to this waterway between Anglesey and the mainland of Wales. There was one particular stretch called the Swellies. They lay – or flowed, or swirled – between the Britannia Bridge, built by the railway engineer, Robert Stephenson, and the Menai Bridge, one of Thomas Telford's masterpieces. The Swellies were treacherous because they were full of rocks and shoals and tidal waters washing around at different speeds. The tide coming down from the Beaumaris end of Anglesey met the tide going up from Caernarfon to make this stretch infamous for its eddies and whirlpools ... and its wrecks.

As we entered the Menai Strait, the wind dropped and we were briefly at the mercy of the currents. We touched the bottom. So, the Meerkats popped through the hatch to take their place starboard amidships with the oars. And for six hours the team rowed, with blistered hands, all the way out of the Menai Strait and into the open waters of Liverpool Bay. I loved that part. Nobody moaned, nobody complained. We were all smiles, laughing and joking and relishing the challenge, encouraging each other and offering support. We gained four places and by the time the good wind had carried us north to Whitehaven on the Cumbrian coast, we were leading the race.

To enter the lock at Whitehaven, we had to reach for the oars again. As soon as we docked at the fuel platform, Jo and I jumped off and got on our bikes. This was the reverse of the first climb, in that Jo was a much more experienced cyclist than me. I had done my triathlons, but Jo, even with a bad back, was quicker, stronger and had the better technique. I on the other hand, was all over the place. She set the pace and I fell in behind her. Because of the varied terrain on this section, we were on cyclo-cross bikes – I could cope with the tarmac but when it came to cycling on the gravel roads towards the mountains, I was soon skidding and falling, with the bike battering my shins on numerous occasions. But Jo was always there, picking me up and helping me through it all. It rained and it blew heavily all the way from the coast to the top of Scafell Pike.

As we reached the peak, we had lost a few places. We stopped and reassessed. The fog was in by now and it was difficult to see the trail.

Two months earlier, I had investigated the route with friends of Pip, Charles and Richard – two brothers who had had success in this race in the past. They were experienced fell runners and their navigation skills were excellent. We spent a weekend recceing the running course. Then, the mountains had been covered in snow. We travelled in convoy and slept in our cars at the foot of mountains. I do enjoy my micro adventures in the car.

Anyway, during the recce on Scafell Pike, because of the deep snow, we ran off route and found a faster line. I decided to follow the same route. On the map, it was nearly a straight line down to the valley. On the tracker, our teammates back in harbour could see what was happening. It was a risk as we followed a stream down. It wasn't as easy as running on the established trails and we were dependent on the map and compass, but it was a faster way down, albeit a slightly more challenging one as my shin found out – hitting a hidden rock on the terrain and receiving a deep cut as a result. However this calculated risk worked in our favour. Without realising it, we passed a few pairs and ran back to our bikes.

By now the wind had increased and the rain was painful on our battered and bruised bodies. I was desperate to get home and so was Jo. With patience running low, I just wanted to get back to the boat. Other than a few words of encouragement here and there, we barely spoke. We would not have been able to hear each other anyway as the howling wind swallowed our voices in the most torrential downpour. There was just no respite. And despite knowing there'd be no warm shower at the end of this stage, the comfort of our temporary home – the cabin – was very inviting. My bike had taken a few batterings after my constant falling earlier in the day but I pedalled hard despite my lack of technique and elegance. It was about keeping warm and getting to that boat to dry and thaw out – that was my only motivation at the time.

When we reached the harbour, the elation of seeing the other three girls was evident. And the relief on our faces when they hauled us into the boats … well, we were exhausted. The cameras caught this all and both of us could hardly show any emotion. There was nothing left in the tank. We had pushed and pushed and as a result had gained a few places. We were back in the chase and leading again.

A few sailors had approached the girls while they were waiting for us. 'Oh, you're quite serious about this race?' No female crew had ever completed the race. Some were surprised that five girls could be competitive. 'Just do your best,' they said at the start of the race. 'We're just really happy to see an all-female group competing.'

We all laughed as the sailors relived the conversations and soon our nine-hour challenge on Scafell Pike was a distant memory.

We left Whitehaven. It was all over to the sailors now to do their job and we could have a few hours rest before rejoining the girls on deck – be it helping with the sailing or with cleaning the area or just making food and teas. Somewhere in all the rowing into Whitehaven and in all that rain and lack of visibility, we lost the lead. The team called Pure Attitude seemed to be six miles ahead of us as we set off north for Scotland.

We overtook Pure Attitude and then were becalmed again. If ultra running had its varying paces, so did sailing, it appeared. Out came the oars again. When the wind did pick up, we sought it out as close to land, with all its rocks and reefs, as we dared. Just when it seemed we could only crash into Scotland at full speed, we'd come about and off we'd go again. Tacking our way north like this, we built up a two-hour lead. We navigated the Corran Narrows and entered Loch Linnhe. Jo and I studied our next 20-mile run and prepared for the final stretch, up Ben Nevis from Fort William. The sailors – Pip, Nikki and Elin – were incredible.

A few hours later we jumped ashore for the last run up to Ben Nevis. Nikki, Elin and Pip left the boat, too, and walked up to the lower slopes of the mountain. Despite being first into Fort William, we were still pushing on the mountain. My maps were full of markings: I had circled every junction and bend with elevation notes, highlighted routes, dangers etc. All cut into a more manageable size, laminated, and clipped onto a lanyard so that when the wind picked up, there'd be no chance of the map flying off out of my hands. I was so glad of my OCD with my map system. The mountain fog came in and with the path invisible under foot with snow, finding the zigzagging path up to the summit was tough. I constantly checked my borrowed altimeter and when we reached a certain altitude, I'd know there'd be a certain change in the route, a sharp left, a dangerous area, a hidden junction. These little things that I had prepared before the race were helping me now. That old saying – by failing to prepare, you're preparing to fail – had proved invaluable again. Jo and I loved it. We could now sense that the finish line was getting closer.

Pip, Nikki and Elin cheered us on and, after the last six miles through industrial and housing estates, they hailed us on the finish line, which we crossed hand in hand, one and a half hours ahead of Pure Attitude. We had won 'line honours' and now waited to see if we had done the double and won the IRC. Once the calculators had churned through the data, we found we had been pipped into second place by Pure Attitude. No double, but by way of compensation, we landed a little treble of trophies: The *Daily Telegraph* Cup (line honours); the Merioneth Cup (for the second yacht to finish under handicap); and The Flicka Cup (winner of the third leg combining IRC sailing and the run). Not bad at all for a team that had met up the day before the race started. We had all got on famously and, well, it just felt good to have done something different, to have felt wind power, oar power and all-woman power.

Moreover, when we crossed that finish line, Team Aparito Digital Health became the first all-female team in the history of the Three Peaks Yacht Race to take line honours.

What had made the difference?

Teamwork! We had battled through the elements, had been there for each other all the time, had worked together as a team from the start. It was all about communication, composure and encouragement – and as a result, our self-worth and self-belief increased. We were encouraged to offer ideas and complement each other's work. We understood the psychology on board – knowing how tiredness could completely ruin our chances and the atmosphere – so we were careful to recognise each other's fatigue. We all spoke after the race about how Elin had built a team based on matching people who added value to one another's skill set. Unity and teamwork spiralled because we got that mix right. There weren't any egos. We were just five athletes with the same goal. I loved it. We all loved it.

The following month, July, I kept this sense of team-effort going by running alongside three friends – Stephen Edwards, Phil 'Tân'

Jones and Alan Owen – on their Anglesey Challenge, to raise funds for the children's cancer charity, *Gafael Llaw* (Holding Hands) and the Alaw Cancer Treatment Centre at *Ysbyty Gwynedd* (Gwynedd Hospital) via the #TeamIrfon campaign. That was the brainchild of Irfon Williams, who, diagnosed with cancer of the colon, set out in 2014 to raise money for the Alaw. Before his death in 2017, Irfon became a legend and our run was in honour of him. It took us on another tour of the island, but unlike the Ring of Fire that went from Holyhead to Holyhead, we would go anti-clockwise from Menai Bridge to Menai Bridge. Nor was our run spread over three days, but concentrated into a single hit of 105 miles in as close to 24 hours as we could manage. Even though we were all experienced runners, we gave ourselves no obligation to meet the 24-hour time-limit. It was an exercise in companionship, in doing something together for the common good. It was made even more emotional when Irfon congratulated us as we crossed the line. Sometimes a run is more than just a run.

I had to quickly leave the group after finishing the challenge, as I had to go straight to a conference in Bangor to talk about my adventures. I asked where my 'clean kit' bag was, which contained my car keys and clean clothes for the presentation. It was in the other support vehicle which was on its way over. I didn't have time to wait. A friend quickly offered me a lift and I arrived at the conference just as I was due to go on stage … still in my very sweaty, smelly running clothes.

I admit, it wasn't the most glamourous of entrances, nor the sweetest of smells, but I had to laugh as I told them, 'You wanted to hear about my adventures, well, now you're getting the full picture!'

I felt great on the run with my friends. We got on and I was surprised at how well I had coped with the twenty-four hours of non-stop running. Actually, I did stop for a little snooze. It was during this run that I mastered the one minute power nap. It makes all the difference to keeping me going. It's like a quick charge of the energy. The one-minute snooze gets me through some tough hours. For example, if I'm running overnight on the mountains and don't want to lose too much time, nor get cold, I'll put the alarm on (I always carry my phone) and will time the shut-eye to where I know, once I close my eyes, I will sleep. The one minute will get me through the night. A full five-minute power boost … well, that feels like an eight-hour sleep. I wish I had learnt these little tricks before going to the Arctic. Before having Gwilym, I really didn't think I could cope on only a couple of power naps every 24 hours. But I've been amazed at what the mind and body can do when pushed.

This 105-mile run helped me on an individual level. It proved to me I could still do it. Knowing I still had what it took was important, for the highlight of 2016 was yet to come. And the low point.

CHAPTER 18

333

Many pages have turned since I last mentioned a FTD. A Failed To Deliver. Ultra running had set me tests and I had passed them. I had performed badly at times, had bad days, but was proud that I had not failed. And yet, I was about to.

In August 2016, I was invited to race the Pen Llŷn Ultra, a one-day 75-mile classic around the tip of the northern peninsular of Wales, which juts out into the Irish Sea and defines the uppermost sweep of Cardigan Bay. The Llŷn was rugged and beautiful, with the sea on three sides and Snowdonia as the backdrop to the east. Perfect for a run in the height of summer. The course followed the twisting coastal path, tarmac for a shortish section and longer stretches of sand, like the beach at Porth Neigwl (Hell's Mouth).

I hadn't been feeling great since the Anglesey Challenge. Those chest infections my childhood pneumonia had left me prone to were not too serious a problem for everyday living, but when it came to running hard with a chest cold, I had to listen to my body and be sensible. Perhaps I had been doing too much all summer. If it hadn't been for the television programme we were making – the pictures promised to be too sumptuous to ignore – I would have withdrawn before the start. Perhaps I thought that a Did Not Finish (the dreaded DNF) might make for good viewing. 'The non-quitter Lowri quits!' Quite how sumptuous I would appear, coughing and spluttering to a halt, I wasn't sure. There was bound to be someone who would think it was all a con, anyway.

I said I would do ten miles. I could hardly speak and when I did, well, it was more of a croak. But it was a beautiful day, I had great company, and I was enjoying. After ten, I said I'd make it to the next point. Ten turned to 20, 20 turned to 30, and the 30 turned to 40. By then, I could feel the wheels coming off. I was going into my reserves. I had lost the flow and was quickly falling out of the overall top ten slot. I saw the camera man at mile 40. I worked out in my head that if I stopped now, I could make it home in time to put Gwilym to bed. That one thought was enough make up my mind. And then I stopped. A DNF. I'm not sure what I felt. This was my first failure in an ultra. I knew for sure my chest was not in good shape, but I was more conscious of the effect it would have on my mind. I had stopped. I couldn't quite believe it. And I didn't feel better for it. I'm not sure it even made very good television. A wheezing, faltering presenter could be only of strictly limited appeal.

Did. Not. Finish. They're an ultra runner's three least-favourite words. Whatever the reason for it, a DNF is often demoralising and can lead to a poor mindset in the ensuing days, weeks, or even months. Since the reasons for dropping out of a race are plentiful and, in some cases, out of our control, it's important to know how to manage the aftermath of such an unrewarding race.

I remembered my mother's words to me before I went into the Amazon. It's not about never falling, it's about the way we rise when we do fall. I soon understood that the ultimate purpose of lining up in a race was to get to the finish line, be it today or in the bigger plan. I still had big goals for the remainder of the year. In my personal experience struggling through a bad race always leaves me worse for wear. I didn't want to be injured post-race. I came to terms with the fact that while the Llŷn Ultra was an important race it was not my be-all and end-all goal. It didn't make or break me as a runner. I had been running competitively for a long time and I knew I couldn't always win, perform well or have a great day. This result forced me to work through my issues and come out stronger on the other side.

I consoled myself with the thought – the-iron-clad, hard-headed thought – that I was saving myself for something much more demanding, something that was approaching very fast. The DNF in the Pen Llŷn was a sacrifice for a greater cause. That's what I told myself. Whether I believed it or not was another matter. I had to put the failure behind me. I had to recover, regain my strength, get rid of the cough and all the congestion. I had a bigger challenge ahead.

We had invented a 'special' for S4C television. We called it the 333 and it consisted of three ultras, averaging 50 miles each, running from North Wales to the south via three of the highest peaks of Wales (Snowdon, Cader Idris above the town of Dolgellau, and Pen y Fan in the Brecon Beacons) in three consecutive days climbing 10,000 metres. Along the way, and as long as I had the breath to speak, I was going to interview a series of inspirational runners.

Just for good measure, I wanted to set an FKT – a Fastest Known Time. For this, I felt I should have increased my training, which was a little fanciful given the state of my lungs. And it was even more unlikely because the logistics surrounding the rotas and travel arrangements of the camera crews and guests, booking everybody's hotels and fine-tuning our routes consumed just about every minute of the day. Compromises had to be made and something had to give. The organiser (me) was so busy that the welfare of the runner (me) wasn't such a priority.

I originally wanted to do it with hardly any sleep, following a similar schedule to the 6633 Ultra. I thought maybe I could do it within 48 hours. Two peaks in one of the days seemed doable. But this wasn't a race. This was an expedition being run in order to make a television series, so we had to take into consideration the guests and above all the crews' working hours. We agreed to adapt it into a three-day event, running 50 miles on the first day, 60 on the second and 40 miles on the final day.

With my compromised training schedule, I was not in the best shape physically or mentally. To be honest, I don't think I have ever started a marathon completely and absolutely prepared, confident that I am going to smash it. There's always something I could have done better, a session I could have pushed at harder, or a nutritional tweak I never quite got round to incorporating (giving up sweets comes to mind). But that is exactly how life is and if I waited for the perfect conditions to attempt the goals I set for myself, I would never get anywhere.

So here I was, about to start the 333, full of doubt and fear. And there was something about the balance between the personal test and the requirements of the camera that niggled away at me. On most ultras, the camera intruded only occasionally. The priority was the race running. Here, the camera controlled the schedule. All in all, I was extremely anxious by the time we started. It was my pet project and I was uneasy about a few aspects of it. Perhaps what affected me most of all was that I was doing it so close to home. Pack up on the Tapajós or on the Mackenzie Delta and there was no escaping the geographical reality that you were still there, in the middle of nowhere. Here, I could easily jump in a car and be home with Gwilym and Siôn in an hour (Point 10 alert).

I loved the 333 but in a completely different way that I had in the past. This was different. With a race, you're in race mode, you have cut-offs to think off, you have pressure. But here, there was nothing of the sort. I knew that even if I plodded through the 24 hours, I could complete the challenge (if all went well and I remained injury free). The pressure was off. And I think that took the edge off what races give you.

I had excellent back-up. My very good friend Matt Ward, whom we'll meet later, arranged the route. I invited the Anglesey Challenge crew to join forces again: Stephen Edwards was managing the logistics; Phil Jones as support; Dewi Ferrero, physio; and Gwyn Griffiths, mountain rescue and paramedic.

Maybe I was naïve or too complacent, but I suppose I didn't expect it to be quite so tough. All those ideas I had had, about doing the 150 miles in 48 hours … well, I'm glad we built in the extra day. And I don't suppose 332 as a title would have had quite the same ring to it.

The landscapes spoke for themselves – we enjoyed amazing views. We received fantastic support along the way, too, with complete strangers donating money to the charity. And the guests were so generous and so forgiving. I didn't think it would be quite so difficult to sustain a conversation during a daily ultra. I had chit-chatted with complete strangers in climates both boiling and frozen, and had never felt short of a word, but I suppose whole minutes – perhaps hours –

passed on those trails without a sentence being uttered. On the 333, I was supposed to be animated and coherent, and all the while remain on the go, under time-pressure to reach the day's destination as quickly as possible. There was always a goal to meet but I was aware that I was now multi-targeting and missing all of them.

My support runners were patience personified. The first was Owen Roberts, whom I interviewed on the way up Snowdon. Owen was a young international mountain runner, recently back from Kenya, where he'd been training at altitude with some of the world's best athletes. I have run up and down Snowdon all the way through this book, but suddenly it felt very difficult. I left Llanberis and within a few hundred metres, I was up on the mountain. I had a shock. My chest cold was still lingering and I struggled with my breathing on the way up, but once you see the summit of Snowdon on the Llanberis path, it gives you a real boost and soon, it wasn't difficult. My emotions were going the way of the challenge: up and down. I was swaying between highs and lows without any of the neutral stages that might last for hours on other multi-stage events. There were none of the miles of mesmerisation that filled in the spaces between the emotional extremes of, say, the Arctic Ultra. Any 'empty' miles were now filled with guests with their amazing stories and inspiration.

I found it hard to rationalise all the contrasts of the 333. By way of illustrating what I was like when I was up, here's what I jotted down by way of a Day 1 log:

1. *There are hours when spirits are so low you feel that there's nothing left in the tank, but having a friend join you, saying 'Go on, Lowri,' can give you such a big lift.*
2. *The weather was warm and we were working our way from checkpoint to checkpoint with relative ease. We knew the terrain from previous recces and our plan to conserve energy early seemed to be working as we hit the first cut-off with over two hours to spare. This was going to be easy.*
3. *If you thought too hard about running 150 miles in three days, it would be enough to make anyone lose their head.*

My second guest, my second friend on Day 1, was Malcolm Jones, who joined me after Snowdon for the leg between Beddgelert and Oakley Arms. Malcolm was in the GB Duathlon (run, cycle, run) team, despite being diagnosed with cancer twenty-five years earlier. In fact, he had run a Snowdon race in the first year of his treatment. A race he has never missed. People like Malcolm would always give me a big lift. During treatment, he would take his running kit with him and fit in a session between treatments. It's what kept him sane, he said. My last interview on Day 1 was with Siân Roberts on the trail from Coed y Brenin to the day's finish in the market town of Dolgellau, built of dark-grey stone and standing on the approaches to the Mawddach Estuary, which leads down to Barmouth, where we started the Three Peaks Yacht Race two months earlier.

Siân had started running back in the 1980s and had represented Wales but, because of an injury, had switched to mountain biking and become UK champion and a world class athlete. This transition from legs to wheels, from running to bikes ... I may have to have another word with Siân.

My chest cold was still evident. My voice was croaky and I was still angry with myself for pushing myself in the Llŷn Ultra three weeks before. I had still not recovered from that. Damn it, I told myself. If I had rested, I would have been much healthier on the start line. The evening rain was not helping matters, either; I was getting cold. The energy was being zapped and as darkness descended, I was getting frustrated with my body. The paramedic pulled me aside – took my pulse, my blood levels. All was fine but you could not ignore my tiredness and frustration at not being able to run the pace I wanted to.

I was then offered an alternative. Stop in Dolgellau to sleep in a hotel. A nice cosy bed for the night. The only downside was that I'd finish at 45 miles instead of 50 and the second day would increase to 65 miles.

I knew if I had any comfort – a warm bed, a shower, proper food – getting up the following morning would be so much harder. If I slept in a bivvy, I'd quickly jump out of bed and be on the trails as soon as possible. I didn't need comfort. But what I did need was sleep. After 45 miles of mountain running in 10 hours, I conceded and did what I was told. Despite not wanting to sleep in a bed nor have supper, I didn't complain. That bed in Dolgellau and the lasagne ... unforgettable!

As expected, getting up from a warm comfortable bed was much harder than getting out of a cold, uncomfortable bivvy. I didn't care about lack of sleep. I could catch up with that after the challenge – I only needed a few minutes here and there anyway. But for filming purposes we needed light and I set off at 7am.

Day 2 went a bit like this. This was the long stretch: 60 miles now increased to 65 miles of climbing along Wales's mountains towards the south. The first big mountain to greet me would be Cader Idris (Idris's Chair) – a stand-alone mountain at the southern end of the Snowdonia National Park, which we would climb first thing. There is a saying that if you fall asleep on Cader Idris you wake up either a poet or a madman. Fat chance of me finding out. I'd had my six hours of sleep in Dolgellau and had to keep moving. Here came the swing of mood the other way. An excerpt from the log of the second day:

1. *This was a section we'd recced but I was struggling to remember any of it. I could hardly visualise any of the sections and it was bugging me.*
2. *It took us ages to get down. We crawled down huge boulders, had to avoid massive holes and heather traps. Again, we were losing time. Late finishes are becoming the theme of the week ...*
3. *... really flagging again, the previous day's lack of sleep catching up with me. This day seemed to go on forever ...*

That was down on paper. In my mind I had another version. I was convinced that this was one of my euphoria days. Running up Cader Idris, we faced howling winds, thick fog and heavy rain. However, as we descended from the summit, the sun blazed down and the views coming off the mountain were second to none. Cardigan Bay was the seascape on one side, Snowdonia rose in the north and the rest of

Wales filled in what was left. I was joined at the bottom of Cader Idris by international mountain biker, and duathlete Ifan Roberts, and we ran together for 15 miles to Bron yr Aur near Machynlleth, which is often shortened to Mach. This Mach has its place in our history as the seat of the parliament set up in 1404 by Owain Glyndwr, the Welsh prince. Ifan had a more recent Welsh history. I had met him on the S4C show, *Ar y Dibyn* (*On the Edge*), that set out to find the next adventurer. He had won the series in 2016 and Ifan was now an international mountain runner. We ran over the mountains making our way towards Machynlleth and then towards Llanidloes.

Ifan and I had a never-ending mountain to run before I said my goodbye to him. I had dreaded this run after the recce. This section would finish after a few hours of hard, endlessly undulating mountains and I feared it. But the award for that particular stage would be worth it, I told myself: at the top I'd see the mountain ranges of Wales from the north to the south in all their glory.

I need not have feared the long climb to the top. My legs had found their rhythm and the conversation flowed. The weather was kind and I felt that my body was getting used to this challenge. I was humbled by the beauty around me – the views were inspirational. This was effortless. I was completely immersed in the run. I felt energised, focused, alive. With each mile, I got faster and faster. I was on automatic pilot. Time seemed to pass quickly. What took me five hours felt like five minutes. I was in the zone, and it felt awesome.

When it was time for Ifan and I to separate, I shed a tear – not because I was sad but because I knew how lucky I have been to have met some truly inspirational people. Sometimes, these meetings have been brief, but they have often left a footprint on my soul.

My support team noticed that my stops at the camera positions were getting longer and longer. Every checkpoint was turning into a rest plus a filming opportunity. I did not realise this. For me, every checkpoint went in a flash, but they were actually 20-minute stops every 8-10 miles. My support team were runners themselves and they knew that I needed to move on; losing a few minutes here and there meant I would be finishing later than expected. I needed to cut down on my talking and concentrate on running! By the time I arrived in Llanidloes I was exhausted and my joints were beginning to hurt. I was still smiling but inside, I was breaking.

In Llanidloes I met Siân Williams, another international mountain runner, and we went all the way to the day's end at Rhayader together. Siân was wonderful company. I needed to apologise to her for my rapidly decreasing pace, but her enthusiasm for life and her experiences on the mountains of the world were inspiring. Her stories kept me going. I could only mutter a few words here and there. In my mind I made sense, but in reality, it came out as a mash of words I'm sure!

I had not recced this part of the course. I knew I was heading towards Rhayader – the end of Stage 2 – but I did not know how far away it was. By now, I was asking the team, 'How much further to Rhayader?' Approximately 10km, a cameraman told me.

OK, I thought to myself. That's 10km or 6.2 miles. Or 2 x 5km. I tried to break it down to smaller chunks.

'How much further?' I asked the director half an hour later.

'3km.'

'Great,' I muttered. I was counting down the miles.

Stephen, Phil and Gwyn caught up with me. Their bouncy gait only highlighted my shuffle.

'How much further?' I again asked. I was struggling now and desperately looking for the street lights of Rhayader to come into sight. About a mile, maybe a mile and a half at the most, I thought.

'Well done,' said Stephen who was unaware of my previous conversations with the cameraman and director 'You're nearly there now. Only five miles to go.'

My heart broke.

I suddenly put the brakes on. 'Stop stop stop,' I said, and pulled out the map. There must be a mistake.

'I'm really sorry, Lowri,' Stephen said, 'but you've another five miles.'

He was right, of course. I had completely miscalculated this part. To be told I had another five miles to go when I thought I had less than a mile left and was mentally preparing to finish really dampened my spirits. Those last five miles felt more like 50, and by the time I shuffled into Rhayader I was too tired to talk to camera. I did mutter something along the lines of the importance of teamwork. My support team had been able to put themselves into my shoes and give me what I needed on both a physical and emotional level in order to keep going. I was the weaker partner, but they knew when and how to push me towards my goal. When I did go to bed, I was given a bowl of pasta to eat. I promptly fell asleep in the bowl after the third mouthful.

Day 3. The last leg. Normally, when I have that sense that I'm going to make it, my spirits lift. This stage from Rhayader to Pen Y Fan was, at 40 miles, the shortest. But here we go again. And here's the log I wrote later:

1. *I felt every bloody mile. This day had the 'slightly less ascent' tag attached to it very quickly, but it was still the third day of running, crawling, climbing and walking up and down mountains. It wasn't going to be easy. This was it, time to finish this thing.*

I'm going to have to sort out the 333 once and for all. So, physically, I wasn't in my best shape. Yes, there was still the lingering effect of the chest infection that had stopped me on the Pen Llŷn Ultra and, no, I had not done enough training. Right, that's out there now. Push it to one side and start running, for goodness' sake. But I was missing my family, especially my 14-month-old boy. Gosh, it would have been so easy to call them and ask them to pick me up. They weren't that far away. If I gave up now, I could be home by lunchtime. How nice would that be.

I followed the River Wye downstream to Llanelwedd, home of the Royal Welsh Show, and crossed the bridge into Builth Wells, where I met Welsh actor Mark Lewis Jones.

I could go into detail about which films and television dramas Mark's been in, but I'll confine myself to two. He was First Order Captain Moden Canady in *Star Wars Episode VIII – The Last Jedi*, to give it its full title. And he was in the television historical drama miniseries *Chernobyl*, based on the 1986 disaster at the nuclear reactor of that name in the Ukraine. Mark played Vladimir Pikalov, commander of the Soviet Chemical Forces. When ordered to find volunteers to drive a truck close to the raging core of the stricken reactor in order to take an accurate reading of the radioactivity, he asked how dangerous it would be. It didn't have to be spelled out. This was a suicide mission. 'Then I'll drive it myself,' said our Mark (Vladimir).

He's also a very good endurance runner. In 2014 he joined fellow Welsh actor and mate, Richard Harrington *(Spooks, Poldark, Hinterland)*, to run the Marathon Des Sables, the epic ultra across the sands of Morocco. How could my spirits not be lifted on our shared run from Builth to Brecon? We sorted out the world, we laughed, joked and had fun but I could not ignore the shooting pains in my legs. By now I was back on the tarmac, and going from running on soft ground to the hard stuff is tough on the joints. Again, I kept apologising to Mark as I had done with the others. 'I'm sorry this run is taking so long for you, I just cannot get my legs working. I'm sure someone has put lead in my shoes.' Mark, just like all the others laughed and said, 'Don't worry. I'm here to get you over the finish line, be it a run, walk or crawl. But I know you'll do it.'

When our time came to an end, I was rewarded with a big *cwtsh* from this wonderful man.

Yes, my spirits had been lifted. And how could they not be raised even higher on the way to Pen y Fan, the highest mountain in South Wales at 886 metres?

It was Nigel's turn next to keep me going. He had been, by his own admission, a right handful in his early days in Bancyfelin, Carmarthenshire in West Wales. He used to smoke and drink to excess. And then he started to sort himself out. He asked Phil Hughes, the butcher up the road in St Clears, time and time again to take him on as an apprentice butcher until it finally happened. He chopped meat at work and had started taking karate classes, but nothing was ever easy because at home his mother had been terminally ill with muscular sclerosis (MS) since he was seven. She died in his arms when he was nineteen.

At the age of 22, he joined the Royal Marines – a slightly unconventional calling for a butcher who couldn't swim. And from there, four years later, he successfully went through the rigorous selection processes and entered the secretive world of the SAS. He left the armed forces when he was 33 and was now running the Blue Mountain Group, offering specialist training for people – operatives – in the security business. And for novice ultra runners, like me.

Having fallen out of a helicopter, had new hips, a knee operation and broken his neck, Nigel was not quite the physical specimen he once had been having just had surgery. But Nigel being Nigel, he relished a challenge. He had cycled from Land's End to John o' Groats on a butcher's bike – 1,149 miles on a one-gear 1940s bike, with a basket carrying his tent and supplies – in memory of his mother and to raise money for MS. He actually saw his mother as he pushed hard on one of the last climbs of the challenge. He did all of this while waiting for a new hip. He should have had it before the cycle ride but he refused the op until after his challenge.

Now he was joining me on the road from the town of Brecon to the base of the highest Beacon. I had not seen him for a long time so it was lovely to see him again. The heavens opened and down came the rain. Heavy rain. And wind. The drone was pulled down. There'd be a camera man on top of the summit waiting but for the next hour, it would just be me and the mountain. And there was something nice about that. A chance to gather my thoughts, to think of the previous 150 miles, lessons learnt and also a chance to think about my family. They'd be there at the bottom of the other side of the mountain waiting. That thought alone was enough to give me some fire power as I found my legs again and powered up the track for one last time.

It didn't matter that the weather had closed in. I left Nigel at the bottom of Pen y Fan and set off with a spring in my step.

Some thought I'd never complete it. Well, I didn't think I truly had it in me either, but the 333 proved to me that I could still do it.

I might not be anything special, but I have achieved more than I thought I was capable of with a lot of hard work and stubbornness.

Finally, I had something positive to log:

1. *Made it … to the castle that marked 5km to the finish. Buzzing … After 10,000 metres of climbing it's all downhill from there. three ultras, three peaks in three days – a first I wonder? … a tear in my eye. It's over. We are done.*

CHAPTER 19

LOOK THE WORLD
STRAIGHT IN THE EYE

I crossed the finish line straight into the arms of my son who didn't care two hoots what I had just achieved. For him, the most interesting thing was the microphone boom hovering above the camera picking up my words; the most important thing was that his Mam was back ... for 24 hours at least. And I was quite happy to reprise my role. The role of mother.

There was no time to dwell on the strange contrasts in my emotions. The day after I finished the 333, I was off again with Green Bay, to Peru. I didn't have time to reflect on what had been. I had time only to move on. Fill the hollowness with work. First, though, I had to buy an outsize pair of flip-flops for my feet, which were ballooning even before we boarded the plane for Lima.

Peru. What a fascinating place. Talk about being humbled. First of all, there was the altitude. I was by now pretty confident when it came to my general fitness, but I was struggling to breathe as we snaked our way up by minibus to the *altiplano* (high plain) of the Andes. The plain lay at an average of 3,750 metres (12,300 feet) above sea level and the high passes over the *cordillera* touched 5,000 metres (16,400 feet). That was up in the death zone. At no higher than 2,000 metres, I was feeling the effects. I struggled to move; I felt constantly sick. I could only watch in awe as we passed farmers of all ages working tirelessly.

We stopped in Cusco, the city called the 'navel' of the Inca Empire, and wandered through its myriad alleyways and peered through its archways to admire the temples and palaces that had survived Spanish conquest in the sixteenth century and the more recent major earthquake of 1950. From the city, we went to the Sacred Valley, where the intricate network of terraces revealed how expert and experimental the Incas were as gardeners and farmers. We visited Pueblo de Chincheros, where a modern kind of experiment was under way. The women of the village had organised themselves into a sort of collective to re-learn traditional weaving skills. Nearly everything they earned was re-invested in the community, the collective family.

Chincheros stood in stark contrast to La Rinconada.

It called itself a city – and at 5,100 metres (16,732 feet) above sea level could claim to be the highest in the world – but in reality, it was a straggling settlement around a dreary gold mine. This was the Klondike of the Andes, whose population between 2001 and 2009 had grown by 230%. There was no sanitation or plumbing here and the soil was contaminated with mercury. Rubbish flowed everywhere. La Rinconada had a smell stronger than the toilets of the Jungle Ultra, but still held out its promise of riches. People continued to pour into the city to seek the one lucky strike that would make their fortune.

We escaped to find some greenery and some oxygen. I thought by now I'd have acclimatised and after going back up again to altitude to film a feature at the world's highest cross-fit centre, I set off for a run. This is nothing, I tried to convince myself – running a 10k is no challenge for someone who had just completed 150 miles (my feet, by the way, had returned to normal and I suffered no blisters. So, no excuses, I told myself).

I knew the crew were tracking my progress with a long lens. I stretched my legs and tried to look strong, but inside, I was desperate to stop. I just could not breathe. I needed to stop, but I didn't want to do that after three minutes of running! And especially in front of the cameras. I had barely covered a mile before I was looking for a tree. A large tree. Large enough for me to hide behind and catch my breath. Eventually, I found one and disappeared behind it. It didn't take long for the camera crew to jump in the car and set off in search of me. As they approached, I suddenly reappeared from behind the tree, looking like a sprinter as I bounced along.

'Nothing to see here,' I shouted. 'I'm fine!'

I should not have told them what I had done, but I did, and we left this beautiful area in laughter. The only consolation came from my dear old GPS watch, which revealed that I was trying to run at 5,052 metres above sea level.

We were invited to a ceremony called *chaccu*, in which the now sacred *vicuñas*, a small relative of the llama, were being gathered for shearing. The beautiful *vicuña* was prized for its wool, but not before nearly going out of existence. It was now a venerated and protected species and part of the *chaccu* held in its honour was to smash a bottle against a fence post to mark the start of the shearing ceremony. Yours truly was invited to perform the task. Most of the wine went all over me.

We said goodbye to the *altiplano* by watching the sun rise over Lake Titicaca, on the border between Peru and Bolivia. There was one lake (frozen) in Canada that I had completely failed to register. There was no way I could ever forget this one, with its high, deep waters reflecting the clearest sky overhead and gigantic mountains all around. It was a balm to the soul.

When I came back, I sat down immediately at my desk to start writing a first draft of the scripts for the 333 series – a kind of voiceover diary of my experience. I was straight back into a less rested side of me. What had I been feeling on the 333? What were these fluctuations in the restless part of me, these rapid changes from high to low and back again? Or was it all part of a new phase of *not* feeling? Was I growing indifferent to all this swaying and swinging within me? Was I doing something wrong? Was it my training? Not enough; too much? Was I stale? Was it something other than my sport? Was it simply an age thing? Was I at a stage of my life where everything needed to be put under review? Were these the first signs of a new found low? If so, shouldn't I be scared? Why wasn't I?

Should I incorporate any of this into the script? I was so busy thinking objectively about myself that I pushed 'whatever' it was to one side. I was too busy writing about me to think about me. No time to think. And then one of those things struck. One of my things. I simply could not squeeze even the tiniest extra into my life, but in it came anyway.

I was writing away, sorting out a timeline and a structure, when I started to have a headache. I had conceded by now that I had to wear glasses. I didn't mind. I was over the threshold of 40; these things happened. So, I went for my first appointment at the opticians. By the way the optician moved in her seat, I knew something was up. I could tell by her silence and her glances at my notes that all was not well.

'Everything all right?' I asked.

'I've seen something but I'm not qualified to assess it. I'm going to arrange for you to see a specialist.'

My family and I had other things on our mind. On that particular day, I received the news that my Aunty Helen, my godmother, had suddenly passed away in the operating theatre.

I went back to work and refused to think about my eye.

I did eventually go to see my GP, a week later, and in front of me, she phoned the ophthalmologist. He would like to see me. When? Straight away.

'Can I drop in later?' I asked. 'I've got three back-to-back meetings today.'

'I'd rather you got out of them if you don't mind. I'd prefer to see you now.'

I went straight to the Eye Clinic at the University Hospital of Wales in Cardiff and sat on a green, very comfortable chair, took out my laptop and got back to work on scripting the 333. I felt fine. I was sure I was about to be told there was nothing to worry about after all. I was soon summoned to the consultant's room. He was very kind:

1. *'No, I haven't been feeling any different.'*
2. *'No, I'm not seeing bright lights.'*
3. *'No, I have no idea what you're talking about.'*

'There's no way of telling, because your eyesight has been good and, because we don't have any notes, we don't know how long you've had this.'

This?

'It's a type of mole and it's very, unusually, large. In fact, I haven't seen one like this before. It's at the back of your eye, sitting very close to your optic nerve.'

I froze for a moment, before all these questions started to form in my head:

4. *'Is it my fault for being out in the sunlight too much / doing the things I do?'*
5. *'Is it growing?'*
6. *'Might I lose my sight?'*
7. *'What is it again?'*

No, it was behind my retina and had nothing to do with light coming into the eye. They didn't yet know if it was benign or malignant, or whether it was growing or not. They couldn't perform a biopsy: it was too risky – I could lose my sight because the mole was tight against the optic nerve. So, they couldn't predict any outcomes.

It was a Friday. I had to return on the Monday for more tests.

To cut a long story short, over the next month I was sent to London and then to Chester to see one of Europe's leading eye specialists. Yes, it was abnormal, and yes, I had to wait a few weeks to find out if it was growing. And if it was, would I be losing my eye? Maybe not, but there was a chance I'd lose my sight.

It was a tough time but I took a lot of solace in thinking back and remembering the lessons I had learnt over the years, especially through running. I had come a long way since shattering my knee. The last twenty-three years had been about baby steps and it might be time to start taking those steps again. I had to remind myself of how important they really are.

Two months later it was officially confirmed that it was a choroidal nevus.

It was then and it is now. I have my choroidal nevus to this day. And it's not growing. But it might, next year or in forty years. So they're keeping an eye on it, excuse the pun. It has in no way put me in the pain cave, but I suppose I am in the waiting cave.

CHAPTER 20

MIND OVER MILES

The 333 series went out on S4C and 2016 turned into 2017. At first I had no grand plan, but I was ticking over. Gwilym was just 15 months old and I was finding it difficult to commit to greater distances because of family and work commitments. But then I began to run more regularly with my friend Janet Ebenezer. It was Janet who introduced me to Siôn back in 2008. She was a fine marathon runner and triathlete, and it was she who converted me to the joys of the regular early-morning start.

I was not always at my best at five o'clock in the morning, but Janet persuaded me to give it a go. I was not convinced I could ever be persuaded, but once we were under way, I had to admit there was something special about being on the move while the vast majority of the nation slept. Turning up for work in the morning having run 20 miles before breakfast was an even better feeling.

Janet was preparing for a road marathon and I was preparing for the 2017 Trail Marathon Wales, a race through the Coed y Brenin (The King's Forest) Park, north of Dolgellau in Snowdonia. There's a visitor centre at the park and a whole series of trails and paths for runners and mountain bikers. I had long wanted to compete in its June marathon foot race, because Coed y Brenin was a place of enchantment. I had run through it during the 333 (the last few miles of Day 1 in the rain and darkness) but I was too tired to really notice the beauty. Snowdonia plays such a big part in my story and even I think of it as this giant open mountain space, a *massif* baring all for those who come to climb or take a ride up its highest peak, Snowdon. It always has to be respected and not just for its steepest slopes. Even the train-takers from Llanberis can go from sunshine to shivery mists in a matter of seconds. Snowdonia is a towering invitation and a giant 'Beware!' sign at the same time, but it has its less obvious secrets, too, and Coed y Brenin is one of them. The forest park sits between the rivers Mawddach and Eden, in an area where once there were gold mines. Yes, Wales had its own mini-Klondike, the Clogau 'rush' of 1862. The pollution that came with the extraction of Welsh gold has been removed and there are trout and salmon in the Mawddach, while the Eden is protected as a breeding ground for rare freshwater pearl mussels.

The race had been founded by my friend Matt Ward, and our friend Steve Edwards was there lending a hand with the organising. Matt and Steve had helped me so often along my way and were so much more than race organisers. They were creators, commentators, pioneers of promoting ultra running in general and, all the while, they found the time and energy to be runners in their own right. I had always wanted to take part in Matt's event but my weekend work on sport and other assorted work projects had come first.

I trained hard for it with Janet now, going on our morning runs that had quickly become a regular part of our lives. We made our separate ways north, though, for the race itself. In fact, my preparations on the eve of the marathon were a little unconventional all the way. I was speaking at the St John Ambulance Summer Ball in Cardiff and was there in the capital, in all my finery, a long way from the start line in Coed y Brenin. I left as soon as I politely could and, still in my best dress, drove up the A470, Wales's Dempster Highway, to the north.

My evening was turning into a story of two halves, of opposite ends, as I awkwardly changed out of my long black evening dress in the car and put on my race gear, plus a couple of layers to keep warm, slept in my Arctic sleeping bag in the car, woke, cleaned my teeth, drank some water and ate some food, did a few stretches, and then began the race.

It was an extremely hot day. But I seemed to revel in the conditions. I had not raced a marathon for a very long time. When I had, it was always as part of my training schedule – a back-to-back long run or a marathon with a weighted rucksack. I asked Stephen before the race for some course advice. 'You run up one forest, down it, then cross to the next forest on the opposite mountain, run up it and then down.' Simple but effective.

I came first and Emma Williams came second.

Here is where I fell into the running company of Emma Williams, whose husband Carwyn, an endurance cyclist, had heard me speak at a function and had introduced himself, and then me to Emma. We found we had a lot in common. We both were mothers, working full-time jobs and we both lived in Cardiff. 'How about we meet early in the morning?' Emma asked. It suited me. Janet had by now moved on to triathlon. Soon, Emma and I were out four or five times a week – getting our 10-15-milers and even 30-milers in before 7.30am.

It was one of the thrills of that summer, but all was not well. Soon afterwards, I found myself really struggling with my motivation and fitness. I was supposed to be training for my second Ring of Fire Ultra on Anglesey, but I couldn't keep up with Emma, who was training for the infamous UTMB race. It wasn't just the once. I was falling behind. And it was happening a lot. As Emma got stronger, I went into reverse. I was going from being the determined plodder to a plodder heading nowhere slowly. I felt dejected. I could not get out of second gear, but there wasn't an option of a higher gear. There was something wrong here. Was it the engine or was it mental? I began to question my reasons for running so far. Should I drop down to the shorter marathon, which had gone well. Did I have the hunger for any of it?

I went north to Anglesey with no expectations, but found that if I wasn't confident about the running part of my sport, at least I was enjoying being back in the company of ultra runners. It was comforting to be back in the multi-stage racing environment which I love so much, exchanging stories, the simplicity of camp life, sharing advice and titbits of information. Although I found it mentally hard hearing my son cry as I left checkpoints. I hadn't prepared for how difficult that would be for me, for Gwilym, and for my parents who were supporting. I knew that once I was out of sight he'd settle back into his joyous self but I could not shrug off the sadness of hearing his calls for 'Mam' as I ran into the distance.

Early on the second day, the longest leg of 100km, I met Adharanand Finn, a journalist at the *Guardian* and author of *Running with the Kenyans* and *The Way of the Runner*. The first of these was shortlisted for the 2012 William Hill Sports Book of the Year award. He would write a third book, *The Rise of the Ultra Runners – A Journey to the Edge of Human Endurance*, and I would get a little mention. We ran together on the second day and got on well as we covered the miles. I chatted away. Actually I chatted … a lot. I thought if maybe I told stories, I would create a distraction from the pain in my stomach. I knew that I was lacking a top gear. However, Adharanand politely listened, asked questions and we talked about our ultra experiences and our love of running. Adharanand was trying to collect points to compete in the UTMB. A very good marathon runner, he was dipping his toes into the world of ultra running and doing extremely well.

On the subject of the rise of ultra runners, it is true that a great deal has changed in the ten years since I started going ultra-long-distance. When it comes to kit, gear, clothing, equipment, training schedule, online coaches, there's a whole industry dedicated to providing runners with everything they should ever need, for all conditions. Everything you might ever want to know about endurance running, plus a vast reservoir of nonsense you would do best to avoid, is available online as blogs, vlogs, podcasts and diaries. My, people are even writing books about themselves! GPS refines the art of navigation more and more each year. No longer are you dependent on compass and map to steer you through a race (although there are still races that ask politely for you to leave your GPS at home). There are more and more events and races taking place on every continent. Instead of being nervous about going into a race underprepared, the danger now is to have your head overflowing with information from all quarters. Instead of a large net to catch what little there is out there, we need a filter to sift the good from the dross. You can be buried by nonsense …

When it came to the Ring of Fire of 2017, I seemed to have a ring of fire in my stomach. I was not feeling good at all. It wasn't a question of feeling generally out of sorts and not being able to keep up with Emma during training. I felt terrible. Was this me unravelling? First, my DNF on the Pen Llŷn, then the eye ... now this. I had already begun to suspect that my head was starting to have doubts about my ongoing suitability for this type of activity. Was my body coming out in sympathy? Was my mind not in it any more? Had I lost that mental strength I had found in the Amazon and Arctic? I was now 43 years old. Was it an age thing? I told myself to pull myself together.

The race started. I set off thinking that I would eventually find the rhythm that would settle me down. You have to be patient sometimes before you hit the groove. Sometimes, regardless of the distance you're running, your legs aren't moving as fast as you'd like, you lose patience and then you lose the flow. I have often thought, 'I can't possibly go any further'. But, as I've said before, the next step will prove me wrong. Relentless forward progress. Whatever the mantra, whatever the motivation, whatever you feel necessary – use it as your motivation.

By the second day, my mantras didn't work. I continued to feel grim. Adharanand let me go ahead. By now I needed to be on my own. In my own pain cave. I wasn't chatty Lowri anymore.

I met my parents and Gwilym at a checkpoint.

I don't always encourage my parents to come to see me during an ultramarathon. Fine at the start or at the end, but during a long race it can be hard for them, watching their daughter go on a rollercoaster of emotions. I've seen other runners hit the wall in obvious distress, or at the top of climbs that leave them on jelly legs. I've seen runners drag themselves to the line covered in blood from a fall. Bites, blisters, broken bones – you see them all and I know that if they saw me going past looking like I sometimes do, well ... I'd also be seriously worried. It is the nature of our game that joy is not always visible. Far from it. Suffering wins on the visibility front any day. In general, I preferred my parents – and now Gwilym – to be spared all that.

However, my parents knew this wasn't my normal suffering. They knew the difference between extreme tiredness and illness.

Even though I didn't. Anyway, Gwilym and they were waiting for me, encouraging me, keeping me going, and getting my support bag ready, and feeding me at the second day's halfway point. 'You're doing well,' they said as I sat in a folding chair with Gwilym on my lap. 'I don't feel it,' I said. 'Come on, Lowri. Dig deep now,' my mother said. I found it hard to motivate myself out of the chair, which was a strange feeling. And after staying with them far longer than I would have in normal circumstances, they knew. They just knew something was up. I doubled over and retched. Something came up.

'What's that, Lowri?' said my father in a flash.

'What's what?' I gasped.

'That. It's blood!'

'No, Dad. It's the gels. Blackcurrant.'

Mam came over. 'Yes, Lowri, it's blood.'

I retched again. Gwilym thought he'd join in next to me as I was doubled over and spat some of his drink out on to the ground. Yes, I do want to inspire my son, but this wasn't quite what I'd had in mind!

'It's blood,' said the doctor. To me, not to Gwilym.

'Gels,' said the obstinate daughter and prepared to move out.

My parents didn't try to physically stop me from continuing, they knew me too well, but Dad texted Steve Edwards, who was further down the line waiting for me. Coincidentally, Steve, being the good friend he is, had noticed that my GPS tracker had stopped. He, being local, came to search for me and he joined me as we ran another ten miles together. He then asked me how important this race was to me. I had completed it before, run an extra four miles, and finished 12th overall. I wasn't collecting points for another race. At the end of the day, it was only a race. Crossing the finish line or not did not define who I was. I had nothing to prove.

I stopped and pulled out at the next checkpoint. It didn't take long for the old ping-pong to start. Mind vs body. I simply refused to believe it was my body that had made me stop. In my mind, it was my mind that was to blame. My mind had failed to win the argument. Mind Failed To Deliver. I was really disappointed in myself. I told myself I should have crawled over the finish line. But, finishing can never be a guarantee. The race will always beat you up, and sometimes it will beat you. This is all part of taking on the challenge in the first place. Although now I questioned whether I still had the motivation and that stubborn doggedness needed to compete in ultramarathons. Maybe I should change distances? Change sport?

I tried not to beat myself up just because the race had. The real me was not in a good place. It was my second DNF. This FTD was becoming a habit.

I went to hospital for a check-up and underwent an endoscopy.

The results showed I had very low iron levels and had a tear to my stomach lining. This body of mine was proving very argumentative. On the other hand, it was a relief to know that there was a reason behind my dip in form pre-race. My stop had an explanation. Recrimination gave way to forgiveness. With a little bit of care and tenderness, my body could be repaired. It was a relief to my mind, which might have taken a bit longer to recover from the disappointment of another DNF.

Reassured and resting, I began to make plans I thought I might be able to salvage something from 2017 by upgrading the 333 to a 777. It had been a quiet goal of mine since 2012. I have always wanted to go to Antarctica and to see more of the world and this seemed a great challenge; one I'd relish. But I didn't want to be away from the family for too long.

There was an event called the 777 World Marathon Challenge, which comprised seven marathons on seven continents in seven consecutive days. For instance, you started on Union Glacier in Antarctica, ran and then flew to Punta Arenas in Chile, ran and flew to Miami, ran and flew to Madrid, ran and flew to Marrakech, ran and flew to Dubai, and ran and flew to Sydney for a run and a rest.

I wanted to customise the 777 and stretch each marathon's course of 26.2 miles up to 32 miles and make it the World Ultra Challenge. Seven ultras in seven consecutive days on the seven continents. It was, I had to admit, a bit expensive but I thought there would be enough interest and enough enthusiasm from the independent production companies to give it a real chance of being commissioned, especially as it would have been a world record. We had a marathon of toing and froing of ideas and budgets, but after a year of prepping and talking to sponsors we fell short of the money and in the end the project was iced.

That ate up 2017, which moved us into 2018.

Now, as a 44- year-old, I changed direction – a little bit. I wanted to see if I could beat my marathon time of 3 hours 08 minutes set when in my 20s. The shorter more intensive training sessions suited my lifestyle. I qualified for a British Championship entry at the London Marathon. I was aiming for sub-three and the training had gone well. My half marathons, 10kms, and Parkruns were showing that if all went well, I could do it. Potentially.

Beginning on 22 February 2018, Great Britain and Ireland were affected by a cold wave, dubbed 'The Beast from the East' by the media and officially named Anticyclone Hartmut, which brought widespread unusually low temperatures and heavy snowfall to large areas. Somehow I developed a chest cold and training was scuppered leading up to the London Marathon in April.

Typically of the British weather, a few weeks after The Beast from the East left, we had the other extreme on race day. The heat of the London Marathon 2018 caught me out and I suffered at the last hurdle. Well, not quite the last hurdle. I crashed into the wall at mile 8!

Everything was going to plan until mile 8. I had run the marathon a handful of times. I had experienced the highs, the amazing atmosphere and wonderful camaraderie that comes with it, and I didn't need to finish it. It was such a hot, humid day. The heat soaked up all of my energy. I hoped that my 'automatic running pilot' would set in, but it didn't, and I went into survival mode. When I knew a sub-three wasn't possible, I moved the goalposts early on.

I wanted to give up but used all the motivation I could muster to literally put one foot in front of another. The thought of my parents making that huge effort, as many others did, to wait patiently along the course for me and then race to the next spot along the route to keep supporting kept me going. '*Diolch* – thank you – *Mam a Dad.*' I told them when I saw them at the end. 'I didn't want to let you down.' And I didn't want to let myself down after all the hours and hundreds of miles of training. I didn't get the time I expected – I was 12 mins slower – but who cares. This was one of the toughest marathons I had run, and despite falling short of my goal, I finished with a smile on my face because I did not give up and could easily have done so.

My A race, however, for 2018 was to run the PTL, part of the UTMB. Sorry about all the capital letters. The Ultra Trail Mont Blanc was a whole series of races, all of them with letters of their own. Bear with me, because it gives an idea of the scale of this world of endurance around the highest massif in Western Europe. There was the MCC (De Martigny-Combe à Chamonix), described as a taster in the Alps. Then came the OCC (Orsières-Champex-Chamonix). And then the CCC (Courmayeur (Italy)-Champex (Switzerland)-Chamonix (France)). Then we went up to seriously ultra, to the TDS (Sur les Traces des Ducs de Savoie), the UTMB being the showstopper and, finally, the PTL. This was the Petite Trotte à Lyon and was a 300-km (188-mile) loop around Mont Blanc, starting in Chamonix and with 25,000 metres of ascent. There were no route markers, just the 'route' itself which changed every year and took runners into France, Italy and Switzerland. We'd be lucky to have 4-6 hours sleep over the five days of racing.

Emma and I had been training hard for this race. Most of our runs were taking place on the mountains of South Wales at 4.30am. It was, by now, a habit. When our schedules got busier and it became harder to fit in our long runs, Emma and I would get a lift, take the train or drive to the Brecon Beacons and run the 60 miles home, over the mountains and overnight, arriving back in time to take our children to school the next morning.

I loved these challenging runs. For me one of the amazing things that happens when people meet for a run, regardless of distance, is everything gets left behind, your background, your job, your age, your gender. None of it is relevant. Running is an open sport for everyone, all you need is a pair of trainers and a passion for running. We are all the same at the start of a run.

When I was offered a chance for the PTL, I wanted to give it another shot. Did I really have what it takes to be an ultra runner any more?

I went for a training run in the Alps in June 2018. I say 'training run', but really, I went with Emma to see how committed I was to the challenge. I had been finding it hard to fit in the training between work and family commitments. My training runs had all been in the dark – either early mornings or overnight runs. Which is an odd feeling. Because they all happened while everyone else was sleeping, my runs all felt like a blur, like a dream. I had not raced for a while so didn't know where I was fitness-wise.

Did I really want to do the PTL? I had read the blurb and loved it, but reading and running were poles apart. I had been a little off the pace. I was no longer punishing myself for the DNFs, but I couldn't say I was in the best form of my life. Could I raise my game? I had known it would take something out of the ordinary to stir my spirits. This might be it. I couldn't shake the PTL out of my head. It was whispering in my ear: 'I dare you … come on, have you got what it takes?' It was writing me a love letter. Here were my favourite bits:

1. *Essential to have good experience of the mountains, the ability to orientate oneself, of being autonomous throughout the day, the know-how to confront difficult conditions (very heavy rain, abundant snow, high winds).*
2. *Often without paths, exposed difficult terrain, tricky grassy slopes, some easy rock-climbing, glaciers and névés (snowfields) with a risk of sliding.*
3. *Very remote itinerary. Altitude >3000m. Intense cold <-10C*

Emma and I headed south to the Alps and met up with another runner who was joining the team. We had to have a taste of it. So, we set off up into the mountains on our 'training run' following much of the Trail Mont Blanc and some of the PTL course, and three days later of 'fastpacking' – running from refuge to refuge – we came down. This is what I wrote in my first flush of stopping when my mind permitted it:

> @_lowrimorgan *We've done it. 120 miles, 10,000 metres ascent w/10kg + on our backs around the Alps in 3.5 days. Training here has been inspiring. My motivation for running (and my mountain legs) have not been at their best lately, but this week I felt stronger and more confident on the mountains. Lots more to be done, but these days on the Alps were needed. Physically and mentally. Merci les Alpes, grazie le Alpi.*

Every word, every metre, every step was drawing me back to them. Every phase had me written all over it. Every obstacle was an invitation. Being on the mountains truly inspired me. I enjoyed every footstep, even when the team of three didn't work out as Emma and I had hoped.

We nearly got there. But within a few weeks of arriving at the start line, and after months of training, mine and Emma's shared dream was quashed, for reasons beyond our control. Just as there was the ever-present danger that some races could never be finished, so there was always the risk that others would never start. My two rules in ultra running – get to the start line and get to the finish line. It went with the territory and I don't suppose Mont Blanc is going anywhere. The PTL, like the 777, will be there, holding out its hand to me. But, oh my, I really wanted to do it. So much. The PTL. You know all those doubts in my mind about my motivation and my age and my work-life balance and my concerns about a diminishing pain threshold? Well, if I could have done the 777 or especially the PTL, I'm sure that those doubts and fears would have evaporated like a park bench on the Ice Road. The PTL … I would have tailored my training for every step it took to do that world-class challenge. Uphill would have been my way. Snow was no problem; ice was a dear friend. High winds? Were they Katabatic? Tricky grassy slopes? I was from Wales for goodness' sake. We have a thousand ways of saying 'wet, slippery grass'. Minus ten degrees? Too warm. I swear, the PTL was made for me.

It was not to be, which left me where? In the bosom of my family, I suppose. No bad place to be at all. Contented with my lot. I mean it. A happy mother, wife and working woman in her mid-40s. You know what's coming, don't you? The but.

It's the waiting cave. It's not always a comfortable place for me. I am restless, I am driven. I need to be doing something that asks me deep down: do you really think, Lowri Morgan, you're up to doing this? Well, try this for size. Let's see what you make of this, or what it un-makes of you.

2018 rolled on. I trained, I raced shorter distances which I enjoyed, but there were no ultras. Where was my Point 12? Where was my chance to pick myself up and make amends for the Did Not Finish? Would there be no deliverance from Failed To Deliver?

It came with the Dragon's Back. The spirit of defiance of the old Welsh dragon, buried deep inside the mountain, came to me. If I have led you prematurely to the *Ras Cefn y Ddraig*, if I have already set off from Conwy Castle before its allotted place on the timeline of my life, it is because this race is so important to me. I have this chance in my precious homeland to rise to the challenge, to ease my fears, as baseless as they may be, and to let my mind tell this ailing body of mine that it cannot fail. I have started the Dragon's Back because I need to get a move on. Time is pressing. I have been warned. The knee, my heart. I may not be able to do this again. I am on borrowed time.

CHAPTER 21

RUN WITH YOUR HEART

I'm standing at the start of the 2019 Berghaus Dragon's Back Race with my fingers crossed. I'm appealing to Lady Luck. I have not been able to prepare as rigorously as I should have liked. You know it and I know it. It's the knee. I could stand here and mill with the others and say to myself I have to have self-belief and faith that I have done everything necessary to succeed in this race. But I don't. I have hardly run for six weeks. Do I have enough residual fitness to see me through? I am nervous – almost like never before. That may be good. Nerves are familiar. All this is familiar. I am in my place. This is where I belong, at the start of the *Ras Cefn y Ddraig* (The Dragon's Back Race). It sounds beautiful in Welsh. It is going to be tough in any language. Come on, Lowri.

Right, here I am, competitor number 314 in the LV class. That's Ladies Veterans – and, if it's all the same with you, I'd rather we didn't mention that again.

A recent MRI scan came back revealing a tear in the cartilage and signs of osteoarthritis. I can race. Maybe for the last time. Most likely for the last time. I have to be realistic and re-set my targets. But I am here. And I must thank a few people, starting with Mr Pemberton who said he couldn't stop me from doing this. I interpret that as a doctor's clean bill of health.

I must thank Siôn for being Siôn. He just laid out the options:

1. *To start and not finish. A DNF.*
2. *Not to start. A DNS?*
3. *To start and finish.*

The choice was mine.

Damn it, it has to be Number 3. Siôn knew exactly what he was doing. Which buttons to press. How to test me. I have to give it a go.

Jo Perkins my physio and pilates teacher came to my rescue when I needed it. And I must say a big thank you, too, to Damian Hall, a champion ultra runner in his own right and for the past five months, my running guru. Once I took the decision to go for it no matter what, I sought a trainer who could make it happen in the real world. Damian has coaxed and encouraged me to the start line. I've enjoyed the last few months of training. He has re-set my racing mind and my training mindset.

When we first spoke at the beginning of 2019, he asked what training I was doing at the time. I proudly told him of my 100-mile week.

'Well done. How much elevation was that in total?' he asked.

'Elevation?' I said, meaning none.

'This is simple,' he said. 'Drop your mileage. We'll increase it again with time, but in the meantime you'll do more elevation. More uphill running. More strength work. More tempo-runs up slopes. More hill-repeats.'

With my free time limited to shorter early morning runs and overnight running, I found myself doubling up with hill repeats later in the day while Gwilym was in nursery. Now it was all about elevation.

Damian's advice has saved and extended my running career by at least one last start. I was going stale, I have discovered. Pounding out the empty miles, thinking it was the only way forward. Damian has taught me that up is my new forward. In fact this way of running has kept me going.

'You have a reserve of fitness. You have enough in the bank,' he has repeated to me countless times.

'You might not be as strong or as fit as you could have been …' Not being able to run nor walk meant me missing out on what I had hoped to have been a month of recceing. '… but you will be at the start line healthy,' said Damian.'Just think peaks from now until the race.'

And so, I have. Uphills are kinder on the knee. Downhills hurt like hell. So I can ease my way down. Only the ups count. His final piece of advice is: 'Think of it as a week-long training session. This is an adventure, not a race. An uphill adventure.' I like the sound of that.

It wasn't just the knee, if truth be told. The Dragon's Back is a mountain race without trails. It offers only recommended routes and mandatory checkpoints, but in between and all over its 200-mile course, it demands a skill set I do not possess. I did not possess. In short, there is an orienteering side to the race that involves reading maps and analysing the terrain, setting courses and believing in them. Sticking with them. Say there is a checkpoint on a peak and between me and that goal is another peak, it is likely the recommended route will take you to that first peak and on to the second. Straight lines rule in recommended routes. But why go up, down and up, when it may be quicker to go around the first peak and give yourself just the one climb? For this, I sought help from another friend and past Dragon's Back finisher, Mike Peckham (who also played a big part in my 777 dream).

I arrived in Conwy a little later than I would have liked. I had to run into registration with only a few minutes to spare before it closed, because I'd been working on the Steelman – a round of the Welsh Triathlon Championship – for television. The three disciplines of swimming, cycling and running, are set against the backdrop of the Port Talbot Steelworks where my extended family once lived. I always enjoyed visiting them in the middle of Port Talbot.

Once the producer shouted 'It's a wrap' my family and I jumped into the car and drove up to North Wales and we arrived there just in time.

I had my photo taken for accreditation and Gwilym enthusiastically joined me in the photo. I could not have been prouder. He was there to witness 450 competitors from all around the world, all with different motivations for being there at the start line of a challenge of a lifetime. And despite our different abilities, backgrounds, ages, we were all there with the same goal. To survive the DBR.

After registration, Shane Ohly, whose company Ourea organises the Dragon's Back, gave a briefing to the 450 runners and 150 marshals, staff and organisers. Well, it was more a speech than a briefing. It was in parts quite stern, laying out in no uncertain terms that we should be aware that the cut-off times would be strictly observed. The Ourea staff had too much to do elsewhere to be waiting around at checkpoints, allowing themselves to be tempted or begged into showing leniency and mercy. Shane's priority was his staff, not the late runner. Miss the cut-off by a fraction and that was it. Race over. And as Shane explained, if that made Shane the Mr Bad Guy, then so be it.

On the other hand, he sold the event superbly. What could rival this togetherness, the sense of adventure, the thrill of the chase ahead? He reminded us that of the 450 starters, half would be out of the race in two days. Fact. A statistic beyond dispute. That sort of concentrated our minds. Fear is always a good element to introduce. The sweeter pill was another fact, the statistic that showed that those among us who finished the first two days would more than likely go on to complete the full set of five. If you survived the third day, you'd be there at the finish line, all being well.

I have to say, here on the start line, that this is an event on a grand scale of organisation. The volunteer effort is enormous. The attention to detail is just so very meticulous.

I am always surprised by the range of people that take up multi-stage challenges and how difficult it is to determine who will, or won't, finish. I look around. You can never tell who are the experienced whippets of the ultra running world, who the newcomers to multi-day running, or who belong somewhere in between. Everybody mixes easily.

I worry about missed sessions, worry that I have made a mistake with my food, putting too much into my drop-bag, that has been taken with military precision down the line to a checkpoint. I'm so used to being self-sufficient, carrying everything I need on me, that I think I've over-compensated and packed too much food and too much first aid and too many socks and spare running shoes into the bag that's meant to be 5kg max. And shouldn't I have kept that waterproof jacket on me?

Stop fretting, Lowri, and breathe it all in. Look up at the ramparts of Conwy Castle and take in the massed crowd that has gathered to see us off. Listen to the male voice choir that's singing us on our way. Listen to your increased heart rate. Let it all sink in. Enjoy the moment and put your nerves to good use. I'm standing with my tent-mates – Caz the Hat, Shan Jones, Mike Evans, Graham Atkinson, Diggory Dalton, Lenny Hughes and Paul Nelson. We all laugh despite the nerves. I see Gwilym and my parents on the castle's walls and think of my husband, who's away with work – they have all supported me. I'm not doing this just for me. They have invested a lot of time, patience and effort into this challenge too. I'm doing this for them. They believe in me. I should believe in me too. Remember what your mother says: 'Follow the leaders. You might not be able to keep up with them but you can learn from them.' But with 450 runners milling about, where are they? What should I ... oh my goodness, we're off.

CHAPTER 22

THE DRAGON'S BITE

No sooner am I out of Conwy than I run straight into mist. Talk about putting a shroud over a sense of excitement. At the start, I lost sight of Gwilym, not because of this mist but because the throng of well-wishers and onlookers and family and runners was so dense that it was useless trying to find individual faces. In a way, it helped. I suddenly went from mother to runner. I put my race-head on. That switch in my head had truly been pushed.

But this mist. It's like setting off in the jungle and having to stop within fifty strides to fix the rucksack. One minute we are 450 runners under the ramparts of the castle with a male voice choir in full song – an echo of times past for me, a marriage of sound and sweat in my present – and the next minute we are barely able to see each other on the trail that is hardly visible at the best of times. Sound, like vision, is suffocated by the cloud. Talk about an anti-climax. The race has started and the mountains ahead and the castle behind have vanished. The disappearing trick … not that again, please … I'm not even out of breath yet.

I'm panicking. I've not recced this part. Oh goodness, I've not recced anywhere near enough of the course. Only Day 2 with a new running friend of mine, Mike Pollard. I'd also recced the first half of Day 4 with Diggory. And the last half of Day 5 with another tent-mate, Mike Evans. But that was nearly three months ago. I can't remember what I did last week let alone three months ago.

Just calm down, Morgan, the voice inside me instructs. Just listen to the body. My knee hurts. Or it is the mind already playing tricks on my body. Calm down. Enjoy the moment. Breathe in. Breathe out. Let the nerves become adrenalin. Use them to your benefit. It'll keep you alert.

I'm a little lost in the mist at the moment. I'm trying to decide whom I should follow.

The mist is clearing. I am back on track, or what little of a path there is. You have to find your own way – make your own path – which is not as frightening as it sounds for an orienteering novice because at this early stage there are always others you can follow, as long as you can see them. And as long as you pick the right group. There are runners everywhere, to the left of me, to the right of me, in front, behind. All trying to find the right path or trot (animal track) on the grassy and gorse-filled terrain.

I have followed a handful of experienced mountain runners, but I've picked the wrong group. Nothing too serious. But we've lost half an hour. We just went in the wrong direction and lost a little time. In the mist, we ran off the summit having clocked our tabs into the checkpoint scanner only slightly off track but we went downhill the wrong way and now we must climb the mountain again to join up with the path. But what is thirty minutes in the grand scheme of things? Nothing … or it could be the difference between making a cut-off or not. We try not to think of that and our panic quickly subsides.

But I can't ignore that frustration deep within the stomach. We've lost valuable minutes and we've only been running for 90 minutes. But all is well now. The sun is out and I am on my way up into the National Park, and up is my thing.

I've been working hard with Damian to be strong uphill. I came second overall and won the women's class in a mountain marathon in April and despite having to walk all the downhills because of my knee, I felt stronger than ever on the ascents. And I'm feeling the effects of all the uphill power walking I did on the treadmill (sometimes wearing a weight vest) prior to the race to replace the fact that I couldn't run. The hours of hiking I did with the family with my 10kg vest was also evident now.

The destination on Stage 1 is Nant Gwynant, but it lies well on the other side of the highest peaks of *Eryri* (Snowdonia) and we have to go up most of them: Glyder Fach, Glyder Fawr, Crib Goch, Garnedd Ugain and *Yr Wyddfa* itself (Snowdon).

They (Welsh geologists, I imagine) say that once upon a time Snowdon stood as tall as Everest, only to be eroded to its size of today, seven times lower than the world's highest mountain. I am glad it has shrunk. Fancy having an Everest in Wales.

Yr Wyddfa as it is, remains so familiar to me, a dear friend that has called me back time after time – sometimes in the wind and rain, as on the day I went up and down it three times; sometimes in glorious sunshine, like now. I am smiling. I am chatting away to Chris Baynham-Hughes and a few others. The conversation flows. We take to its slopes. Crib Goch is next. The magnificent and the dreaded Crib Goch. As mountain climbs go for runners, this is one of the most challenging.

'Forty minutes it took me from here to the summit last time,' Chris says.

That's exactly what I wanted to hear. Forty minutes – what is 40 minutes in one's life? When I break it down like that, it sounds achievable. I feel so free going up that mountain. I even stop before reaching her summit to look around. Sometimes you're so caught up in racing and getting to the top, you forget to look around. To see the view and the path we have taken from early in the morning now that the clouds have risen is a humbling experience. I can see dots of runners from far away. How small we look on this amazing planet. I stop to listen. It is peaceful, except for my heart pumping away, working the body to its limit. It's a good feeling. I feel alive.

And I am in a good place. Who knows, perhaps this is it – my last time in a competitive race. I savour every moment. I am literally going from checkpoint to checkpoint. I might not make it to the end of the day with this knee. It is hurting on the downhills, hurting on the flat, but I remember the surgeon's words. It can't get worse. If you can cope with the pain, then smile and get the job done. Just do it, Lowri. And only after that can I rest.

'What's with the strapping?' runners asked.

'Oh, just a torn cartilage,' I say.

'And that's confirmed?' A raised eyebrow, as if I've self-diagnosed.

'Oh, yes, it's confirmed.'

'Fair play to you ...' they say as they run off.

There is a mutual respect in this race. Whether you're in the front pack, middle or in the back, everyone there has a goal. The Dragon can bite. It doesn't matter how strong, fast or experienced you are, this race takes many casualties – from elite runners to the plodders like me.

Once I am at the summit of Snowdon, the vast majority of the 3,560 metres (11,679 feet) of ascent on this first day have been done. It is more or less downhill all the way to the end of the 30-mile stage. Not that my knee likes running downhill. The good news is that the gravity-assisted slopes are so steep that a more cautious pace is the wiser option. Slow doesn't blow the joint. Anyhow, I have my sticks in my pack in case I need the extra support.

The camp at Nant Gwynant is visible from a long way out, a masterpiece of tented accommodation in serried rows for all the runners. Or those that make it this far. The organiser's words about the drop-out rate are chilling. One step at a time, but take care with each one, too.

I am ten metres from the finish line of Stage 1. I'm just about to check out of the stage alongside another runner. And that's when I realise – I have made a mistake. Goodness knows how, but having seen the tented village from afar, I have sailed past the last checkpoint without performing the one thing for which this CP exists. Checking in. There's a small electronic tagging process you have to go through and somehow, I manage to miss it. Perhaps it has something to do with the mirage of Tuk's lights or Alter do Chão's. You see them and they are real, but also an illusion – visible but, as yet, out of reach. Perhaps I've thought that the tented village, like a shimmering oasis, must be further from me than I think. Head down. Don't be fooled. Keep going. It was most probably the relief of seeing the tented village that caused me to take my eye of the game. Straight past the CP that stands between the illusion and me. To be fair, this last check-in is tucked into a gateway just to the side of another gateway, but it's no excuse. I have run on, oblivious to it, and reached the end before realising my error.

Now, what am I to do? I have been running the Carneddau, Glyderau and Snowdon massif for 9 hours and 50 mins. 50km and 3,600 metres of ascent. I have already lost time in the mist. And I know that each time I have consulted my map I have wasted valuable seconds. Old hands read maps on the go. I have to stop. The seconds tot up and it's frustrating. And now this. I try to remember Damian's words, that this is an adventure not a race. But today I'm a racer and now an irritated racer. If I had an ice pole with me, I'd be click-click-clicking it into the ground. I turn around and run back to the checkpoint, clock myself in and run back. I have lost another 45 minutes. Runner 314 is in 74th place overall after Day 1 and is not consoled at all by being the leading LV (if I really must – but this is the last time – that's Ladies Veteran). Just as mortifying is the discovery that missing the checkpoint is not serious. I could have taken it as a 'strike', of which we are allowed two without penalty. A third, and you're eliminated. Three strikes and you're out. I could have saved myself the bother of running back up the mountain to check in and just taken a first strike; it would have been my lucky strike …

The race marshals (who are amazing) take my bag, as they do with all the athletes, to my tent and I try to relax by going through my post-run routines. I lay out my lightweight sleeping bag and put on my kit for the next day, adding an extra layer because the temperature is surprisingly cold. I mean, it's hardly Arctic withering, but, no question, it's chilly. I prepare my recovery meal and settle down. My body needs calories now. I tell myself that it is good to be frustrated. I say in my head that to have gone back to the CP is to respect the integrity of my participation. It is my homage to honesty. No short-cuts, no easy options. But still annoying. I console myself that what I am feeling is not pain or doubt, just the desire to do better. I am cross at myself and maybe that's not a bad thing. At least I care.

My frustration aside, it's great to be at the athlete's village. There's a buzz here. Despite the tiredness, people are exchanging stories and inspiration. I feel tempted to stay in the food tent to meet more like-minded folk, but I know I must rest. I must get my kit ready for tomorrow. Rest is just as important as the running. I must go back to my inviting sleeping bed, using my stuffed sports bag as a pillow on the floor.

Day 2: A slightly longer stage at 34 miles (55km) with slightly less elevation – 3,042 metres (10,000 feet). We are heading for Dolgellau, where we have been before. First, though, I have to negotiate the Rhinogydd range. These are ancient volcanic peaks that rise above man-made Lake Trawsfynydd, whose waters used to feed the one and only nuclear power station ever to be built inland in Britain. In the United Kingdom, we build nuclear power stations on the coast. Except for Trawsfynydd, built in the middle of the Snowdonia National Park. Even if it was designed by Sir Basil Spence – the architect of the new Coventry Cathedral that arose next door to the old one, destroyed by bombing in 1940 – it was asking a lot to make a nuclear power station blend into the scenery of Snowdonia. Trawsfynydd was shut down in 1991 after being operational for 25 years, although it won't be fully decommissioned for another 100 years. One hundred years ...

The peaks of the Rhinogydd range are not as well-visited as the neighbouring Snowdon *massif*, but they are so much harder on the feet. And there is a different symmetry to their ups and down. Or asymmetry. They are extremely tough. There is no easy way around them, I find.

This is the day I had recced with Mike Pollard, who I had met on the Trail Marathon Wales race. When they heard of my plan to recce Day 2, Mike and his lovely wife, Lesley, offered to help out. It was wonderful to have company especially from a local. He told the story of his route into ultra running. I was blown away and hugely inspired by Mike's journey. At 27 years of age he had Hodgkin lymphoma. He underwent chemo, went into remission, but then suffered a pulmonary embolism and ended up in HDU fighting for his life. Three years after recovering, he tried a 5km trail run and struggled.

However, his love of being out on the trails had been born and he realised that despite being a footballer and sprinter in his youth, he enjoyed running far more. This was his way of keeping cancer at bay. In 2003 he tried his first marathon in London. He was a recent convert to ultra running, having been inspired by the *Ras yn Erbyn Amser* and the 333 series.

He saw similarities in our mindset and wanted to keep challenging himself to succeed in the same way that he had battled and overcome cancer and all the challenges that illness had thrown at him.

We spent a day and a half recceing the route. During the race, we'd have a day. It was horrendously difficult to navigate but Mike, like millions of others around the world, was constantly challenging the perception that only extraordinary people do extraordinary things. Actually, quite often it's the ordinary folk who do the most remarkable of things ... and this is so evident in the case of ultramarathon running.

Back in the race, I join forces with Paul, who is sharing a tent with me and another five. (We've sadly already lost Shan and Mike, both incredible runners, to injuries.) Paul was with me on Day 1 when we got lost. We were both determined to not place a foot wrong on this day. Well into his 50s, Paul moves like someone half his age. And before long we're off the map and have found another way – a path less travelled. Soon, we are alone. We're going around the mountains. While most of the runners are going up and down over never ending boulders, we're going further away from the route. (I find out later that my friends at home are shouting, 'You're going the wrong way!' as they track our movements on the race's website.) But we're moving faster covering ground with less ascent. The only downfall of taking this risk is the last ascent up Rhinogs; it is the most direct one and the steepest. But I can cope with 45 minutes of steep, painful incline rather than hours and hours of stumbling over rocks.

We eventually join the recommended route and see some of the front runners. They are amazing to watch at work. Just to let you know, the faster you are, the more time you have in the evening (like in the jungle) but also in the morning. It's a staggered start, to ensure that most runners arrive at the end of the stage at roughly the same time. So the slowest would start at 6am, with the fastest having the option to lie in and start after 8am. I did have the option to start later but never took it up. I was not going to be complacent on this race. Every day started at around 6am for me. I never knew if or when my knee would blow. I was taking no chances.

The front runners, Galen Reynolds and Jim Mann, run past us. At first, they appear to be just another part of the long queue that is winding its way upward, but then they ease to the side and start a new trail and begin to overtake. It's not some great surge of pace, just a cadence that develops and before you know it, they're out on their own and out of sight. They pass us and shout their encouragement. I appreciate that.

I'm carefully observing my own, more cautious speed. This is a brutal day of climbing and even when we come down, I find it tough. We hit a proper road, but tarmac is just as bad for the you-know-what as downhills on the mountainside. I am grateful for the support of Paul for the last, long section into Dolgellau, and for the support of people along the way. This cannot be the London Marathon, where crowds line the streets from start to finish, but there are supporters in North Wales, including Mike and his wife Lesley, at regular intervals on the road and they cheer us along. I am a loner; I love company.

I go through my spartan routines again at camp. There is an opportunity to have a shower (which has a long queue outside) but I choose to use my time wisely; instead I wash in the river and have a twenty-minute nap. I know it sounds as if I prefer a punishment-beating to a caress, but there's something about letting yourself be totally absorbed by the great outdoors that appeals to me. I am not a total masochist, but I do like to leave the man-made world behind. If I had to be honest, I also find it difficult to walk the 800 metres to the showers.

I've started having an unsettling feeling in my stomach (similar to motion sickness) but I have made it to the end of Stage 2. The odds are in my favour. I have risen up the table to 42nd place overall.

Day 3. From Dolgellau to Ceredigion, over the last high mountain of Snowdonia and into the Cambrian Mountains of Mid-Wales. It's the longest section at 42 miles (69km) and the second hardest in elevation, 3,341 metres (11,000 feet). We go through two towns: Dolgellau and Machynlleth. Dark-stoned Dolgellau at the base of Cader Idris and Mach. Familiar places and familiar routes. Cader Idris featured in the 333 and Nigel and I did Pumlumon, the highest in the Cambrian range, while training for the jungle. I know these places. I love them, even though my affection for Pumlumon is bruised by getting lost near it.

I do not like them at all today. I tell myself to be sensible with my knee. The descents on Days 1 and 2 were kinder by being steep and awkward to get into a rhythm. I had to take them slowly. These downhills are gentler, easier to stretch the legs and just let loose. I feel I should be breaking into a stride. I enjoy running downhill but now, fast makes me gasp. This is the toughest stage for me. If Shane Ohly pops up to remind us that we're statistically sound and well on course to finish the Dragon's Back, I'll give him a piece of my mind.

I run with another incredible lady. She tells me that she, like Mike, ended up for years in critical care and wasn't expected to survive – she, because of anorexia. This strong runner is now inspiring others, including me today, to run strong. Another was bullied terribly at school. The persecution led to depression and failed suicide attempts before they even finished college. As life took its course, this athlete discovered running and never looked back. Their presence reminded me of the inspirational people that I've met through this sport.

We separate as we arrive into mid-point at Machynlleth, while some stop at the local shops for some fresh food and cold drinks, I decide to pass them all so as not to lose my rhythm or stride (not that I have much rhythm by now). I am desperate to sit down at the halfway point. Looking back, I'm not sure if pushing on was the wisest move. A bit of fresh food and an ice cold can would have been much better, I think as I sit, looking awful, on a camping chair.

I am rescued from my thoughts by former Royal Engineer Sean O'Connor. We have mutual friends and I am pleased to meet him now. I know he (as an RE) has not only recced the course this year, but has also run this race before. When you're grumpy and on a bad knee and you've suddenly hit an extended section of tarmac and the sun is beating down, it helps to share a mile or ten in good company.

At the moment, I'm not sure what Sean thinks of me. It's not just the knee (same old). I'm having real problems with my food and drink. I am truly disciplined when it comes to replenishment. Part of the reason I don't sleep for long at night while racing is because I'm constantly drinking from the water bottles by my side. And I'm very good at taking small amounts of food at regular intervals. I am a responsible eater and drinker. As usual, I have my bottles – one for water and two for blackcurrant-flavoured electrolyte – and my supply of my edible favourites: chocolate brioches and Nutella sandwiches, crisps, salt and vinegar nuts, and sweets. Just as in the past, stomach issues are returning and I'm finding it hard to digest food and liquid. It's very similar to the feeling I had in the Ring of Fire when I DNF'd. I try to erase that memory from my mind. I don't need any negative thoughts in my mind now.

Think of the body as a vehicle, Nigel once told me. 'Think of your feet as tyres. It doesn't matter if you have the strongest engine – if you have a puncture, you're not going anywhere far or fast.' My feet and toes thankfully are not a problem. But my engine is a problem. I am not putting enough fuel into it. Today, I just cannot face eating my food. My electrolytes – even the smell is turning my stomach. Every sip today makes me want to gag and every mouthful is like chewing dust. I've been stopping at little streams to fill my bottles but I've been careful and I'm not getting cramps because of dodgy water. I'm sure Sean thinks I am a little peculiar, what with the most unpleasant sounds I'm making.

Regardless, we stay together. The running rhythm seems more important than my noises. We seem to synchronise well. When one starts to run, the other joins in. We slow together and we pick up the pace together. We finish together with a high five.

Although I do pick up a strike for not checking in at one checkpoint, I know I have checked in at all of them today. This one especially, because I was with Sean at the time. But I must have been so exhausted that I had not waited for the beeps to confirm my check-in. Oh dear, that's my second strike. One more and I'm out of the race … Or is this my first? I can't remember. I need to concentrate. I need to sleep.

We go our separate ways. I'm OK, but the difficulty in swallowing food and drink is accompanied by a slight nausea. All my post-stage rituals are abandoned. I go to my tent (still beautifully prepared by the organisers) and flop down in an untidy heap. Matt Ward knocks on the door. He was at Pumlumon summit and saw me. In hindsight, Sean and I had taken a more challenging route up the mountain. I was deep in my pain cave but according to him, I looked strong. Looks can be deceiving. It's amazing the difference ten red and black fruit pastilles, all at once, can make to an exhausted ultra runner.

'Looks can be deceiving,' I tell him as I sit on the floor, completely spent. He has a huge smile on his face and gives me a big *cwtsh*. 'You're doing so so well, Lowri. We really didn't think you'd get this far with your knee. But you're here and you're flying. We're all so proud of you.' I have tears in my eyes. 'Thank you, Matt.' It's what was needed – a gentle reminder to myself that I was doing OK. I was pushing my own limits. And finding new ones.

I write in my diary:

To call this race tough is an understatement but its an awesome adventure. Every pat on the back and cheer of support from fellow runners got me through today. We're all tired but sticking at it. Two days to go.'

I turn the airplane mode on my phone off (I was trying to save the battery in case I needed to use my phone as a map or ring someone in an emergency) and am surprised to have signal. I quickly FaceTime Siôn and Gwilym.

'You're doing great,' Siôn says in his chilled-out way. 'It's about getting the job done now. You're making us both very proud. Isn't she, Gwilym?'

Gwilym replied, 'Go, Mam, go. And remember, if you don't try your best, you won't win.'

I throw them a kiss, laugh and go to sleep with Gwilym's words in my head.

Day 4. I have not slept well on the third night. In my diary I write:

'Today was the first time I actually thought about not getting out of my sleeping bag and throwing in the towel. I didn't sleep much, it was v cold, my knee was throbbing, toenails throbbing and I'm struggling to consume all the food that I have to consume. I'm finding it hard to eat and drink constantly to keep the energy up. As I lay in my sleeping bag, I had to remind myself about discipline ... it's about knowing what you want now and what you want the most. I've come so far in this race. I've exceeded my expectations. I'm feeling emotional. But I'm still plodding on. Just.'

When I wake up, I am in no mood to leap from my sleeping bag. I want to curl up and let the world run on without me. The thought of food makes me gag again. I surprise myself by overcoming my reluctance quite easily. How many times has my body asked for a lie-in and been ordered instead to shake a leg and move? It goes with the territory and I am soon up and about. A little short of fuse, perhaps, but ready to face the day's 42 miles (67 km) and 2,133 metres (7,000 feet) of elevation. It's a sub-8,000ft day. Well, that's something to look forward to. We're going through the Elan Valley. Maybe today I'll find a footprint I left last time I was here. Round and round and up and down Wales I go. Surely I'll find a trace of myself somewhere.

I meet up with Sean again early on in the day. He doesn't seem to have been put off by my retching noises yesterday. The stage passes as well as can be expected. Towards the end, on the last 10-kilometre stretch of road, Sean wants to press on. He knows this downhill road section and knows the constant pounding will be unkind to my knee. I think he's a bit concerned that if he leaves me behind I'll stop for good. 'Keep my cap in sight,' he says kindly. I have not the slightest intention of stopping but am not really in any fit state to answer him. I just wave him off and carry on, thinking that his invitation to keep his cap in sight echoes what Carwyn Phillips told me on Day 1. Carwyn is 'Caz the Hat'. 'Follow the hat,' he said. I think it's a term of encouragement in mountain running. Possibly a little safer than 'Break a leg.'

I'm struggling on this horrible tarmac section. It's six miles of undulating road – mostly downhill. Normally I would have been relieved to hit this part of the stage and then suddenly I remember my son's words from the night before. If you don't try your best, you won't win.

I tried to explain that I was not going to win the race; he was not having any of that. But then, when I thought about it, winning is not necessarily about being the first to cross the finish line. Winning is about being the best version of yourself. I witnessed impressive mind over matter. Even when people were slowed to a hobble due to injuries – one man was even seen walking downhill backwards because his knees were so sore – they still found the will to keep going. Repeatedly, I saw people in tears and agony, who then told me they would make it because they had the strength of determination to do so. I was impressed by the mental resolve of so many runners. They are winners, too.

Sean's little surge has taken him up to 37th overall. In the process he passes Caz the Hat. I seem to have slipped down to 46th. I am fourth in the women's race. I tell myself that Damian, who has competed in this race himself, has stressed that the adventure comes before the race, and it's absolutely true that I have benefited from not putting my knee through hell on the downhills. I do want to carry on running post-Dragon's Back Race. I desperately don't want this part of my life, which has been such a huge part of who I am, to come to an end. I know I have other passions, but running has made me the person I am today. It shaped me way before I met Siôn and became a mother. I am a better person thanks to running and the way it has helped me overcome some of life's challenges. I start to get emotional. Tears again, but this time I stop myself. Come on Lowri. You've got this.

Part of me, however, still flares up at the wasted hour at the CP on Day 1. The minutes lost in the mist. The seconds that slipped away as I consulted the map. I can't help it.

Repeat to self: I am pleased to be annoyed. The fact that I am annoyed shows that I still care. I still have it – that doggedness that I thought I had lost all those years ago. I wonder if there is the slightest chance of me making the podium in the women's race.

After the race, Sean sends me a text saying how much he has enjoyed the last two days on the trail. It seems I have given him some advice of my own. 'Thank you for what you said,' he writes. 'You're absolutely right. From now on, I'm going from conservative to balls-out.' Well, I don't think those are the exact words I used, but I'm pleased he, like me, found that he had more in his tank than originally thought.

I appreciate that I am not anatomically able to put Sean's interpretation of my advice to my own use, but on Day 5, I decide to go for it. Even on the downhills, I'm going to stretch my legs. I'm tired of being tired. I need to push on. There are 40 miles (64km) to go and 1,954 metres (6,400 feet) of climb, before the finish line near Carreg Cennen Castle, not far from Llandeilo, where my mother is from. Mam will be there at the finish line with my family to greet me home. And as I run high on the mountains, I'm reminded of happy times spent with my grandparents in this area.

My relationship with my mother's family, just as with my father's, has always been close. Mam is one of seven children born to Trefor and Gwladys Thomas, who ran The Refresh – a hugely popular and successful tavern in Llandeilo, a busy vibrant town surrounded by farms. My memories of being there are still vivid. It was always busy, full of singing and laughter.

My grandparents were very hardworking publicans and my grandmother was also a determined pioneer in her day, establishing a catering business in the area. My grandparents on both sides have sadly long passed, but I am told that I have developed their passion, determination and the perseverance which made them successful in their chosen professions. I think about them a lot on the last day and I'm sure they would have been proud to see me get there. My mother's sisters and two brothers have always played an important part in my life and today some of them are hoping to make it to the finish line.

With my family in the forefront of my mind, I am ready and happy to go. Off I go, then, letting loose today. My reasoning is that even if I have to hobble home it doesn't matter, but I will make it. The knee, touch wood, has held up. Just. The pain has not disappeared, not for one second, but I have embraced it. It has become a part of the rhythm by now. It has earned a gallop. And if it flares up, well, it can have a good elevated lie-in tomorrow.

I stand at the start line, on my own. I'm cheered away by the wonderful crew, who have been a constant support to me all week. 'I just can't believe I'm here, on the last day. I really didn't think I'd get to mid-point Day 1,' I cry.

'Well, you are here … And we will see you at the end,' they shouted as I ran off.

I think of Gwilym. I really hope that one day he too will come to believe that he can do something incredible. I am just an average runner running incredible races. And as I gaze in wonder across the beautiful valley, I ask myself, Why? Why do these things in the first place? I do not need to prove to myself that I can run distances. I can. But one of my reasons is quite simple: I just don't want to be rubbish at life. I don't want to waste the opportunity I have been given to live a life full of adventure and possibility. As we get carried away with GPS, PBs, SBs, WRs, etc., sometimes we forget the reasons why we run. With my son, we're chasing dinosaurs. They have hiding spots and caves and they are really adept at sneaking past you and going the other way, so you have to turn around and chase them all over again. Whatever keeps you going. Here on the mountains I'm visualising the end of the race, just like a toddler's mental trick is to chase dinosaurs. Imagination is a beautiful thing when it comes to finding motivation on the run. And I'm running happy. It's my passion. That is, for me, the thing that keeps me going when I've used up all other motivation. I just, quite simply, enjoy running. It is what makes me feel like me. It's integral, an innate feeling. It is in my blood.

I must check myself. Don't get carried away. I've been talking away with other runners and I'm worried I have missed another checkpoint. Three strikes and I'm out. And I'm too tired to recall whether I've already gained one or two. I would be devastated to run all this distance only to be eliminated because of my chattiness. I phone Siôn. 'Check my GPS,' I mumble into the phone. 'Have I checked in at the last checkpoint?'

'Hang on,' he says. 'I'm in a meeting in work but I'll check now and get back to you … By the way. Looking forward to seeing you tonight. You're nearly home now.'

Those ten minutes felt like ten hours.

The phone rang … 'You're OK. You've checked-in.'

Phew. But there was still a whole day in front of me. Right, less of the talking and more concentrating. We have been warned: beware the sting in the tail of the Dragon's Back. *Y Mynydd Du.* The Black Mountain. After Llandovery we climb towards it. I am not to be stung by any wasps on the Dragon's Back. I take the Black Mountain in my stride. I reach its peak and continue along the ridge that runs westward from it. Having run and climbed and gone gingerly down through the sparsely populated highlands of North and Mid-Wales, suddenly the South is below me. I see a very different Wales.

Do you remember right at the very beginning, when I had been inspired by the London Marathon but was in the waiting cave before running my first marathon? How the most effervescent man I know, Alun Wyn Bevan, conjured up entries for the New York Marathon, because he couldn't find many takers in the Amman Valley, where he was working? Well, here I am now, right back where opportunity first arose, and here it is, the Amman Valley, far below me: the river Amman itself and the string of old mining villages that follow its downhill run from Brynamman to Ammanford. Anthracite villages. Steam coal for the Royal Navy. And for the Titanic.

I'm six miles away from Llandeilo. I'm getting closer to the finishing line. My grandfather used to walk six miles to see my grandmother when they were courting; a 12-mile round trip. Amazing what one is willing to do to see a loved one.

I see more friends along the route who have come to support – PT instructor Dai Watkins and Ironman coach Dylan Morris come out to cheer me on. 'Come on Lowri – it's a sprint home now. It's all in the mind now.' Both are former Royal Marines and although they don't know each other, they know these mountains like the backs of their hands and shout support to all who pass them on their way to the finish line. Hearing their words has given me another boost. To experience this is a powerful feeling, strong enough to have me coming back, again and again, for more. Because completing these challenges reminds me of how powerful we really are. The mind is the most powerful tool we own and there's nothing more valuable than proving to yourself how strong yours really is.

So, I keep telling myself – Keep at it, Lowri, and never give up. Life is not perfect and I will never be perfect, but I will always try to better myself. Because when the time comes, I want to be able to tell my little boy that I was training for the best race of all – Life.

Yes, life is good. I am feeling good. I am in the flow. I am lucky enough to tap into the runner's high and it now feels easy, exhilarating, even euphoric.

I am confident enough to try a few 'lines' of my own. Forget about the GPS, read the map this time. Look ahead and read the trail ahead instead of looking down at a watch. 'Follow the leaders,' Mam says, 'and learn from them.' I don't know whether I'm good enough as a solo course-charter for this to make any difference, but I am feeling great. I have spoken to the very best of the mountain runners and have confessed that I have so much to learn about this type of running without markers and paths.

Carreg Cennen is in sight at last, still imposing as a ruin tiptoeing on the edge of a sheer 100m high cliff.

Not far from the finish, Dad, Mam, Gwilym and my trusted running buddy Nel are here to welcome me home. Just.

In typical Lowri Morgan fashion, I underplayed my ETA. I had picked up the pace on the second half of the day. With 5km to go, I phoned home to let them know I was nearly there.

'Oh dear. We've not left the house yet.' I could hear the three of them rushing to the car. They had a twenty-five-minute journey to get to the finish.

And as I turn the corner onto the home straight, they've just parked the car. They nearly miss my finish but make it just in time. My father opens the car door. 'Go go go!' he shouts and out runs Gwilym and Nel. Nel smiling (she does smile, honestly) on my one side and Gwilym on the other. My mother, with her sister Anne and husband Warren, look proudly on. Seeing them there makes the finish line even sweeter: they, too, have a connection with the place; the place of their birth and upbringing. They have my grateful thanks.

I ask Gwilym if he wants to run alongside me to the finish. He shakes his head. No. He doesn't want the fuss and starts running in the opposite direction. Not towards the banners and the finish line. Does he want to go on my shoulders? He nods.

When I first started running again, two weeks after giving birth, it was my dream that one day I'd run with Gwilym on days like this. Well, it might have been just 50 metres but this is a start. I hoist him aboard and he holds on tight to my head. He and I cross the line together. Nel beats us to it. I do not make the podium in the women's race. I stay in fourth place. But I am a Dragon's Back finisher.

Sean finishes in 36th place overall. Caz the Hat surges up to 26th. I am 44th. I feel great. I am, by the way, the LV champion. I don't have time to dwell too much on what has just happened. Within seconds of crossing the line, I'm back again to being Mam, Gwilym's mam, and he needs my attention. I gladly give it to him.

And now? What am I going to do now? I tell you what I'm going to do right now. I'm going to leave Carreg Cennen near Llandeilo and head straight for Cardiff. Siôn has bought tickets for us to see Noel Gallagher tonight in Cardiff Castle with my brother-in-law and sister-in-law. I am going to drown out stories with rock and roll. I am going keep any post-race blues at bay, fill any hollowness with music.

And maybe a glass, or two, of fizz. But most importantly I'm going to enjoy my time with my family. They've helped me through the highs and lows and they've never stopped me from doing what I love.

And then? What next? I don't know, yet. I refuse to go into the waiting cave. I'm not sure about that place. I prefer to enter the reassessing chamber. I must think of my knee, although I have to say it has come through its latest ordeal pretty well. I wonder …

I find myself saying out loud, like one single point on my big list of things to do in my life, this:

I really don't want it to come to an end.

That's what my head is telling me. My knee, my eye, my any-other-bit-of-me may say something entirely different. I suppose I shall have to be patient, but I think I know (and that may be the clue) which part of me will win the argument. If my toenails haven't put you off and if you feel tempted in even the tiniest way to run, then this may help:

1. *Make the target small. Not 350 miles …*
2. *… But the one, first step is the most important. And take all the ones that follow, with all their ups and downs …*
3. *… One step at a time.*
4. *Sometimes the best way to learn is to go beyond limits and set your own rules.*

And so we come, a few thousand miles, several toenails and a couple of pulks after setting out, to the point where illusion and reality meet, the last checkpoint, the place to … no, not to stop … the place to pause, to take stock … the place where new plans begin.